Text & Tests

for Transition Year

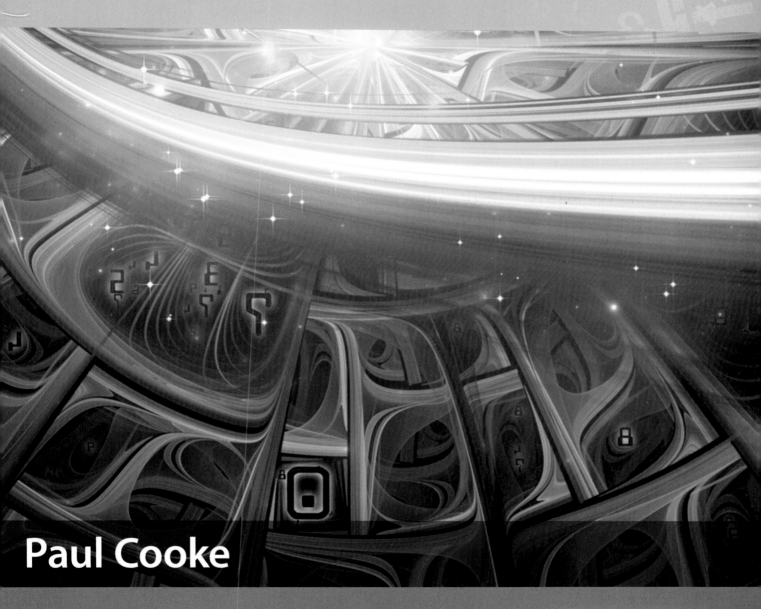

Paul Cooke

The Celtic Press

Available **FREE** as an
eBook
www.cjf.ie/code

Published by
Celtic Press
Ground Floor – Block B
Liffey Valley Office Campus
Dublin 22

First Edition March 2021

ISBN: 978-0-7144-2997-7

© Paul Cooke

All rights reserved.
No part of this publication may be reproduced, stored in a retrieval
system or transmitted in any form or by any means, electronic,
mechanical, photocopying, recording or otherwise, without the prior
written consent of the copyright holders.

Contents

Preface

This book is designed as a bridge between Junior Cycle and Leaving Certificate mathematics. It presents eight modules central to the study of mathematics. Its main aim is to focus on key concepts within these modules and to revisit work already undertaken at Junior Cycle level (**Looking back <<**) and to show how these topics will develop (**Looking forward >>**) into senior level mathematics.

- Each module includes a timeline development over the centuries for this branch of mathematics at the beginning of the chapter.

- The modules are broken into parts, each of which revises a specific topic. They are written in a simple easy-to-understand style. Emphasis is placed on enabling students to recognise and connect mathematical ideas as well as to relate mathematics to the real world.

- A worked example with a short, focused exercise (**Check-up**) is a key element of each part.

- Every effort has been made to graduate the level of difficulty of the questions in each check-up.

- **Talking points** are included to add clarity, suggest other approaches or stimulate discussion of the topic.

Finally, each chapter concludes with a **Test** covering all the mathematical topics covered in that module.

Paul Cooke

1 Algebra *through history*

- A mathematical method for solving problems
- Using symbols, particularly x, to represent an unknown quantity
- A system that creates a balancing statement, *an equation*, to represent a problem
- A set of manoeuvres that adapts *the equation* until the unknown is isolated and found.

250 AD	**Diophantus** of Greek origin, spent most of his life in Alexandria, Egypt. He wrote many books of mathematics, the most famous of which is *Arithmetica*, which deals with solving algebraic equations.

800 AD

Al-Khwarizmi was a Persian mathematician who worked most of his life in the Baghdad House of Wisdom, a major library and place of learning in the Middle East.
His book on algebra,
> The Compendious Book on Calculation by
> Completion and Balancing,
contains the word **al-jabr** in the Islamic title, from which we derive the modern word, **algebra**.

The library was destroyed by a Mongol invasion in 1258 and the books destroyed. It is said that the Tigris ran black due to the ink from the books that were thrown into its waters.

1843 AD

William Rowan Hamilton, the famous Irish mathematician, was vexed by the problem of trying to multiply or divide points in 3-dimensional complex space.
As he walked along the Royal Canal towards Broombridge in Cabra, Dublin 7, the answer came to him and he immediately carved the solution on the bridge.
His solution needed a 4th dimension $\{1, i, j, k\}$ which gave rise to 'quaternions'.

$$i^2 = j^2 = k^2 = ijk = -1$$

The algebraic properties of quaternions are especially used today in computer graphics, robotics and orbital mechanics (satellite motion).

1850–today

Modern algebra, sometimes called *Abstract Algebra,* is not interested in specific outcomes or solutions.
It is interested in the behaviour of sets and mappings of the elements of those sets.
In modern algebra we study:
Groups, Rings and Fields.

A **group** consists of a pairing between a set and an operation. The set of integers with the operation of addition is a *group*.
$$Z, +$$

Algebra

Part 1: Working with equations

- 6 is a **constant**, its value cannot change.
- $4x = 4 \times x$, is a **term** whose value changes, depending on the value of x.

  If $x = 5$, $4x = 4 \times 5 = 20$.

  If $x = -2$, $4x = 4 \times (-2) = -8$.
- $4x = 6$, is an **equation**, a balance between the value of $4x$ and 6.
- To **solve** for x, change the equation to get the unknown (x) on its own, on the left-hand side of the equation.

$$4x = 6$$

$$\frac{4x}{4} = \frac{6}{4} = 1.5 \text{ ...dividing \textbf{both} sides by 4}$$

$$x = 1.5 \text{ is the \textbf{solution} (the value of } x \text{ that makes the equation true)}$$

Example

What value of x satisfies the equation $\frac{3x}{2} - 4 = 5$?

Answer:

$$\frac{3x}{2} - 4 = 5$$

$$\frac{3x}{2} - 4 + 4 = 5 + 4$$

$$\frac{3x}{2} = 9$$

$$\frac{3x}{2} \times 2 = 9 \times 2 \text{ ...multiplying both sides by 2}$$

$$3x = 18$$

$$\frac{3x}{3} = \frac{18}{3} \text{ ...dividing both sides by 3}$$

$$x = 6$$

Check:

$$\frac{3 \times 6}{2} - 4 = 5$$

$$9 - 4 = 5 \checkmark$$

1.1 Check-up

Find the value of the unknown in each of the following equations.
Verify your solution by substituting it into the original equation.

1. (i) $4x + 5 = 13$ (ii) $3x - 9 = 12$ (iii) $6x - 3 = 12$

2. (i) $\frac{x}{4} + 6 = 8$ (ii) $\frac{2x}{3} - 5 = 3$ (iii) $4 + \frac{5x}{6} = 9$

3. (i) $\frac{2}{x} = 10$ (ii) $\frac{3}{x} + 2 = 17$ (iii) $\frac{24}{x} - 10 = 2$

4. (i) $\frac{y}{4} + 2y = 18$ (ii) $\frac{9}{t} - 4t = 0$ (iii) $\frac{4}{3x - 2} + 1 = 5$

Example

<<

Solve the equation $\frac{x}{5} + 2x = 22$

Answer:
$$\frac{x}{5} + \frac{10x}{5} = \frac{110}{5} \text{ ...common denominator 5}$$

$$\frac{x + 10x}{5} = \frac{110}{5}$$

$$11x = 110$$

$$x = 10$$

Check:
$$\frac{10}{5} + 2 \times 10 = 22$$

$$2 + 20 = 22 \checkmark$$

1.2 Check-up

<<

Find the value of the unknown in each of the following equations.
Verify your solution by substituting it into the original equation.

1. (i) $\frac{2x}{3} + x = 15$ (ii) $\frac{5x}{4} - 2x = -6$ (iii) $4x + \frac{2x}{6} = \frac{13}{3}$

2. (i) $\frac{x}{4} - 6x = \frac{23}{4}$ (ii) $\frac{x}{8} + \frac{1}{16} = \frac{x}{4}$ (iii) $4 + \frac{5x}{6} = 9$

3. (i) $\frac{2t}{7} + 5 = 6$ (ii) $\frac{y}{12} - 5 = 3y$ (iii) $4 + \frac{5s}{6} = 9$

Part 2: Manipulating and evaluating expressions

Looking back

<<

- To **change the subject** of an equation we perform the same operation on both sides of the equation at each step.
- To **factorise** an expression, divide by the highest common factor.
- To **evaluate** an expression, substitute the value given for each unknown and calculate a total.

Example

<<

Make x the subject of $h - cx = d$ and
hence find the value of x when $h = 2$, $c = 4$ and $d = -10$

Answer:
$$h - cx = d$$
$$h - h - cx = d - h \text{ ... subtracting } h \text{ from both sides}$$
$$-cx = d - h$$
$$cx = -d + h \text{ ...multiplying both sides by } -1.$$
$$x = \frac{h - d}{c} \text{ ...dividing both sides by } c$$

When $h = 2$, $c = 4$ and $d = -10$
$$x = \frac{2 - (-10)}{4}$$
$$\therefore x = 3$$

Check:
$$h - cx = d$$
$$2 - 4(3) = -10$$
$$-10 = -10 \checkmark$$

2.1 Check-up

<<

Make x the subject in each of the following equations.
Hence find the value of x using the data given.

1. (i) $y + dx = c$ (ii) $a = h - gx$ (iii) $a + b = c - dx$

2. (i) $a^2 - bx = d$ (ii) $y + \dfrac{h}{x} = y^2$ (iii) $a(b - x) = c$

3. (i) $\dfrac{h}{(m + x)} = b$ (ii) $g + (ax)^2 = b$ (iii) $y^2 - \dfrac{c}{x} = g^2 + 3$

Data, $y = 3, d = 2, c = 5, a = 1, h = 6, g = -1, b = 4, m = \dfrac{7}{4}$

4. $v^2 = u^2 + 2as$.

Make a the subject of this equation.
Find the value of a when $u = 5$ m/s, $v = 60$ m/s and $s = 500$ m

5. A heavy bob swings as shown in diagram.
The time for a complete cycle is given by the equation,

$$T = 2\pi\sqrt{\dfrac{l}{g}},$$

where g represents the acceleration due to gravity.
Make g the subject of this equation.
Find a value for g, correct to 1 place of decimals,
when $T = 1.85$ s and $l = 0.85$ m

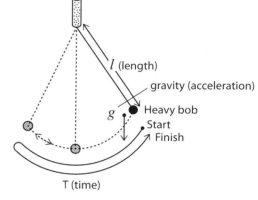

6. $\dfrac{1}{f} = \dfrac{1}{u} + \dfrac{1}{v}$.

Write v in terms of f and u and hence find a value for v when $u = 0.85$ m and $f = 0.65$
correct to 2 places of decimals.

7.

In a heat pump, electrical work (W) is done to extract an amount of heat, Q_c, from the cold air
outside and deliver heat energy, Q_h, into the house.
The Coefficient of Performance of a heat pump is given by

$$\text{CoP} = \dfrac{Q_h}{W} \text{ where } W = Q_h - Q_c$$

(i) Calculate the CoP value given that $Q_h = 20J$ and $Q_c = 15J$.
(ii) Explain why the coefficient of performance is always greater than 1.
The thermal efficiency (η) of a heat pump is given by

$$\text{Thermal efficiency } (\eta) = \dfrac{W}{Q_h}$$

(iii) Explain why η is always less than 1.

(iv) Show that $\eta = 1 - \dfrac{Q_c}{Q_h}$

(v) Find the thermal efficiency of the heat pump above in percentage terms.

(vi) If a heat pump is 75% efficient and $Q_h = 500J$, find a value for Q_c

Example

Factorise: (i) $8a^2 + 2a$ (ii) $6x^3 + 12x^2 - 6x$

Answer:

(i)

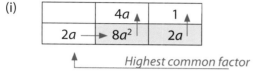

Highest common factor

$$\therefore 8a^2 + 2 = (2a)(4a + 1)$$

(ii)

Highest common factor

$$\therefore 6x^3 + 12x^2 - 6x = (6x)(x^2 + 2x - 1)$$

2.2 Check-up

Factorise the following expressions:

1. (i) $24x + 84y$ (ii) $12a - 6b + 9c$ (iii) $9x + 6xy - 3x^2$

2. (i) $\pi r^2 + 2\pi r$ (ii) $4\pi r^2 + \pi rh$ (iii) $20x^2 - 15y^2$

3. (i) $3t + 9t^2$ (ii) $4x^3 + 12x^2 + 8x$ (iii) $axy + bxy^2$

Example

Factorise $2x^2 - 5x - 12$ and hence find values of x that satisfy $2x^2 - 5x - 12 = 0$

Answer: $2x^2 - 5x - 12 = (2x + 3)(x - 4)$

$\therefore (2x + 3)(x - 4) = 0$

$\therefore (2x + 3) = 0$ | $(x - 4) = 0$

$\therefore 2x = -3$ | $x = 4$

$x = -\dfrac{3}{2}$ The solutions are $x = -\dfrac{3}{2}, 4$

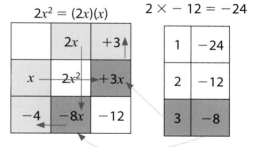

2.3 Check-up

Solve each of the following equations using factorisation:

1. (i) $x^2 + 2x - 8 = 0$ (ii) $x^2 - 8x + 15 = 0$ (iii) $2y^2 + 9y + 4 = 0$

2. (i) $3x^2 + 11x - 4 = 0$ (ii) $2x^2 + 3x - 5 = 0$ (iii) $2t^2 + 9t - 18 = 0$

3. (i) $5x^2 - 3x - 2 = 0$ (ii) $8t^2 - 14t + 3 = 0$ (iii) $2v^2 - 10v - 72 = 0$

4. Simplify each of the following algebraic fractions by factorising the numerator and denominator.

(i) $\dfrac{x^2 + 4x + 3}{x^2 + 6x + 5}$ (ii) $\dfrac{x^2 + 2x - 8}{x^2 + 5x + 4}$

Part 3: Linear equations

- $y = mx + c$ is the **equation of a line**, m is the slope and c is the y-intercept.
- $ax + by + c = 0$ is the **general** equation of a line.
- A point (x_1, y_1) is on a line if it satisfies the equation of the line:
  - $y_1 = mx_1 + c$ or
  - $ax_1 + by_1 + c = 0$

Example <<

Show that the line $k: y = 3x + 4$ contains the points $A(1, 7)$ and $C(-2, -2)$ and does not contain the point $D(3, 4)$.

Answer:

$$y = 3x + 4$$
$$(x, y) = (1, 7) \Rightarrow 7 = 3(1) + 4$$
$$7 = 7$$
$$\therefore (1, 7) \in k$$

$$(x, y) = (-2, -2) \Rightarrow -2 = 3(-2) + 4$$
$$-2 = -2$$
$$\therefore (-2, -2) \in k$$

$$(x, y) = (3, 4) \Rightarrow 4 = 3(3) + 4$$
$$4 \neq 13$$
$$\therefore (3, 4) \notin k$$

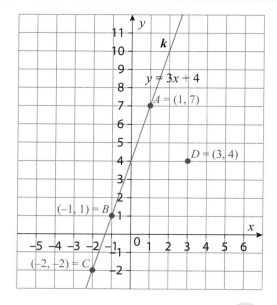

3.1 Check-up <<

Determine which points of each set are on the given line:

1. $l: y = 4x - 2$, $\qquad \{A(1, 1), B(4, 12), C(-1, -6), D(3, 10)\}$

2. $k: 2y = 5x + 2$, $\qquad \{A(0, 1), B(-2, -4), C(6, 16), D(-1, -2)\}$

3. $m: 2x + 4y - 5 = 0$, $\qquad \left\{A(2.5, 0), B(4, 1), C\left(5, \dfrac{-5}{4}\right), D\left(0, \dfrac{5}{4}\right)\right\}$

4. $t: x - 2y + 6 = 0$, $\qquad \{A(2, 4), B(0, 2), C(4, 5), D(-6, 0)\}$

5. Which of the following lines pass through the point $(1, -4)$?

   $l: 3x + y + 1 = 0$, $\quad m: 6x - y - 5 = 0$, $\quad n: 3x + 2y + 5 = 0$, $\quad k: 5x - y - 9 = 0$

6. Finn collected the following data from his spiral spring experiment.

W(N)	1	2	3	4	5	6
l(cm)	12.5	16	18	20	22.5	25

   He claimed that all of his data belonged to the linear equation $5W - 2l + 20 = 0$. Was he correct?
   Explain your answer.

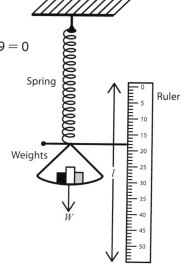

Spring

Ruler

Weights

Example

Given that the point $A(8, 4)$ is on the line $y = ax$,
find the value of a.

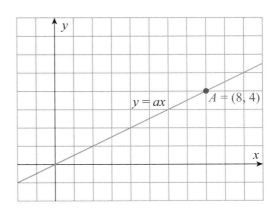

Answer: $y = ax$

$(x, y) = (8, 4) \in$ of the line

$\Rightarrow 4 = a \times 8$

$8a = 4$

$\Rightarrow a = \dfrac{4}{8} = \dfrac{1}{2}$

$\therefore y = \dfrac{1}{2}x$

$a = \dfrac{1}{2}$

3.2 Check-up

Find the value of the unknowns given the following information:

1. The point $(3, 9)$ is on the line $y = ax$, find the value of a.

2. The point $(2, -4)$ is on the line $y = 5x + c$, find the value of c.

3. The line $2x - by + 1 = 0$ contains the point $(2, 1)$, find the value of b.

4. The point $(10, f)$ is on the line $x + 4y - 2 = 0$, find the value of f.

5. The point $(g, 3)$ is on the line $2x - 4y - 6 = 0$, find the value of g.

6. The point $(1, 10)$ is on the curve $y = 3x^2 + bx + 4$, find the value of b.

7. The curve $y = ax^3 + 4x^2 + 2x + 1$ contains the point $(-1, 2)$, find the value of a.

8. The point $(-2, -2)$ is on both lines $ax + 4y = 6$ and $3x + ay = b$.
Find the value of a and b.

9. Explain why the line $cx + 2y - 9 = 0$ cannot contain the $(0, 3)$, for all values of c.

10. Determine which of the given points are on the curve,
$y = 2x^3 - 4x^2 - 5x + 3$
  (a) $(0, 2)$ (c) $(3, 5)$
  (b) $(1, -4)$ (d) $(-1, 2)$

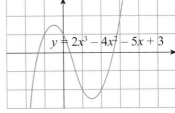

11. The curve $y = 2x^2 - 5$ is shown.
Prove that the point $C(4, 3)$ is not on the curve.
Prove that the points $A(-2, 3)$ and $B(1, -3)$ are on the
curve.

A second curve $y = x^2 + a$ passes through the point
$C(4, 3)$.
Find the value of a.

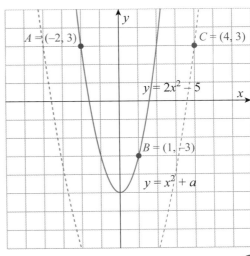

Part 4: Simultaneous equations

- $3x + 2y = 5$
  $2x - y = 1$ are examples of simultaneous equations.
- Simultaneous equations have one point (x, y) in common.
- To solve simultaneous equations (To find the common point):
  - Equate the coefficient of x or y in both equations.
  - Add or Subtract the equations to **eliminate one of the variables**.
  - Solve the resulting equation for the remaining variable.
  - Using the value found and one of the original equations, find the value of the second variable.
  - Check that the values obtained satisfy both original equations.

Example   <<

Solve the simultaneous equations $3x + 2y = 5$ and $2x - y = 1$

Answer: $3x + 2y = 5$ $3x + 2y = 5$

          $2x - y = 1$ $\times 2$ $\underline{4x - 2y = 2}$

                                    $7x \quad = 7$ ...adding both equations

                                     $x \quad = 1$ to eliminate y.

$$3x + 2y = 5$$
$$\Rightarrow \ 3(1) + 2y = 5 \quad ...x = 1$$
$$2y = 5 - 3 = 2$$
$$\therefore y = 1$$

Check: (1,1) is the common point by substituting it into the original equations.

        $3x + 2y = 5 \Rightarrow 3(1) + 2(1) = 5$ and $2x - y = 1 \Rightarrow 2(1) - (1) = 1$

                      $\Rightarrow \quad 5 \quad = 5$ ✓ $\Rightarrow \quad 1 = 1$ ✓

        $\therefore (1,1)$ is a point on both lines.

4.1 Check-up   <<

Solve the following pairs of simultaneous equations using the elimination method:

1. $3x - 5y = 4$
     $x + 2y = 5$

2. $2x + 3y = 1$
     $3x - 4y = 10$

3. $7a + b = 10$
     $2a + 3b = -8$

4. $3m - 2n = 12$
     $5m - 3n = 21$

5. $a + b = 0$
     $a - b = 9$

6. $5x - y = 20$
     $4x + 3y = 16$

7. $(-2, 4)$ and $(4, 1)$ are two points on the line $y = ax + b$ as shown.

Using these points, form two simultaneous equations in a and b.

Solve these equations to find the values of a and b.

Verify that the points A and B are on the line $y = ax + b$.

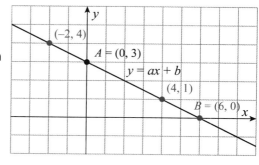

8. The line $y = mx + c$ contains the points $(0, 4)$ and $1, 1$. Find the values of m and c.

9. Find the equation of the line $y = mx + c$ containing the points $(2, 8)$ and $(-1, 2)$.

10. Two lines AB and AC pass through the points

$A(4, 3)$, $B(6, 0)$ and $A(4, 3)$, $C(-1, 0)$.

By forming simultaneous equations using the equation of the line $y = mx + c$, find the equation of AB and AC.

Write each equation in the form $ax + by + c = 0$, where $a, b, c \in Z$.

Show that the point $A(4, 3)$ is on both lines.

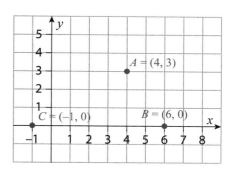

Talking Point

From the work above, we can conclude that to find the values of **two** unknowns in an equation we need to have **two** simultaneous equations.

Part 5: Working in 3-Dimensions

Looking ahead >>

- The equation, $2a + 5b - c = 1$, has 3 unknowns a, b and c (3-dimensions).
- To solve an equation with 3 unknowns we need 3 equations:
  - Taking the equations 2 at a time, one of the unknowns is eliminated.
  - We then have two equations with two unknowns.
  - Finally, we use the **elimination method** again to solve for one of the unknowns.
  - Using this value, the other unknowns are found from the original equations.

Example

>>

Solve the equations:
$$a + b + c = 0 \quad \text{...A}$$
$$3a - 2b - 5c = 9 \quad \text{...B}$$
$$5a + 4b - 3c = -11 \quad \text{...C}$$

Answer:

$$\text{A} \times 5 \rightarrow 5a + 5b + 5c = 0$$
$$\underline{\text{B} \qquad \rightarrow 3a - 2b - 5c = 9}$$
$$\mathbf{8a + 3b \qquad = 9} \quad \text{...adding both lines we get an equation in } a \text{ and } b.$$

$$\text{A} \times 3 \rightarrow 3a + 3b + 3c = 0$$
$$\underline{\text{C} \qquad \rightarrow 5a + 4b - 3c = -11}$$
$$\mathbf{8a + 7b \qquad = -11} \quad \text{...adding both lines we get a second equation in } a \text{ and } b$$

$$8a + 3b = 9$$
$$8a + 7b = -11 \text{ ... subtracting both lines, } a \text{ is eliminated.}$$
$$-4b = 20$$
$$4b = -20$$
$$b = -5$$

$$\therefore 8a + 3(-5) = 9 \qquad \qquad \therefore a + b + c = 0 \qquad \qquad \therefore a = 3$$
$$8a - 15 = 9 \qquad \qquad 3 + (-5) + c = 0 \qquad \qquad b = -5$$
$$8a = 24 \qquad \qquad -2 + c = 0 \qquad \qquad c = 2$$
$$a = 3 \qquad \qquad c = 2$$

Check: the results by substituting the values for a, b and c, back into all three original equations:

A: $a + b + c = 3 - 5 + 2 = 0$ ✓
B: $3a - 2b - 5c = 3(3) - 2(-5) - 5(2) = 9 + 10 - 10 = 9$ ✓
C: $5a + 4b - 3c = 5(3) + 4(-5) - 3(2) = 15 - 20 - 6 = -11$ ✓

5.1 Check-up

In each of the following questions, find the value of the unknowns using the elimination method. Verify your answers by substituting your answers into the original equations

1. $a + b + c = 7$
$2a + b - c = 0$
$a + 3b + c = 11$

2. $x + 2y + z = 1$
$2x - y + z = 6$
$x + y + z = 2$

3. $2r + s - t = 5$
$r + 2s - t = 4$
$r - s - 2t = 1$

4. $a + 2b - c = 7$
$2a - 2b + c = 5$
$a + b - 2c = 7$

5. $x + y + z = -1$
$2x - y + 2z = 13$
$x + 2y - 3z = -10$

6. $2r + s - t = 15$
$r - 2s - 2t = +5$
$3r + s + t = 8$

7. A curve $y = ax^2 + bx + c$ passes through the points $A(0,1)$, $B(2, -3)$, $C(3, -2)$.

By substituting the points into the equation, form 3 equations in a, b and c.

Solve the equations to find values for a, b, c.

Verify that the points are on the curve.

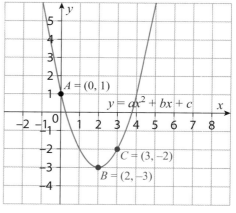

8. By selecting 3 suitable points on the curve, find the coefficients a, b, c of the curve shown using 3 simultaneous equations.

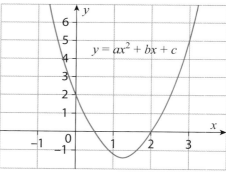

9. In a Christmas maths test, the students were asked to solve the equations
$2d + e + f = 8$
$d + 3e + 2f = 5$
$3d - 2e - 3f = 1$
Patrick said he got $\{d, e, f\} = \{-3, 2, 4\}$,
Marcus got $\{d, e, f\} = \{3, -2, 4\}$,
and Ava got $\{d, e, f\} = \{3, 2, -4\}$.

Check if any of the three students got the correct answer.

Algebra 2: Solving word problems using algebra

Part 6: Linear equations with one unknown

Looking back <<

- A symbol x (or any suitable letter) is used to represent the unknown quantity.
- An equation is formed using the symbol x and the information in the question.
- The equation is solved for x.
- The answer is checked.

Example

<<

The sum of three consecutive integers is 99.
Find the three integers.

Answer: Let n be the first integer.
$\Rightarrow n + 1$ is the second integer.
$\Rightarrow n + 2$ is the third integer.
$\Rightarrow n + (n + 1) + (n + 2)$ is the
   sum of the three integers.
$\therefore n + (n + 1) + (n + 2) = 99$
$\therefore 3n + 3 = 99$
$\therefore 3n = 96$
$\therefore n = \dfrac{96}{3} = 32$ ...the first integer
$\therefore n + 1 = 33$ ...the second integer
$\therefore n + 2 = 34$ ...the third integer

Consecutive numbers follow one another. For example, 3, 4, 5.

Talking Point

Since the numbers are *consecutive*, if we divide 99 by 3 we will get the mean or middle number,

$$\frac{99}{3} = 33$$

$\therefore$ the numbers are 32, 33, 34

(Would this approach work if four numbers were involved?)

Check: **32 + 33 + 34 = 99** ✓

6.1 Check-up

<<

Use algebraic reasoning to find the unknown in each of the following:

1. The length of a rectangle is 1 cm less than twice the width of the rectangle.
    If the perimeter measures 22 cm, find the dimensions of the rectangle.
    (Hint: let the width be x.)
    Check that your dimensions add up to a perimeter length of 22 cm.

    Length = 1 cm less than twice the width

    Width

2. A second number is 5 more than three times the first number.
    If the sum of the numbers is 45, by letting x be the first number, find the numbers.

    Check that the two numbers add to 45.

3. Travelling by train a first-class ticket costs two and a half times as much as a second-class ticket. If the total cost of 6 first-class tickets and 10 second-class tickets is €187.50, write an equation to show this information. Solve the equation to find the price of a first-class ticket.

4. A rectangle has dimensions as shown.
Write and solve an equation to find x.

Find the area of the rectangle.

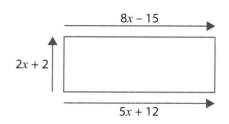

$8x - 15$

$2x + 2$

$5x + 12$

5. The denominator of a fraction is 4 more than the numerator.
If 2 is added to the numerator and 1 subtracted
from the denominator then the fraction becomes $\frac{5}{6}$.

$\dfrac{numerator}{denominator}$

Find the fraction.

6. Pat's parents had promised her new runners if she
got a mean score of 80 in her four maths tests.
Her scores in the first three tests were 74%, 88% and 82%.
What minimum percentage must she get in her last test
to be sure of getting the new runners?

$$\text{Mean (of } a \text{ and } b) = \frac{a + b}{2}$$

7. From geometry we know that the sum of the angles in a
parallelogram add to 360° and that opposite angles are equal.
If the larger of the angles of the parallelogram shown is 30° less than
2 times the smaller angle, find the measure of each angle.

Verify that the angles add up to 360°.

8. If n represents an 'odd' number write an expression for the next consecutive 'odd' number.
The sum of two consecutive 'odd' numbers is 248.

Find the numbers.

9. Damien wants to line the
side of his lawn with sleepers.
The width of the lawn is 3 m
and its area is 42 m².
Three sleepers are needed for the
side but 1 m needs to be cut off the
third one.
If x be the length of a sleeper, write an equation
for the length of a sleeper.

Solve the equation to find the length of a sleeper.

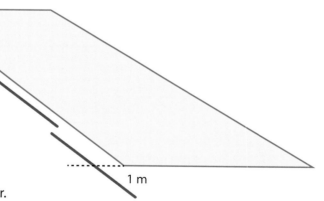

1 m

Part 7: Problems involving rates

Looking ahead >>

- When a problem involves a rate, isolate a single unit of time.
    - John and Terry paint a wall at different rates, how much of the wall will they each paint in 1 hour?
    - Emma cycles to work at 20 km/h, she travels 20 km in 1 hour.

Example   >>

Terry can paint a large wall in 20 hours.
John can paint the same wall in 15 hours.

Working together, how long will it take them to paint the same wall?

Answer: In 1 hour, Terry paints $\frac{1}{20}$ of the wall.

In 1 hour, John paints $\frac{1}{15}$ of the wall.

In 1 hour together they paint $\frac{1}{20} + \frac{1}{15} = \frac{3}{60} + \frac{4}{60} = \frac{7}{60}$ of the wall.

Together they paint $\frac{7}{60}$ of the wall in 1 hour

$\frac{1}{60}$ of the wall in $\frac{1}{7}$ hours

$\frac{60}{60}$ of the wall in $\frac{60}{7}$ hours

They paint the wall in $8\frac{4}{7}$ hours.

7.1 Check-up   >>

1. Marie can dig a row of potatoes in 6 hours.
   Anna can dig the same row of potatoes in 8 hours.
   Working together, how long will it take them to dig the same row of potatoes?

2. Kevin cycles to work at 18 km/h (with the wind).
   Kevin cycles home at 16 km/h (against the wind).

   His work is d km from home.

   The total time for a return trip is $4\frac{1}{4}$ hours:

   (i) Write an equation in terms of d for the time Kevin takes to cycle to work.
   (ii) Write an equation in terms of d for the time Kevin takes to cycle home.
   (iii) Show that Kevin cycles 36 km to work.

3. Tap A can fill a tank in 60 minutes.
   Tap B can fill a tank in 90 minutes.
   (i) If both taps work at the same time, find what fraction of the tank is filled in 1 minute.
   (ii) With both taps working, the tank fills in t minutes. Find t.

4. A farmer decided it was time to bring his melons to market.

He gathered 100 kg of melons and put them in a crate.

He tested the melons before he set off to market and found that the water content of the melons was 99%.

It was a very hot day as he drove to market.

When he got to the market, he tested the melons again and found that the water content had decreased to 98%.

He was to be paid per kg, by the market, however there was no scales to measure the mass of the melons!

Use algebra to find the mass of the melons. (You will be surprised at the answer!)

(Hint: Water content of 99% implies that 1% was pith or fibre and the heat has **no** effect on this)

(Hint: Let x kg, be the mass of the water in the melons at the market)

Part 8: Problems with two unknowns

Looking back
<<

- Symbols x and y (or other suitable letters) are used to represent the unknown quantities.
- Two simultaneous equations are formed, using the symbols x and y, from the information in the question.
- The **elimination method** is used to reduce the two equations to one.
- This equation is solved for x.
- The second equation is used to find the value of y.
- The answers are checked with the original information.

Example   <<

> The difference between two numbers is 21.
> The sum of the two numbers is 95. Find the two numbers.

Answer: Let n be the first number and m be the second number.

$$\therefore n - m = 21$$
$$\text{Also } \underline{n + m = 95}$$

Adding the equations .... $2n \quad = 116$

$$\therefore n = \frac{116}{2} = 58$$

If $n = 58 \Rightarrow 58 + m = 95$ *Check:* $58 - 37 = 21$ ✓
$$\therefore \quad m = 95 - 58 = 37$$ $58 + 37 = 95$ ✓

8.1 Check-up

<<

1. The sum of two numbers and twice a second number is 14.
   When the second number is subtracted from the first number, the difference is 2.

   Let x be the first number and y be the second number.
   Write two equations linking both numbers.
   Solve the equations to find the two numbers.

2. The sum of the ages of Sophie and Max is 38 years.
   Seven years ago, Max was twice as old as Sophie.

   Let x years be Sophie's age and y years be Max's at present.
   Write two equations linking the ages now and seven years ago.
   Solve the equations to find Max's age at present.

Example

<<

Aidan bought 12 small shrubs and 5 packets of seeds
costing €116 in the local garden centre.
Anna bought 8 small shrubs and 12 packets of seeds
costing €112 in the same garden centre.
Assuming each of the shrubs and each of the packets
of seeds were priced equally, find the price of a shrub
and the price of a packet of seeds.

Let x be the price of a shrub and let y be the price of a packet of seeds.

Answer:
$$12x + 5y = €116 \quad \text{.... } A$$
$$8x + 12y = €112 \quad \text{.... } B$$

$$2 \times A: \quad 24x + 10y = €232$$
$$3 \times B: \quad 24x + 36y = €336$$
$$-26y = -€104$$
$$y = €\frac{104}{26} = €4$$

$$\therefore 8x + 12(4) = €112$$
$$8x = 112 - 48 = €64$$
$$x = €\frac{64}{8} = €8$$

Check: $12(8) + 5(4) = 96 + 20 = 116$ ✓
$8(8) + 12(4) = 64 + 48 = 112$ ✓

8.2 Check-up

<<

Solve each of the following for the two unknowns:

1. In the local hall, there are 25 seats in some rows and 15 seats in the remaining rows.
   There are 25 rows altogether.
   When the hall is full, it holds 545 people.

   25 per row

   15 per row

   Let x be the number of rows with 25 seats
   Let y be the number of rows with 15 seats.
   Write down two equations for x and y.
   Solve the simultaneous equations to find the number of
   rows of 25 seats and the number of rows of 15 seats.

2. An equilateral triangle has sides $(10x - 7y)$cm, $(6x + 3y)$cm and 36 cm.
   Find the value of x and y.

3. A local football club's admission charges are €12 for an
   adult and €8 for a student.
   On a particular Saturday, 800 tickets were sold.
   The total receipts amounted to €8540.
   Let m be the number of adults and n be the number of
   students who attended the match.
   Find the number of adults and the number of students
   who attended the match.

4. Find a pair of numbers satisfying $9x - 2y = 68$ given that one number is 4 times the other.

5. A bakery was asked to supply the local supermarket
   with a number of loaves of bread (y) over a certain
   number of days (x).
   If the bakery supplies 160 loaves of bread each day,
   the manager says that he is short 50 loaves.
   If the bakery supplies 180 loaves each day, the manager
   says that he will have 50 loaves too many.
   Write two equations in x and y.
   Solve the equations to find (i) the number of loaves asked for (ii) the number of days.

6. A fraction $\frac{x}{y}$ is equivalent to $\frac{2}{7}$.

   If the numerator and denominator are both increased by 3, the fraction is equivalent to $\frac{3}{10}$.
   Find both fractions.

7. A gardener has 26 m of wood to construct a
   rectangular frame for a raised bed.
   If the length of the frame is to be 3 m longer than
   the width, find the area of the frame.

8. A final of a club championship had 2500 spectators.
   For those who paid online in advance, there was a certain discount on the admission fee.
   If the number of people who got a discount was 622 less than the number who did not,
   find the number of people who paid the full price.

9. Peter's bank balance was twice as big as Zoe's yesterday.
   When Peter lodged an extra €15 into his account, his bank balance was €100 more than Zoe's.
   How much did Peter have in his bank account yesterday?

10. 3A added to 9B gives a total of 120.
   5A added to 5B gives a total of 90.
   Find the total of 5A and 7B.

Part 9: Solving word problems requiring 3 unknowns

Looking ahead
>>

- A linear equation in three variables (unknowns, x, y, z) will be of the form $ax + by + cz = d$, where a, b, c and d are constants.
- Three equations linking the unknowns are needed to solve for x, y, z.
- Using two of the equations at a time, one of the variables is eliminated, resulting in two equations with two unknowns.
- Finally, one unknown is eliminated using the simultaneous equation method and the value of the last unknown is found.
- The value of the other unknowns can be found by substitution.

Example

The sum of three numbers is 6.
Twice the first number added to the second number is one greater than the third number.
Four times the first number added to twice the third number is four greater than three times the second number.
Find the numbers.

Answer: Let x, y, z represent the three numbers.

$A...$	$x + y + z = 6$	$\rightarrow$ $x + y + z = 6$
$B...$	$2x + y = z + 1$	$\rightarrow$ $2x + y - z = 1$
$C...$	$4x + 2z = 3y + 4$	$\rightarrow 4x - 3y + 2z = 4$

$A...$ $x + y + z = 6$		$2 \times B...$ $4x + 2y - 2z = 2$
$B...$ $\underline{2x + y - z = 1}$		$C...$ $\underline{4x - 3y + 2z = 4}$
$D...$ $3x + 2y \quad\;\; = 7$ ...adding $A + B$		$E...$ $8x - y \qquad = 6$ ...adding $2B + C$

D and E are equations in x and y only, z has been eliminated.

$$
\begin{aligned}
D \qquad\quad 3x + 2y &= 7 \\
2 \times E \quad \underline{16x - 2y} &= \underline{12} \\
19x \;\;\;\;\; &= 19 \\
x \;\;\;\;\; &= 1
\end{aligned}
$$

$\Rightarrow \quad 3(1) + 2y = 7$ ...using equation D

$\qquad\qquad\quad 2y = 4$

$\qquad\qquad\quad\; y = 2$

$\Rightarrow (1) + (2) + z = 6$ ...using equation A

$\qquad\qquad\quad\; z = 3$

$\qquad\quad (x, y, z) = (1, 2, 3)$

Check: $A: 1 + 2 + 3 = 6$ ✓

$\qquad\qquad B: 2(1) + 2 - 3 = 1$ ✓

$\qquad\qquad C: 4(1) - 3(2) + 2(3) = 4$ ✓

9.1 Check-up

If we know three points on a quadratic curve, we can use
the simultaneous equation technique above to find the coefficients as seen in **Check-up 8**:

1. A quadratic curve of the form $y = ax^2 + bx + c$
passes through the points A (1, 2), B (2, 4), C (3, 8).

By letting $(x, y) = (1, 2)$ write an equation in a, b, c.
Repeat for $(x, y) = (2, 4)$ and $(x, y) = (3, 8)$

Solve the equations formed to find the values of a, b, c.

Show that the point (2, 5) is not on the curve.

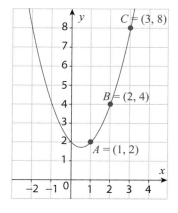

2. 50c, 20c and 10c coins were collected from a coin machine and
counted.
The total value of the coins was €32.
When counting the coins, the cashier made piles of similar coins.
She noticed that:
  (i) twice the number of 20c coins, added to the number of 10c coins
       equalled three times the number of 50c coins.
  (ii) four times the number of 50c coins added to the number of 10c coins equalled six times the
       number of 20c coins.
Find the number of each type of coin by:
letting $x = $ the number of 50c coins,
letting $y = $ the number of 20c coins,
and letting $z = $ the number of 10c coins in the machine.

3. The circle shown has the equation
  $$x^2 + y^2 + ax + by + c = 0.$$
Using the points: $A\ (x, y) = (1, 2)$
                  $B\ (x, y) = (2, 1)$
                  $C\ (x, y) = (1, 0)$
form three equations in a, b, c.
Solve the equations to find the equation of the circle.

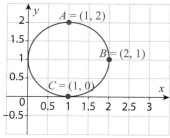

Using your result show that the circle also passes through the point (0, 1).

4. Denise wrote three numbers on the back of her copy and asked Damien to work out the numbers
given the following three clues:
  (i) the sum of the three numbers was 13
  (ii) the third number was twice the second number
  (iii) the sum of the first and second number was 2 less than the sum of the second and
       third numbers.
       Find the three numbers.

Part 10: Perfect squares / Completing the square

Looking ahead

>>

- Some quadratic expressions have two identical factors
  - these expressions are called **perfect squares**.
  - $x^2 + 8x + 16 = (x + 4)(x + 4) = (x + 4)^2$ is a perfect square.
  - $x^2 - 10x + 25 = (x - 5)(x - 5) = (x - 5)^2$ is a perfect square.
  - Graphs of $y = x^2 + 8x + 16$
    and $y = x^2 - 10x + 25$

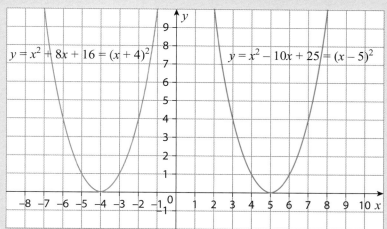

- Equations containing perfect squares are easily solved
  - $x^2 + 8x + 16 = 5$
    $\therefore (x + 4)^2 = 5$
    $x + 4 = \pm\sqrt{5}$
    $x = -4 \pm \sqrt{5}$ (this answer is written in *surd form*)
- All quadratic equations can be solved by ***completing the square***.
- Given $x^2 + 16x$, to complete the square
  add and subtract half the coefficient of x squared.
  - $x^2 + 16x = x^2 + 16x + 64 - 64$ .... (half of 16 = 8 and $8^2 = 64$)
    $= (x^2 + 16x + 64) - 64$
    $= (x + 8)(x + 8) - 64$
    $= (x + 8)^2 - 64$

Example   **>>**

Write down the equation for the graph of the function shown.

Answer: The graph has two equal roots at $x = 3$
$\therefore$ the factors are $(x - 3)(x - 3) = (x - 3)^2$
$\therefore y = (x - 3)^2$

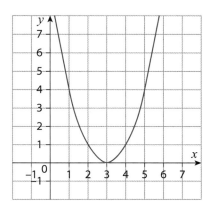

10.1 Check-up

1. Write an equation for each of the graphs shown.

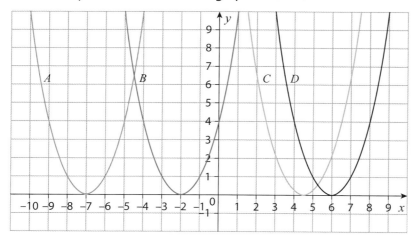

2. Identify each of the following graphs:

$y = (x - 6)^2$

$y = (x + 1)^2$

$y = (x - 2.5)^2$

$y = -(x - 3)^2$

$y = -(x + 4)^2$

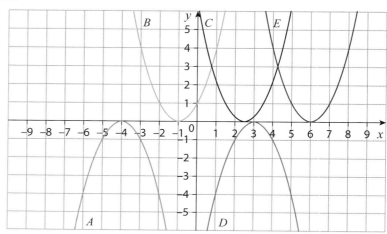

Example

Complete the square of $x^2 + 10x$ and hence solve the equation $x^2 + 10x = 9$.

Answer: $x^2 + 10x = x^2 + 10x + 25 - 25$ ... add and subtract the coefficient of x divided by 2 and squared.

$$x^2 + 10x = (x + 5)^2 - 25$$

$$\therefore (x + 5)^2 - 25 = 9$$

$$(x + 5)^2 \quad = 9 + 25$$

$$(x + 5)^2 \quad = 34$$

$$x + 5 = \pm\sqrt{34}$$

$$x \quad = -5 \pm \sqrt{34}$$

Talking Point

Answers in *surd form* are exact (uncorrected) answers

If $x^2 = 40$ $\qquad x = \pm\sqrt{40}$

10.2 Check-up

1. By taking the square root of both sides, find the value of x in each of the following:
   (i) $(x - 3)^2 = 49$
   (ii) $(x + 2)^2 = 4$
   (iii) $(x - 1)^2 = 25$
   (iv) $(2x + 3)^2 = 36$
   (v) $(3x - 4)^2 = 16$
   (vi) $(2x - 1)^2 = 5$

2. Solve the following equations and verify your answers:
   (i) $(x - 5)^2 = 36$
   (ii) $(5x + 1)^2 = 100$
   (iii) $(4x + 7)^2 = 49$

3. Complete the square for each of the expressions, writing your answer in the form $(x + a)^2 + b$:
   (i) $x^2 + 4x$
   (ii) $x^2 - 4x$
   (iii) $x^2 + 16x$
   (iv) $x^2 + 12x$
   (v) $x^2 - 20x$
   (vi) $x^2 + 5x$

Example

Solve $x^2 - 8x + 5 = 0$, by completing the square, leaving your answer in surd form.

Answer:
$$x^2 - 8x + 5 = 0,$$
$$x^2 - 8x = -5,$$
$$x^2 - 8x + 16 - 16 = -5 \quad \text{... add and subtract the coefficient of } x \text{ divided by 2 and squared.}$$
$$\therefore (x - 4)^2 - 16 = -5$$
$$(x - 4)^2 = -5 + 16$$
$$(x - 4)^2 = 11$$
$$x - 4 = \pm\sqrt{11}$$
$$x = 4 \pm \sqrt{11} \quad \text{i.e. } x = 4 + \sqrt{11}, \text{ and } x = 4 - \sqrt{11}$$

10.3 Check-up

1. By completing the square, solve each of the following equations leaving your answers in surd form:
   (i) $x^2 + 4x = 5$
   (ii) $x^2 - 4x = 1$
   (iii) $x^2 + 12x = 6$
   (iv) $x^2 + 8x = 2$
   (v) $x^2 + 4x + 1 = 0$
   (vi) $x^2 - 4x - 2 = 0$
   (vii) $x^2 + 5x - 1 = 0$

2. Copy and complete the following lines by filling in the brackets.

$$ax^2 + bx + c = 0$$
$$\Rightarrow ax^2 + bx = -(\quad)$$
$$\Rightarrow a\left(x^2 + \frac{(\;)}{(\;)}x\right) = -(\quad)$$
$$\Rightarrow \left(x^2 + \frac{(\;)}{(\;)}x\right) = -\frac{c}{a}$$
$$\Rightarrow \left(x^2 + \frac{(\;)}{(\;)}x + \frac{b^2}{4a^2} - \frac{(\;)}{(\;)}\right) = -\frac{c}{a}$$
$$\Rightarrow \left(x + \frac{b}{2a}\right)^2 - \frac{(\;)}{(\;)} = -\frac{c}{a}$$
$$\Rightarrow \left(x + \frac{b}{2a}\right)^2 = \frac{b^2}{4a^2} - \frac{c}{a}$$

$$\Rightarrow \left(x + \frac{b}{2a}\right)^2 = \frac{b^2 - (\quad)}{4a^2}$$
$$\Rightarrow x + \frac{b}{2a} = \pm\sqrt{\frac{b^2 - (\quad)}{4a^2}}$$
$$\Rightarrow x + \frac{b}{2a} = \frac{\pm\sqrt{b^2 - (\quad)}}{2a}$$
$$x = \frac{-b}{2a} \pm \frac{\sqrt{b^2 - (\quad)}}{2a}$$
$$x = \frac{-b \pm \sqrt{b^2 - 4ac}}{2a}$$

ALGEBRA TEST

1. Simplify: $4(3 - 5x) - 3(2 - 7x)$

2. Find the factors of the expression $3x^2 - 10x - 8$.
Hence find functions $g(x)$ and $h(x)$ so that:
  (i) $(x - 4) \times g(x) = 3x^2 - 10x - 8$
  (ii) $(4 - x) \times h(x) = 3x^2 - 10x - 8$

3. Find the point of intersection of the lines:
$3x + 4y - 20 = 0$ and $2x - y - 6 = 0$.
Find also the points where the lines intersect
the x-axis. (Note, the x-axis has the equation
$y = 0$)
Hence find the area of the triangle enclosed
by the lines and the x – axis.

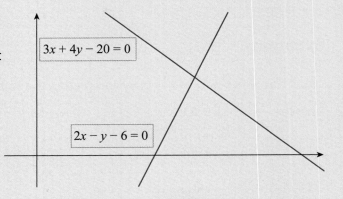

4. Show that $x^2 + 10x + 7 = (x + 5)^2 - 18$
Hence solve the equation $x^2 + 10x + 7 = 0$, giving your answer in surd form.

5. The curve $y = ax^2 + bx + c$ passes through the
points $A(1, 1)$, $B(2, 3)$ and $C(4, 1)$ as shown.

Using the points write 3 simultaneous equations with
the unknowns a, b and c.

Solve the equations for a, b and c.

Show that the point $(3, 3)$ is also on the curve but that the
point $(5, -2)$ is not on the curve.

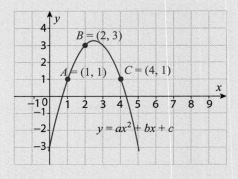

6. Seán's dad is 30 years older than Seán.
In four years time, Seán's dad will be three times as old as Seán.
Write an equation connecting Sean's and his dad's age in four years time.
How old are Seán and his dad now?

7. By completing the square, solve the equations:
  (i) $x^2 - 2x = 5$
  (ii) $x^2 - 10x - 3 = 0$
  (iii) $2x^2 - 10x - 2 = 0$ (Factorise the 2 before proceeding to complete the square)

8. Find the y-axis intercept (where $x = 0$) of each of the following and hence draw a rough
sketch of each equation.
  (i) $y = (x + 2)^2$ (ii) $y = -(x - 3)^2$

2 Geometry *through history*

- The mathematics of *lines, shapes and spaces*
- A point in space has three dimensions $\{x, y, z\}$
- A point on a plane has two dimensions $\{x, y\}$
- A point on a line has one dimension $\{x\}$

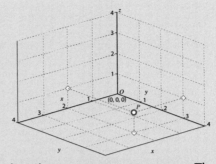

2000 BC	***Egyptian Rhind Papyrus*** contains the earliest known text on geometry. The principles outlined in these books were used to address questions arising from surveying, construction and astronomy.
300 BC	***Euclid of Alexandria*** wrote one of the most successful textbooks in the history of mathematics. His book called *Elements* consists of 13 books on proportions, the theory of numbers and geometry theorems in two and three-dimensional space. After the invention of the printing press in 1440, it was one of the first books printed and more than 1000 editions have been published since.

250 BC	***Archimedes*** was born in Syracuse on the island of Sicily. He was a renowned scientist and mathematician, credited with deriving an accurate approximation for π (*pi*), enabling him to calculate the area of any circle quickly.

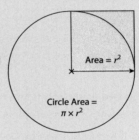

1637 AD	***René Descartes*** (1596–1650), a French mathematician, devised a coordinate system to locate points on a plane. This meant that lines and curves could be represented using algebraic equations. The plane is called the Cartesian plane after the Latin version of his name, *Cartesius*.

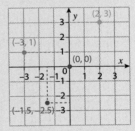

2020s	***Modern Geometry*** has many applications particularly in the fields of architecture, engineering, physics and art.

Calatrava Bridge

Geometry 1: Coordinate geometry of the line
Part 1: Equation of a line

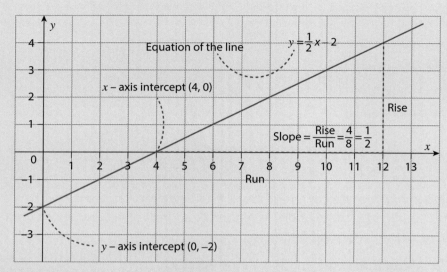

- Equation of a line is a rule linking the x and y coordinates of every point on a line:
  - $y = mx + c$, is the slope (m) / intercept (c) equation of a line.
  - $ax + by + c = 0$, is the general equation of a line.
  - $y - y_1 = m(x - x_1)$, is the equation of a line with slope m passing through the point (x_1, y_1).
- Slope of a line is defined as,

$$\text{Slope} = \frac{\text{Rise}}{\text{Run}} = \frac{y_2 - y_1}{x_2 - x_1} \text{ for any two points } (x_1, y_1), (x_2, y_2) \text{ on the line.}$$

Example

Find the equation of the line that passes through the point (8, 2) and has a slope of 2.

  (i) Find the point where the line crosses the x – axis.

 (ii) Find the point where the line crosses the y – axis.

(iii) Find the angle the line makes with the x – axis.

Answer: $y - y_1 = m(x - x_1)$

$y - 2 = 2(x - 8)$… where $(x_1, y_1) = (8, 2)$

$y - 2 = 2x - 16$

$y = 2x - 16 + 2$

$y = 2x - 14$, is the equation of the line.

 (i) Let $y = 0$,

$0 = 2x - 14$.

$2x = 14 \therefore x = 7 \Rightarrow (7, 0)$ is the point where the line crosses the x – axis.

(ii) Let $x = 0$,

$y = 2(0) - 14$.

$y = -14$

$\Rightarrow (0, -14)$ is the point where the line crosses the y – axis.

Talking Point

From trigonometry we note that,

$$\frac{\text{Rise}}{\text{Run}} = \tan\theta = m$$

where $\theta =$ the angle the line makes with the positive sense of the x – axis.

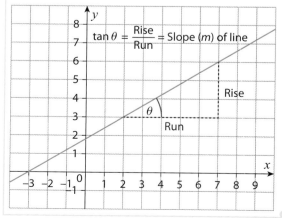

(iii) The slope of the line $= \tan\theta = m$

$$\therefore \ \tan\theta = 2$$
$$\therefore \quad \theta = \tan^{-1} 2 = 63.43°$$

1.1 Check-up

<<

Write each of the following equations in the form $y = mx + c$:

1. $4x - y = 12$ **2.** $2x - 4y = 18$ **3.** $3x - 6y = 12$

4. $2x + \dfrac{y}{2} = 8$ **5.** $\dfrac{2y}{3} - 4x = 6$ **6.** $4x + 2y = 9$

7. $2x - y - 6 = 0$ **8.** $x - 3y - 15 = 0$ **9.** $3x + \dfrac{y}{2} - 4 = 0$

1.2 Check-up

<<

Find the slope of each of the following lines:

1. $y = 2x + 2$ **2.** $y = -3x - 18$ **3.** $y = \dfrac{x}{2} + 1$

4. $x + \dfrac{y}{3} = 8$ **5.** $\dfrac{y}{5} - x = 6$ **6.** $4x - y = 7$

7. $x + 5y - 5 = 0$ **8.** $10x - 2y - 7 = 0$ **9.** $3x + \dfrac{y}{4} - 1 = 0$

1.3 Check-up

<<

By finding the coordinates of two points (M and N), find the slope and the y – axis intercept of each line shown in the diagram.

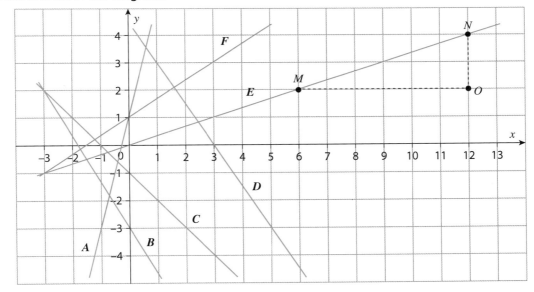

1. Line A **2.** Line B.   **3.** Line C.   **4.** Line D.   **5.** Line E.   **6.** Line F.

1.4 Check-up

<<

Using the information given, find the equation of each of the following lines.
Give the answer in the form $ax + by + c = 0$.

1. Line A has a slope of 3 and a y – axis intercept of $(0, -2)$.

2. Line B has a slope of -1 and contains the point $(0, 3)$.

3. Line C has a slope of $\dfrac{1}{2}$ and contains the point $(1, 1)$.

4. Line D has a slope of 5 and a y – axis intercept of (0, 2).

5. Line E has a slope of 3 and contains the point (2, 5).

6. Line F has a slope of $\dfrac{2}{3}$ and passes through the point (5, 0).

7. Line G has a slope of $\dfrac{-1}{6}$ and contains the point (0, −3).

1.5 Check-up

<<

Using the coordinates of the points in the diagram, find the equation of each line.
(Note: find the slope of each line first)
Give the answer in the form $ax + by + c = 0$

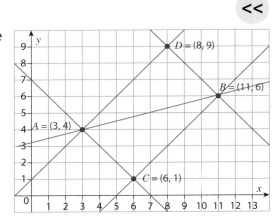

1. Line AD
2. Line AB
3. Line AC
4. Line DB
5. Line BC

Part 2: Parallel and Perpendicular lines

Looking back

<<

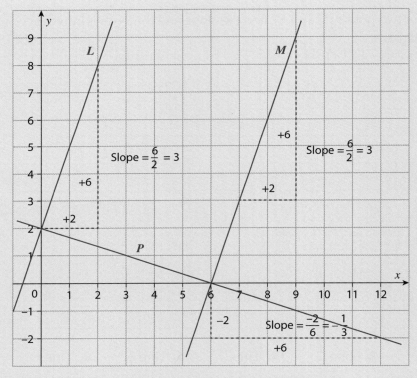

- L is parallel to M, written as $L \parallel M \Rightarrow$ they have the same slope, $m_L = m_M$.

- P is perpendicular to M (and L), written as $P \perp M \Rightarrow m_P = \dfrac{-1}{m_L}$

$$\Rightarrow m_P \cdot m_L = -1$$

- If the product of two slopes $= -1$, then the lines are perpendicular.

Example

$2x + y - 4 = 0$ is the equation of line L.

(i) Find the equation of the line K parallel to L that passes through the point (3, 2).

(ii) Find the equation of the line M perpendicular to L that passes through the point (3, 2).

Answer: $2x + y - 4 = 0$

$$y = -2x + 4$$

The slope of $L = -2$

(i) The slope parallel to $L = -2$

$$y - y_1 = m(x - x_1)$$

$$y - 2 = -2(x - 3) \ldots \text{using point (3, 2)}$$

$$y - 2 = -2x + 6$$

$$2x + y - 8 = 0 \ldots \text{equation of } K$$

Talking Point

Slope	Perpendicular slope
4	$\dfrac{-1}{4}$
$\dfrac{1}{3}$	-3
-5	$\dfrac{1}{5}$

To find a perpendicular slope,
'Invert the slope and
change the sign'.
Test for perpendicular lines,
$$m_P . m_L = -1$$
i.e. Slope $\times$ Perpendicular slope $= -1$
$$-5 \times \frac{1}{5} = -1$$

(ii) The slope perpendicular to $L = \dfrac{1}{2} \ldots - \left(\dfrac{1}{-2}\right)$

$$y - y_1 = m(x - x_1)$$

$$y - 2 = \frac{1}{2}(x - 3)$$

$$2y - 4 = x - 3$$

$$x - 2y + 1 = 0 \ldots \text{equation of } M$$

Talking Point

If $l = ax + by + c = 0$

$$\Rightarrow by = -ax - c$$

$$\Rightarrow y = -\frac{a}{b}x - \frac{c}{b}$$

$\therefore$ Slope of line $l = -\dfrac{a}{b}$

$\therefore$ Slope of $\perp$ line $= \dfrac{b}{a}$

Equ of $\perp$ line $= bx - ay + k = 0$

2.1 Check-up

<<

Find the equation of each of the following lines.
Give the answer in the form $ax + by + c = 0$.

1. Line A parallel to $2x + y - 3 = 0$, passing through the point $(2, 0)$.

2. Line B parallel to $x - 2y + 4 = 0$, passing through the point $(0, 5)$.

3. Line C parallel to $4x - y + 1 = 0$, passing through the point $(1, 1)$.

4. Line D perpendicular to $x + 4y - 1 = 0$, passing through the point $(2, 2)$.

5. Line E perpendicular to $2x - y + 6 = 0$, passing through the point $(0, 1)$.

6. Line F perpendicular $x + y + 1 = 0$, passing through the point $(1, 4)$.

2.2 Check-up

<<

Examine the following list of equations of lines.
State which lines are parallel and which are perpendicular.

A: $2x + y - 3 = 0$

B: $x - 2y + 4 = 0$

C: $4x - y + 1 = 0$

D: $x + 4y - 1 = 0$

E: $2x - y + 6 = 0$

F: $x + y + 1 = 0$

G: $x - y + 6 = 0$

H: $8x - 2y + 4 = 0$

I: $3x + 6y + 1 = 0$

J: $5x + y + 4 = 0$

K: $x - 5y - 1 = 0$

L: $x + 2y + 5 = 0$

2.3 Check-up

<<

1. A tangent line is a line that touches a circle at one point only and is perpendicular to the radius at that point. Find the equation of the tangent at the point $(8, 2)$ on a circle with centre $(5, 5)$ as shown.

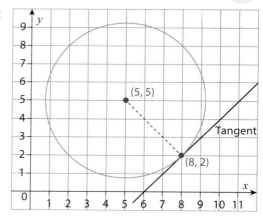

2. Show that a line segment joining C to A is $\perp$ to the line segment AB.
Find the equation of a line, l, through C parallel to AB.
Find the equation of a line, k, through B perpendicular to AB.
Find the point of intersection of l and k, call this point D.
Prove that $ABDC$ is a square.

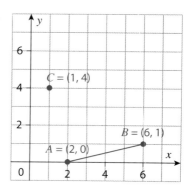

Part 3: Distance of a point from a line

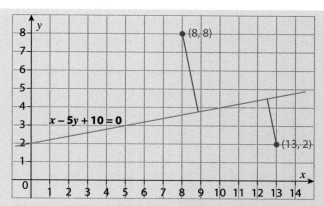

- To find the (perpendicular) distance from a point to a line.
    - Let the point be (x_1, y_1)
    - Let the line be $ax + by + c = 0$
    - The distance $d = \left| \dfrac{ax_1 + by_1 + c}{\sqrt{a^2 + b^2}} \right|$

$$\dfrac{(x_1, y_1)}{\substack{ax + by + c \\ \sqrt{a^2 + b^2}}}$$

Example   >>

Find the distance (d) from the point (i) (8, 8) (ii) (13, 2) to the line $x - 5y + 10 = 0$

Answer: (i) Point: $(x_1, y_1) = (8, 8)$

Line: $x - 5y + 10 = 0$

$a = 1, b = -5, c = 10$

Distance: $d = \left| \dfrac{ax_1 + by_1 + c}{\sqrt{a^2 + b^2}} \right|$

$d = \left| \dfrac{(1)(8) + (-5)(8) + 10}{\sqrt{(1)^2 + (-5)^2}} \right|$

$d = |-4.3| = 4.3$

(ii) Point: $(x_1, y_1) = (13, 2)$

Line: $x - 5y + 10 = 0$

$\therefore a = 1, b = -5, c = 10$

$d = \left| \dfrac{ax_1 + by_1 + c}{\sqrt{a^2 + b^2}} \right|$

$d = \left| \dfrac{(1)(13) + (-5)(2) + 10}{\sqrt{(1)^2 + (-5)^2}} \right|$

$d = |2.5| = 2.5$

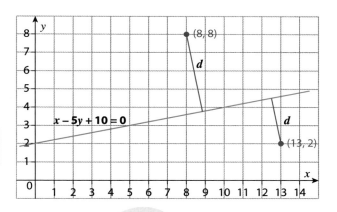

Talking Point

Distance has no direction or sign (+ or −).
Magnitude signs (||) are used to get the absolute value of the distance, d.

3.1 Check-up

Find the distances from the given points to the lines, correct to 1 place of decimals:

1. From $(2, 0)$ to the line $2x + y - 3 = 0$

2. From $(4, 1)$ to the line $x - 2y + 4 = 0$

3. From $(1, 5)$ to the line $x + 4y - 1 = 0$

4. From $(0, -3)$ to the line $2x - y + 6 = 0$

5. From $(0, 0)$ to the line $x + y + 1 = 0$

6. From $(3, 0)$ to the line $x + y + 1 = 0$

7. From $(0, -4)$ to the line $x + y + 1 = 0$

8. From $(-2, -2)$ to the line $x + y + 1 = 0$

Talking Point

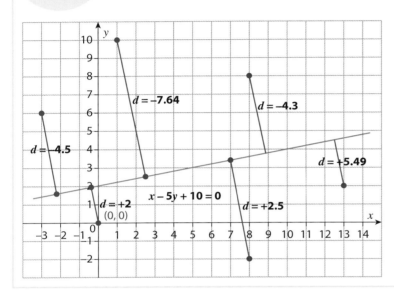

We note that points on the same side of a line have the same **sign** before the magnitude is taken.

9. The flight path between airports A and B is shown.
The coordinates on a Cartesian (x, y) plane of A are $(-2, 1)$ and B $(13, 7)$.
   (i) Find the slope of the flight path.
   (ii) Find the equation of the flight path between A and B, giving your answer in the form of $ax + by + c = 0$
   (iii) The residents of the town Carraig, C $(2, 5)$, claim that they suffer from greater noise pollution than their neighbours in Daingean, D $(9, 3)$, due to air traffic because the flight path is closer to their town. Determine if they are correct.

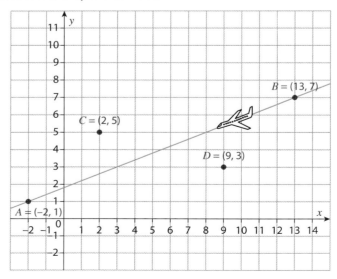

Geometry 2: Coordinate geometry of the circle
Part 4: The equation of a circle

Looking ahead >>

- A circle is a set of points all equidistant from a fixed point called the *centre* of the circle.
- The distance from the centre to any point on the circumference is called the radius.
- Every point on a circle has coordinates (x, y).
- If the centre of the circle is $(0, 0)$, using the theorem of Pythagoras,

$$x^2 + y^2 = (\text{radius})^2$$

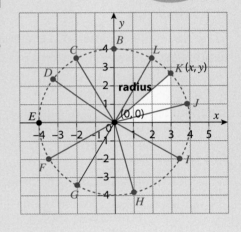

Example

>>

A circle with centre $(0, 0)$ contains the point $(3, 4)$.

Find the equation of the circle.

Answer: The distance from $(0, 0)$ to $(3, 4)$ is the radius of the circle.

$$\therefore r = \sqrt{(x_2 - x_1)^2 + (y_2 - y_1)^2}$$
$$r = \sqrt{(4 - 0)^2 + (3 - 0)^2}$$
$$r = \sqrt{16 + 9} = \sqrt{25} = 5$$

The equation of the circle is $x^2 + y^2 = (5)^2 = 25$

Talking Point

If a point (x, y) is on the circumference of a circle with centre $(0, 0)$ then

$$x^2 + y^2 = (\text{radius})^2$$

e.g. $(3, 4)$

$$3^2 + 4^2 = (\text{radius})^2$$
$$25 = (\text{radius})^2$$
$$5 = \text{radius}$$

Example

>>

Find the radius of each of the following circles:

(i) $x^2 + y^2 = 100$ (ii) $x^2 + y^2 = 12$ (iii) $4x^2 + 4y^2 = 9$

Answer: (i) $x^2 + y^2 = 100$ $\Rightarrow (\text{radius})^2 = 100$
$$\Rightarrow \text{radius} = \sqrt{100} = 10$$

(ii) $x^2 + y^2 = 12$ $\Rightarrow (\text{radius})^2 = 12$
$$\Rightarrow \text{radius} = \sqrt{12} = 2\sqrt{3}$$

(iii) $4x^2 + 4y^2 = 9 \quad \Rightarrow x^2 + y^2 = \dfrac{9}{4}$

$\qquad\qquad\qquad\quad \Rightarrow (\text{radius})^2 = \dfrac{9}{4}$

$\qquad\qquad\qquad\quad \Rightarrow \text{radius} = \sqrt{\dfrac{9}{4}} = \dfrac{3}{2}$

4.1 Check-up $\quad$ >>

Write down the equation of a circle with centre $(0, 0)$ and the given radius.
Express each answer in the form $ax^2 + ay^2 = b$, where $a, b \in Z$.

1. Radius $= 2$ $\qquad$ **2.** Radius $= 5$ $\qquad$ **3.** Radius $= 3.5$ $\qquad$ **4.** Radius $= \sqrt{3}$

5. Radius $= \dfrac{1}{2}$ $\qquad$ **6.** Radius $= 2\dfrac{1}{3}$ $\qquad$ **7.** Radius $= 3\sqrt{2}$ $\qquad$ **8.** Radius $= \dfrac{\sqrt{5}}{3}$

4.2 Check-up $\quad$ >>

Write down the radius of each of these circles:

1. $x^2 + y^2 = 25$ $\qquad$ **2.** $x^2 + y^2 = 1$ $\qquad$ **3.** $x^2 + y^2 = 48$

4. $4x^2 + 4y^2 = 25$ $\qquad$ **5.** $9x^2 + 9y^2 = 4$ $\qquad$ **6.** $25x^2 + 25y^2 = 12$

4.3 Check-up $\quad$ >>

Find the equation of the circle with centre $(0, 0)$ and passing through the given points:

1. Circle A, centre $(0, 0)$ and passing through the point $(-4, 1)$

2. Circle B, centre $(0, 0)$ and passing through the point $(5, 2)$

3. Circle C, centre $(0, 0)$ and passing through the point $(3, 3)$

4. Circle D, centre $(0, 0)$ and passing through the point $(-2, -2)$

4.4 Check-up $\quad$ >>

1. The equation of circle C is $x^2 + y^2 = 9$.
If the area of circle S is twice the area of circle C,
find the radius of S, in surd form.
Hence find the equation of S.

Note: Area of a circle $= \pi r^2$.

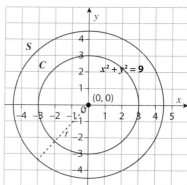

2. Sandra wants to program the robotic painter her
local club has bought to mark the lines of
the football pitch.
She lets the centre of the centre-circle on
the pitch have the coordinates $(0, 0)$ and
a point, C, on the circle therefore has
coordinates $(4.5, 0)$.
What equation does she need to insert into
the program for the robot to paint the circle
as shown?

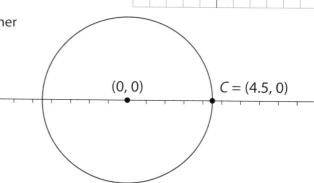

Part 5: Tangent to a circle

Looking ahead
>>

- A tangent to a circle is a line that touches the circle at **one point only**.
- The distance (d) from the centre of the circle to the tangent is the radius.

$$d = \text{radius} = \left| \frac{ax_1 + by_1 + c}{\sqrt{a^2 + b^2}} \right|$$

where $(x_1, y_1) = (0, 0)$, the coordinates of the centre of the circle.

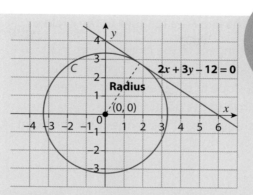

- It can be shown that a line drawn perpendicular to a tangent at the point of contact will go through the centre of the circle.
  ⇒ the slope of the line from the centre of the circle to the point of contact is **perpendicular** to the slope of the tangent.

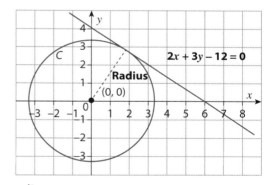

Example   >>

The line $2x + 3y - 12 = 0$ is a tangent to circle C, with centre $(0, 0)$.

(i) Find the length of the radius

(ii) Write down the equation of the circle.

Answer:

(i) $2x + 3y - 12 = 0$

$\Rightarrow a = 2, b = 3, c = -12$

$(x_1, y_1) = (0, 0),$

$$d = \text{radius} = \left| \frac{ax_1 + by_1 + c}{\sqrt{a^2 + b^2}} \right|$$

$$= \left| \frac{2(0) + 3(0) - 12}{\sqrt{(2)^2 + (3)^2}} \right|$$

$$r = \left| \frac{-12}{\sqrt{13}} \right| = \frac{12}{\sqrt{13}} = \text{the length of the radius.}$$

(ii) $x^2 + y^2 = (\text{radius})^2$

$$x^2 + y^2 = \left(\frac{12}{\sqrt{13}} \right)^2 = \frac{144}{13}$$

$$13x^2 + 13y^2 = 144$$

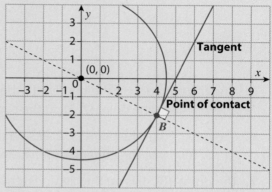

5.1 Check-up   >>

1. The line $2x + y - 5 = 0$ is a tangent to the circle with centre $(0, 0)$
   (i) Find the length of the radius of the circle.
   (ii) Write down the equation of the circle.

2. The line $4x - 3y - 25 = 0$ is a tangent to a circle c, with centre $(0, 0)$.
   Find the equation of c.

3. Find the equation of the circle, s, with centre $(0, 0)$ and radius $2\sqrt{5}$.
   t is the line $x - 2y + 10 = 0$.
   Determine if the line t is a tangent to the circle s.

4. The line t is a tangent to the circle $x^2 + y^2 = 20$.
   (i)   Show that $(4, -2)$, is a point on the circle.
   (ii) Find the slope of the line joining the centre
         of the circle to the point $(4, -2)$.
   (iii) Find the equation of the tangent t at the point $(4, -2)$.

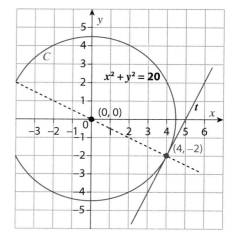

5. Find the equation of the tangent to the circle
   $x^2 + y^2 = 8$ at the point $(2, 2)$ on the circle.

6. Show   (i) that the point $(5, 2)$ lies on the circle $x^2 + y^2 = 29$.
          (ii) that the equation of the tangent to the circle at this point is $5x + 2y - 29 = 0$.

7. The point $A(3, 4)$ is on the circumference of a circle as
   shown.
   (i)   Write down the equation of the circle.
   (ii) Find the equation of a tangent to the circle at
         the point $(3, 4)$
   (iii) Find the equation of a line through $(0, 0)$
         parallel to the tangent.

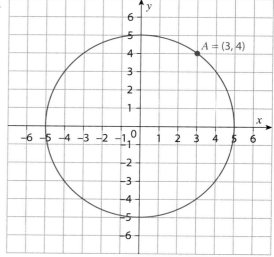

8. (i)   Find the equation of the circle, s, with centre $(0, 0)$
         that passes through the point $(3, 0)$.
   (ii) Show that the line $18x + 24y - 90 = 0$ is a
         tangent to the circle s.
   (iii) Find the y – axis intercept of the tangent
         $18x + 24y - 90 = 0$.
   (iv) The line l is a tangent to the circle s and is parallel
         to the line $18x + 24y - 90 = 0$.
         (a) By symmetry find the y – axis intercept of the
             line l.
         (b) Find the equation of l.
   (v)   The lines m and n are perpendicular tangents to
         $18x + 24y - 90 = 0$.
         Given that m intercepts the y – axis at the point $(0, 5)$, find the equations of m and n.

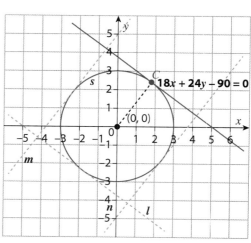

Part 6: Plane Geometry

- The sum of the angles in any triangle is 180°.
- An **equilateral** triangle has 3 equal sides and 3 equal angles each 60°.
- An **isosceles** has two equal sides and equal base angles.
- The **exterior angle** of any triangle is equal to the sum of the opposite and interior angles.
- The **interior angles** of a quadrilateral add up to 360°.
- The **diagonals of a square** are equal and bisect each other at right angles.
- The **diagonals of a rectangle** are equal and bisect each other.
- The **diagonals of a parallelogram** bisect each other.
- For **parallel** lines with a transversal, alternate angles are equal and corresponding angles are equal.

Talking Point

Vertically opposite angles are equal
$\angle x° = \angle y°$

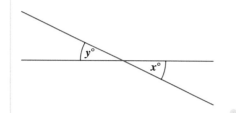

Talking Point

We show parallel lines with arrows.
AB is parallel to CD.

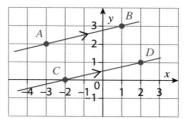

6.1 Check-up

<<

1. Find the size of the angles marked x and y in the following diagrams:

(i)

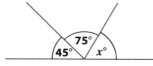

(ii)

(iii)

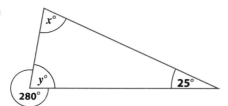

(iv)

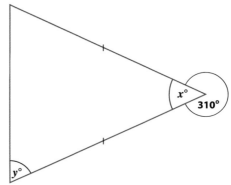

2. Find the size of the angle $a°$.

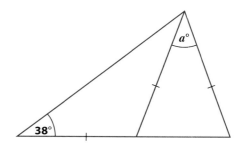

3. Find the angles marked $c°$, $d°$ and $x°$ in the following diagrams:

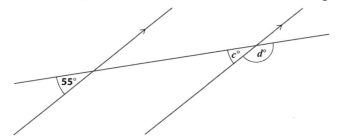

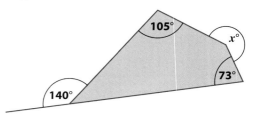

4. l and m are parallel lines and
$|AB| = |AC|$
Use this information to find the value
of the angles marked $a°$ and $c°$.

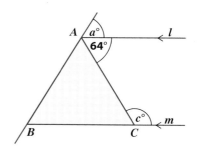

5. $ABCD$ is a rectangle leaning on an equilateral triangle
at an angle of 34°.

Find the size of $\angle ADG$.

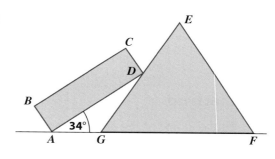

6. In this construction, ABC is a straight line.
BCD is an equilateral triangle.

Show that triangle BDE is isosceles.

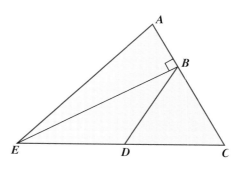

7. In the triangle ABC,
$|AC| = |AB|$

In the triangle CFB,
$|CF| = |CB|$

Calculate the value of $x°$.

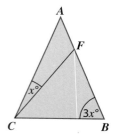

Talking Point

All quadrilaterals have four sides.
There are many *special* quadrilaterals with extra properties. These include, square, rectangle, parallelogram, rhombus, trapezium, and kite.

6.2 Check-up

<<

1. Accurately draw each of the following diagrams.

Use your diagram to complete the sentences given:

(a)

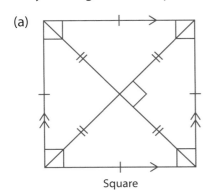

Square

- ✓ All sides have the same _____.
- ✓ All angles are _____°.
- ✓ Opposite _____ are parallel.
- ✓ Diagonals are _____ in length.
- ✓ Diagonals _____ each other at _____°

(b)

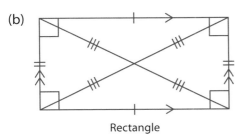

Rectangle

- ✓ All angles are _____.
- ✓ Opposite sides are _____ in length.
- ✓ Opposite sides are _____.
- ✓ Diagonals are equal in_____.
- ✓ Diagonals _____ each other.

(c)

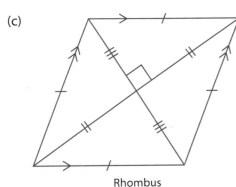

Rhombus

- ✓ All _____ are _____.
- ✓ _____ sides are _____.
- ✓ Opposite angles are _____.
- ✓ Diagonals _____ the angles of the rhombus.
- ✓ Diagonals bisect each other at _____°

(d)

Parallelogram

- ✓ Opposite _____ are _____ in length.
- ✓ _____ sides are parallel.
- ✓ Opposite angles are _____.
- ✓ Diagonals _____ each other.
- ✓ Adjacent angles add up to _____°

(e)

Trapezium

- ✓ One pair of opposite _____ are _____.

(f)

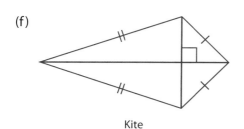

Kite

✓ Two pairs of adjacent sides are _____ in length.
✓ Two _____ triangles are formed by a diagonal.
✓ Diagonals intersect at _____.

2. Are each of the following statements *always* true?
Give your reasons for agreeing or disagreeing with each of the statements.
(a) A rhombus is a square.
(b) A square is a rhombus.
(c) A rectangle is a parallelogram.
(d) The diagonals of a parallelogram intersect at right angles.
(e) A rhombus is a parallelogram.
(f) A trapezium is a parallelogram.

3. Find the value of each unknown in the following diagrams

(a)

(b)

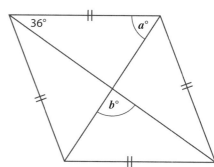

(c)

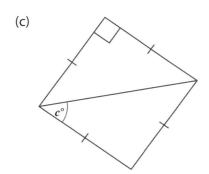

(d)

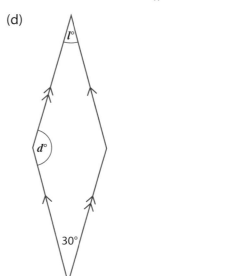

(e)

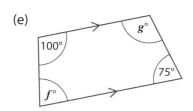

(f)

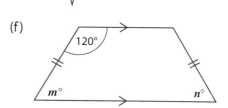

GEOMETRY TEST

1. Find the equation of the line that has a slope of 3 and that contains the point (2, 4).

2. Find the equation of the line passing through the points $A(-1, 4)$, $B(2, 3)$.

3. The line l is parallel to the line $3x - y + 4 = 0$ and passes through the point (1, 1)
   Find the equation of l.

4. Find the slope of a line perpendicular to the line $5x + 2y + 1 = 0$.

5. Use the formula, $d = \left| \dfrac{ax_1 + by_1 + c}{\sqrt{a^2 + b^2}} \right|$, to find the distance from the

   point (4, 3) to the line $x - 2y + 1 = 0$.
   Give your answer correct to 1 place of decimals

6. Write down the equation of the circle with centre (0, 0) and radius 5.

7. Find the equation of the circle with centre (0, 0) that passes through the point (2, 4).

8. Find the slope of the radius from $B(4, 4)$ to $C(3, 7)$.
   Hence find the equation of the tangent l.

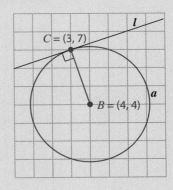

9. $ABCD$ is a rectangle.

   Using the information in the diagram
   find the size of the angle marked $x°$.
   Show all your work.

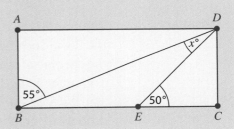

10. Write down the coordinates of the points A, C, E, F.
    Prove that these points are the vertices of a square.

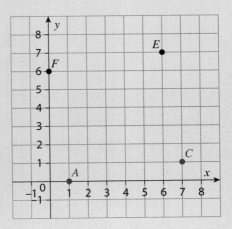

3 Probability *through history*

- The mathematics of *chance*.

- When the *chance* of something happening is certain, we say that it has a probability of 1.

- A probability of 0, means that there is no *chance* of it happening.

- $P(E)$, the probability of an event E, is always in the range

$$0 \leq P(E) \leq 1.$$

2500 BC

Dice: The oldest known dice were excavated from the legendary *Burnt City* in the south of Iran, a city that was destroyed many times by fire, over generations, before being abandoned in 2100 BC. Dice were originally made from the anklebones of hoofed animals. They were the first known ways of producing random numbers.

1650 AD

Blaise Pascal and ***Pierre de Fermat***, two French mathematicians, discussed certain gambling problems and this discussion laid the foundations for the modern theory of probability. They were particularly interested in the gambling dice game which asked you to bet on (i) getting a six on four throws of a die or (ii) getting two sixes on twenty-four throws of two dice.

At the time, most gamblers opted for 24 throws of two dice because of the large number of throws involved but it can be shown that

P(one 6 in four throws) = 0.518 while
P(two 6's in twenty four throws) = 0.491

There is a slightly better chance of rolling a 6 in 4 rolls of the die.

1760 AD

Thomas Bayes, a minister of religion in the southeast of England and a member of the Royal Society in London wrote, in 1763, an '*Essay towards solving a problem in the doctrine of chance*'. This essay led to the development of Conditional Probability. Container A has 3 blue and 2 gold stars and container B has 4 blue and 1 gold star, if a gold star is chosen at random from any one of the containers, conditional probability enables us to find the probability that it came from a particular container A or B.

Bayes theorem is used to find the probability that the gold star came from A and is written as: P(A | gold) = [P(gold | A) × P(A)] / P(gold)

Today

Modern Probability: Probability today is used in risk analysis in the insurance industry. It is also used in engineering, disease control, sociology, finance and many other areas wherever *chance* is involved.

Probability

Part 1: Elementary probability

Looking back
<<

- An **outcome** is the result of an activity.
  - When a coin is tossed, there are two possible outcomes, *heads* or *tails*.
  - When a die is rolled, there are 6 possible outcomes.
- An **event** may be a single outcome or a collection of outcomes.
  - When a die is rolled, getting an even number is an event.
  - The event of picking an ace from a deck of cards has 4 possible outcomes.
- The **Probability scale** goes from 0 to 1. $0 \leq P(E) \leq 1$
  - If $P(E) = 0$ the event is *impossible*.
  - If $P(E) = 1$ the event is *certain*.
- **Theoretical probability** $= \dfrac{\text{The number of favourable outcomes}}{\text{The number of possible outcomes}}$

- If $P(E) = \frac{1}{5}$, the probability of E **not** occurring, $P(\text{not } E) = \frac{4}{5}$

Example

<<

A bag contains 5 blue, 7 red and 8 black counters. A counter is drawn at random from the bag.
  (i)   What is the probability of drawing a black counter?
  (ii)   What is the probability of drawing a red or black counter?
  (iii)   What is the probability of drawing a white counter?

Answer: Total number of counters $= 5 + 7 + 8 = 20$
The number of black counters $= 8$
The number of red or black counters $= 7 + 8 = 15$
The number of white counters $= 0$

$P(\text{black}) = \dfrac{8}{20} = \dfrac{2}{5}$

$P(\text{red or black}) = \dfrac{15}{20} = \dfrac{3}{4}$

$P(\text{white}) = \dfrac{0}{20} = 0$

Example

<<

Sylvia brings a box home from the bakery, containing
raspberry(R) and cream(C) doughnuts.
When a doughnut is taken at random from the box, the
probability of her picking a raspberry doughnut, P(R), = 0.2

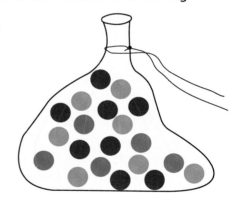

  (i)   What is the probability that a doughnut chosen at random
     is cream?
  (ii)   Mark takes a doughnut from the box and it is a raspberry doughnut.
     What is the smallest number of cream doughnuts that could be in the box?
  (iii)   After Mark, Anna takes a doughnut at random from the box, she also gets a raspberry
     doughnut.
     Now what is the smallest number of cream doughnuts that could be in the box?

Answer: (i) $P(\text{raspberry}) = 0.2$ ∴ $P(\text{cream}) = 0.8$ …there are only two possible outcomes cream or raspberry and the $P(\text{cream}) + P(\text{raspberry}) = 1$.

(ii) $P(\text{raspberry}) = 0.2 = \dfrac{2}{10} = \dfrac{1}{5}$ is the simplest fraction possible

∴ if there is a total of 5 doughnuts, there is 1 raspberry doughnut.

⇒ 4 out of 5 would be cream doughnuts.

(iii) Anna takes a second raspberry

1 raspberry doughnut ⇒ 4 cream doughnuts

2 raspberry doughnuts ⇒ 8 cream doughnuts …. $P(\text{raspberry}) = 0.2 = \dfrac{2}{10}$

Therefore, the smallest number of cream doughnuts is 8.

1.1 Check-up

<<

Calculate the probability of each of the following events.
Express your answer in its simplest form.

1. A box contains 2 red balls and 8 black balls.
A ball is chosen at random from the box.

What is the probability that the ball is (i) black (ii) red?

2. A letter is chosen at random from the word BRIDGE.

What is the probability that the letter is (i) an R (ii) a vowel?

3. Each letter of the word "AMBASSADOR" is printed on a card and placed in a box. A letter is chosen at random from the box.

What is the probability that the letter chosen is:
(i) an A (ii) a vowel (iii) a consonant?

4. 6 red marbles, 3 black marbles and 11 green marbles are placed in a bag. A marble is chosen at random.

What is the probability that the marble chosen is:
(i) green (ii) not red
(iii) red or green (iv) black or red?
(v) A marble is chosen at random and **not** returned to the bag, what is the probability that a second marble chosen at random is red if the first marble was also red?

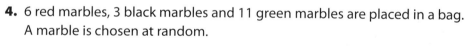

5. Numbers from 1 to 50 are written separately on pieces of card.
The numbers are placed in a box and shuffled. A number is chosen at random from the box.

What is the probability that the number chosen is:
(i) a prime number (ii) an even number (iii) an odd number
(iv) is a multiple of 6 (v) a multiple of 5 **or** a multiple of 8?

6. Copy and complete the eight possible outcomes that occur when three coins are tossed. (Heads/Tails)

Using the table find the probability that:
(i) exactly one head shows up
(ii) all three coins show the same face
(iii) at least two coins show tails up.

Coin 1	Coin 2	Coin 3

7. There are 5 white beads and an unknown number, (x) of silver beads in a box.
Write the probability of picking the silver bead at random from the box, as a fraction, in terms of x. i.e. P(silver bead) = ?

If the probability of picking a silver bead is $\frac{2}{3}$, use algebra to find x.

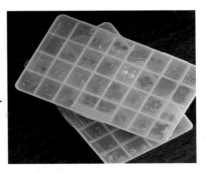

8. One of the three letters, a, b and c is chosen at random then a second and finally the third letter is chosen.
Copy and complete the **tree design** to show the number of possible outcomes.

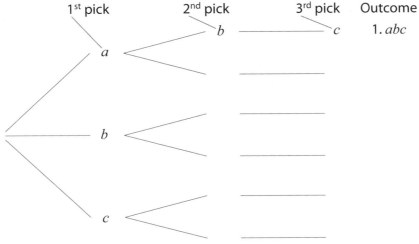

Find the probability that:
  (i)   the last letter chosen is a
 (ii) the letter order spells the word (cab)
(iii) b is the second letter chosen.

9. In an exam-centre, 200 girls and 300 boys are about to sit their final exams.

120 girls and 260 boys have already taken their seats.

If the queue is arranged at random, find the probability that the next student to enter the exam hall is a girl.

10. A certain gambling game has four possible outcomes a, b, c and d.
a, b and c are equally likely outcomes but d is twice as likely as a or b or c.
What is the probability that a would occur?

Part 2: Probability and Sets

- If two sets of data **A, B** are given, they can be represented by a Venn diagram as shown.
- The 5 regions of the Venn diagram are:
  - The elements in *A* **and** *B* $\Rightarrow A \cap B$
  - The elements in *A* **or** *B* $\Rightarrow A \cup B$
  - The elements in *A* **only** $\Rightarrow A|B$
  - The elements in *B* **only** $\Rightarrow B|A$
  - The elements **not** in *A* **nor** *B* $\Rightarrow (A \cup B)'$

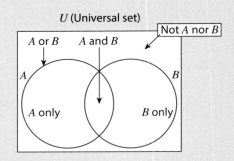

- The probability of an event is calculated by getting the cardinal number of each section of the Venn diagram.

$$\text{e.g. } P(A \textbf{ and } B) = \frac{\#(A \cap B)}{\#U}, \quad P(A \textbf{ or } B) = \frac{\#(A \cup B)}{\#U}, \quad P(A \textbf{ only}) = \frac{\#(A|B)}{\#U}$$

Example

<<

In a class of 36 students, 24 know how to play draughts, 17 know how to play chess while 6 know how to play both games.
If a student is chosen at random from the class, find the probability that he/she:
 (i)   can play both games
 (ii) can only play chess
 (iii) can play neither game.

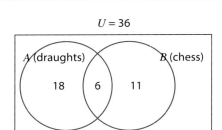

Answer: (i) The number of students who play **both** games = #$(A \cap B)$ = 6

$$\therefore P(A \cap B) = \frac{\#(A \cap B)}{\#U} = \frac{6}{36} = \frac{1}{6}$$

  (ii) The number of students who play **chess only** = #$(B|A)$ = 11

$$\therefore P(B|A) = \frac{\#(B|A)}{\#U} = \frac{11}{36}$$

  (iii) The number of students who play **draughts or chess**
  = #$(A \cup B)$ = 18 + 6 + 11 = 35
  ∴ The number of students who do **not** play **draughts nor chess**
  = #$(A \cup B)'$ = 36 − 35 = 1

$$\therefore P(A \cup B)' = \frac{\#(A \cup B)'}{\#U} = \frac{1}{36}$$

Chess: 17
Draughts and Chess: 6
Chess only:
17 − 6 = 11

2.1 Check-up

Examine each of the Venn diagrams given and work out the following probabilities.

1. 30 students replied to a survey asking them to decide on Rugby or Football as the ball sport for the term.

The results of a survey are shown in Venn diagram form. Find the probability that if a student is selected at random he chose:
   (i) Rugby **only**
   (ii) Rugby **and** Football
   (iii) **Neither** Rugby **nor** Football.

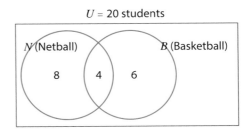

2. Using this Venn diagram if a student is chosen at random, find the probability that she plays:
   (i) Netball **or** Basketball
   (ii) Basketball **only**
   (iii) Netball **and** Basketball

3. This Venn diagram shows the language choices made by a group of students at the start of Fifth Year.
If a student is chosen at random, find the probability that he/she: (i) chose French and German
   (ii) chose German only
   (iii) chose German
   (iv) did not choose French
   (v) did not choose French or German.

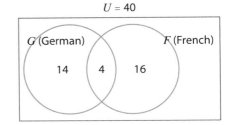

4. Claire did a quick survey of her maths class of 24 students to find out how many students had a cat or a dog.
Her results were as follows:
- 15 had neither a cat nor a dog at home
- 6 had a dog and 5 had a cat

Draw a Venn diagram to show the results of her survey.
Find the probability of picking a student at random who had a dog **and** a cat at home.

5. The Venn diagram shows the number of students who study modern languages, German, French and Spanish in First Year.

How many students are in First Year?
Find the probability that a student chosen at random studies:
   (i) None of these languages
   (ii) French
   (iii) French only
   (iv) French and German
   (v) French and German only
   (vi) French and German and Spanish
   (vii) French or German or Spanish
   (viii) French and Spanish but not German
   (ix) French or Spanish but not German.

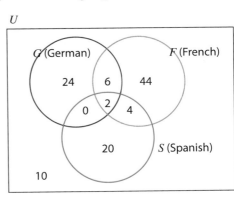

Part 3: Mutually exclusive events (Or)

Looking ahead

- An **event** may be a single outcome or a collection of outcomes:
  - When a die is rolled, getting an even number is an event.
- **Mutually exclusive events** are events that cannot occur at the same time:
  - Picking an Ace or a King from a deck of cards
  - Picking an odd number or a multiple of 4 from the number 1 to 16.
- Venn diagram of mutually exclusive events / not mutually exclusive events:

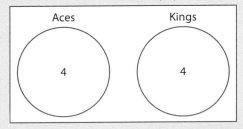

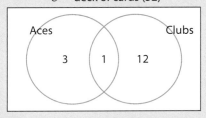

An Ace and a King cannot be picked at the same time

An Ace and a Club can be picked at the same time (the ace of clubs is common to both sets)

- If A and B are **mutually exclusive events** then $P(A \text{ or } B) = P(A) + P(B)$.

Example
>>

A card is selected at random from a deck of 52 cards.
What is the probability that the card chosen is:

    (i) a red card   (ii) a club   (iii) a red card or a club?

Answer: (i) Number of red cards = 26
                  Number of cards = 52

     (ii) Number of club cards = 13
                  Number of cards = 52

$$P(\text{red card}) = \frac{26}{52} = \frac{1}{2}$$

$$P(\text{club card}) = \frac{13}{52} = \frac{1}{4}$$

     (iii) Red cards and clubs are *mutually exclusive* events,

$$\therefore P(\text{red card or a club card}) = \frac{1}{2} + \frac{1}{4} = \frac{3}{4}$$

Talking Point

There are 13 club cards + 26 red cards in a full pack of cards = a total of 39 cards.

$$P(\text{red or club}) = \frac{39}{52} = \frac{3}{4}$$

- If two events A and B are **not** mutually exclusive, then $P(A \text{ or } B) = P(A) + P(B) - P(A \cap B)$
- $P(\text{an Ace or a Club}) = P(\text{Ace}) + P(\text{Club}) - P(\text{Ace of clubs})$

$$P(\text{Ace or Club}) = \frac{4}{52} + \frac{13}{52} - \frac{1}{52}$$

$$= \frac{16}{52}$$

$U = 52$

A number is selected at random from the integers 1 to 12 inclusive.
Find the probability that the number is:

  (i)   even   (ii)   a multiple of 3   (iii)   even or a multiple of 3.

Answer: (i)   There are 6 even numbers from 1 to 12 $P(\text{even number}) = \frac{6}{12} = \frac{1}{2}$
            Total number of numbers = 12

  (ii)   There are 4 multiples of 3 from 1 to 12 $P(\text{multiples of 3}) = \frac{4}{12} = \frac{1}{3}$
            Total number of numbers = 12

  (iii)   (even or a multiple of 3) since there are 2 numbers (6, 12) which are both even
            and multiples of 3, the probability of these occurring must be subtracted.

$$\therefore P(\text{even } \textbf{or} \text{ multiple of 3}) =$$
$$= P(\text{even}) + P(\text{multiple of 3}) - P(\text{even } \textbf{and} \text{ a multiple of 3})$$
$$= \frac{1}{2} + \frac{1}{3} - \frac{2}{12}$$
$$= \frac{6}{12} + \frac{4}{12} - \frac{2}{12} = \frac{8}{12} = \frac{2}{3}$$

Talking Point

It is possible to **list** the numbers in the sample space {1, 2, 3, 4, 5, 6, 7, 8, 9, 10, 11, 12}
that are <u>even</u> **or** <u>multiples of 3</u>. Note: 6, 12 are in both sets but are counted only once.

{2, 3, 4, **6**, 8, 9, 10, **12**}

⇒ 8 out of 12 numbers are even **or** multiples of 3.

3.1 Check-up

Find the probability of each of the following events:

1. John drives to work.
   The probability that he finds a parking space on Thomas street = 0.3
   The probability that he finds a parking space on Stevens street = 0.1
   Find the probability that he finds a parking space on either Thomas Street **or**
   Stevens Street.

2. A card is drawn at random from a pack of 52 cards.
   Find the probability that the card chosen is an Ace **or** a Jack.

3. A number is chosen at random from the integers from 1 to 25.
   Find the probability that the number chosen is a multiple of 5 **or** a multiple of 6.

4. A card is drawn at random from a full deck of cards (52 cards).
   Find the probability of each of the following possible outcomes:
   (i)   A club   (ii)   A king   (iii)   A queen of clubs
   (iv)   A red card   (v)   A ten   (vi)   A ten **or** a jack **or** a queen **or** a king

5. A Venn diagram with a sample space S is shown.
   The #S = 36
   Find the probability of each of the following events:
   (i) $P(A)$
   (ii) $P(A \text{ or } B)$
   (iii) $P(A \text{ and } B)$
   (iv) $P(A \text{ only or } B \text{ only})$

S = 36

A   B

6   2   12

6. As relaxation, Maurice plays chess two days out of the 5 days Monday to Friday and goes to the gym on the other weekdays. List the 10 possible outcomes in this event. What is the probability that he goes to the gym on Wednesday?

7. The number of outcomes in two events A and B in a sample space S, are shown in the Venn diagram given.
Find the following probabilities:

  (i) $P(A)$ (ii) $P(B)$ (iii) $P(A \cup B)$.

Now verify that $P(A \cup B) = P(A) + P(B) - P(A \cap B)$

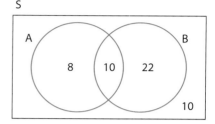

8. A survey of the type and colour of the cars parked in a local shopping centre car park is shown.
Use the data to find the probability that a car chosen at random is:

  (i) a white estate car

  (ii) a saloon car

  (iii) a black car **or** a white car

  (iv) a black car **or** an estate car

  (v) a white car **or** a saloon car.

	Saloon	Estate
Black	68	62
White	26	32
Green	6	6

9. Copy and complete the table showing the number of possible outcomes when two coins are tossed.
Find the probability of tossing two heads **or** two tails.

Coin 1	Coin 2

10. Two fair dice (a green and a blue) are thrown.
What is the probability of getting:

  (i) the same number on both dice

  (ii) a total of 8

  (iii) the same number **or** a total of 8

  (iv) the same number **or** a total of 7?

	1	2	3	4	5	6
1						
2						
3						
4						
5						
6						

11. In casinos the game of 'craps' is played by throwing two dice on a table and betting on the outcome.

You win if the dice total 7 **or** 11.

  (i) Use the table in Q10, to find P(a win)

     You lose if the dice total 2 **or** 3 **or** 12
     (This is called crapping out!)

  (ii) Use the table in Q10, to find P(a loss).

     If the total is 4, 5, 6, 8, 9 **or** 10 the game moves to another stage

  (iii) Use the table in Q10, to find P(game moves to the next stage).

  (iv) Use your answers to find P(win **or** the game moves to the next stage)

Part 4: Independent events (And)

Looking ahead >>

- An **event** may be a single outcome or a collection of outcomes:
  - When a die is rolled, getting an even number is an event
- **Independent events:** Event A and event B are independent if the event of A happening does not affect the event of B happening:
  - Tossing a coin and rolling a die are independent events
  - Rolling two dice A and B
  - Picking two cards from a deck **if** the first card is replaced before the second card is drawn
  - Shooting a number of times at a target as in archery or darts or penalties in rugby or frees in football.
- If A and B are **independent events** then $P(A \text{ and } B) = P(A) \times P(B)$

Example >>

A coin is tossed and a die is rolled.
Find the probability of getting a Tail (T) **and** a 4.

Answer: $P(T) = \dfrac{1}{2}$

$P(4) = \dfrac{1}{6}$

$P(T \text{ and } 4) = \dfrac{1}{2} \times \dfrac{1}{6} = \dfrac{1}{12}$

Dice/Coin	Head	Tail
1	1, H	1, T
2	2, H	2, T
3	3, H	3, T
4	4, H	**4, T**
5	5, H	5, T
6	6, H	6, T

As can be seen from the grid, there are 12 possible outcomes to this event.
(4 and T) is one of the 12 possible results.

4.1 Check-up >>

1. (i) A coin is tossed, what is the probability of a head?
    (ii) A coin is tossed twice, what is the probability of getting a head on the first toss **and** a head on the second toss?

2. The weather forecasters say that the probability of rain:
    (a) next Monday is 0.4 (b) next Tuesday is 0.4.
    What is the probability that it will rain next Monday **and** Tuesday?

3. A die is rolled and a coin is tossed:
    (i)   What is the total number of possible outcomes in this event?
    (ii) What is the probability of rolling an even number, $P(\text{even})$?
    (iii) What is the probability of tossing a head, $P(\text{head})$?
    (iv) What is the probability of rolling an odd number **and** a tail, $P(\text{odd number and tail})$?
    (v)   What is the probability of rolling a prime number **and** a head, $P(\text{prime and head})$?

4. A die is rolled twice. Find the probability of rolling a six on the first **and** the second throw.

5. A coin is tossed 3 times. Find the probability of getting 3 heads
i.e. $P(H \textbf{ and } H \textbf{ and } H)$

6. A die is rolled. What is the probability of **not** rolling a 6?
A die is rolled a number of times. Find the probability of rolling a 6 on:
   (i)   the 2nd roll, i.e. $P($ not a 6 **and** a 6)
   (ii) the 3rd roll, i.e. $P($not a 6 **and** not a 6 **and** a 6)

7. A card is drawn from a pack of 52 cards and then replaced.
A second card is then drawn.
What is the probability that:
   (i)   both cards are black
   (ii) both cards are kings
   (iii) the first card is a black ace **and** the second card is a diamond?

8. Three friends Chris, Mia and Jessica sit a summer maths test.
Chris has a probability of 70% of passing.
Mia has a probability of 80% of passing.
Jessica has a probability of 90% of passing.
   (i)   Find the probability that all three will pass the test.
   (ii) Find the probability that all three will fail the test.

9. Ben throws a fair coin 3 times.
Draw a tree diagram for the 3 throws showing the outcomes.

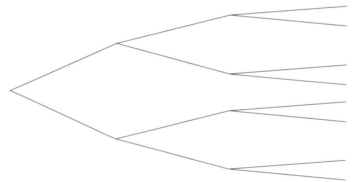

Write the probabilities of each event along each branch.
Find the probability of getting 2 heads **and** 1 tail.

Talking Point

- **Mutually exclusive** events A, $B \Rightarrow P(A \textbf{ or } B) = P(A) + P(B)$.
- **Independent** events A, $B \Rightarrow P(A \textbf{ and } B) = P(A) \times P(B)$

Sometimes an event might be broken down into a set of '*independent events*' that are in turn '*mutually exclusive*'.

Throwing a die 2 times, find the probability of rolling **at least** one 6.

Consider [1st throw and 2nd throw], the possibilities are:
$$[P(6 \textbf{ and } \text{not } 6)] \quad \textbf{or} \quad [P(\text{not } 6 \textbf{ and } 6)] \quad \textbf{or} \quad [P(6 \textbf{ and } 6)] =$$
$$[P(6) \times P(\text{not } 6)] + [P(\text{not } 6) \times P(6)] + [P(6) \times P(6)]$$

An archer shoots at a target. He has a 20% chance of hitting the gold area.
If he fires two arrows at the target, find:
- (i) the probability that both arrows hit the gold area
- (ii) the probability that only one arrow hits the gold area

Answer:
(i) First arrow hits gold **and** second arrow hits gold.
$= P(\text{gold})$ **and** $P(\text{gold}) = 0.2 \times 0.2 = 0.04$

(ii) (First arrow hits gold **and** second arrow does not hit gold) **or**
(First arrow does not hit gold **and** second arrow hits gold)
$= P(\text{gold}) \times P(\text{not gold}) + P(\text{not gold}) \times P(\text{gold})$
$= 0.2 \times 0.8 + 0.8 \times 0.2 = 0.16 + 0.16 = 0.32$

4.2 Check-up   >>

Use the **AND** and **OR** probability rules to find a value for each of the following events.

1. A die is rolled twice.
Find the probability of getting a 4 on only one of the throws.

2. A bag contains 4 red discs and 6 blue discs. A disc is drawn at random and then replaced.
A second disc is then drawn. Find the probability that:
- (i) both discs are blue.
- (ii) the first disc is blue **and** the second disc is red.
- (iii) the first disc is red **and** the second disc is blue.
- (iv) both discs are red.
- (v) both discs are the same colour.

3. A slot machine has three independent reels and pays the
Jackpot when three lemons are obtained.
Each reel has 12 pictures.
The first reel has 4 lemons, the second reel has
3 lemons and the third reel has 2 lemons:
- (i) Find the probability of winning the Jackpot.
- (ii) Find the probability of losing on the first attempt
and winning on the second attempt.
- (iii) Find the probability of losing twice **and** winning on the third attempt.
- (iv) Find the probability of winning on the first **or** second **or** third attempt.
give all answers correct to 3 places of decimals.

4. During a penalty competition:
The probability of A scoring is 0.5
The probability of B scoring is 0.7
The probability of C scoring is 0.8
Each player takes 3 penalties:
- (i) Find the probability that they all score on their first attempt.
- (ii) Find the probability that B scores on his second attempt only.
- (iii) Find the probability that A does not score on his first two attempts.
- (iv) Find the probability that C scores exactly once on his first three attempts.

5. The probability that it will rain tomorrow is $\frac{2}{3}$.

The probability that Sarah will forget her umbrella tomorrow is $\frac{3}{4}$.

Find the probability that it will rain tomorrow and Sarah will remember her umbrella.

6. A fair die is rolled three times.
Find the probability that there will be:

(i) no sixes   (ii) exactly one six   (iii) at least one six

Find also the probability that the three throws show the same number.

7. Three people selected at random were asked what day of the week their next birthday was falling.
Find the probability (correct to 3 places of decimals) that:

(i) none of the birthdays fall on a Sunday.

(ii) only one of the birthdays falls on a Sunday.

(iii) at least one of the birthdays falls on a Sunday.

8. Mary takes a multiple-choice test with 3 questions.
There are 4 answer choices (a), (b), etc for each question.
If she guesses each answer, what is the probability that:

(i) she gets all 3 correct

(ii) she gets the first two wrong but the third answer correct

(iii) she gets **only** one correct answer?

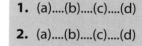

9. Three friends decide to enter a marathon race.
The probabilities that they will complete the marathon are 0.9, 0.7 and 0.6 respectively.
Assuming that the performance of each is independent of the performance of the others, find the probability that at least two of them will complete the marathon.
[Hint: By naming the runners A, B and C, list the possible outcomes for this event]

PROBABILITY TEST

1. 168 people were surveyed and asked if they owned a cat or a dog. In the survey, 79 did not own either a cat or a dog, 34 owned a cat and 69 owned a dog:

   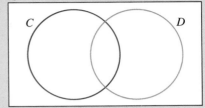

   (a) Complete the Venn-diagram (find the number who had both a cat and a dog by letting x be the number who had both and solving for x or otherwise)

   (b) If a person is chosen at random from the survey, what is the probability that the person owns (i) a cat only (ii) a cat and a dog?

2. A bag contains 6 red counters and 8 black counters. A counter is drawn at random from the bag, the colour is noted and the counter is returned to the bag. A second counter is then drawn.
   Find the probability that the first counter is red **and** the second counter is black.

3. In a basketball match, when Jack takes his **first** free throw, the probability that he is successful is 0.7
   For all following throws in the game, the probability that he is successful is:

   - 0.8 if he has been successful(S) on the previous throw.
   - 0.6 if he has been unsuccessful(U) on the previous throw.

   (a) In a game, find the probability that Jack is successful (S) with **all** of his first three throws, considering the probabilities above.

   i.e. that Jack is successful with his first **and** second **and** third throw
   i.e. $P(S, S, S) =$

   (b) Find the probability that Jack is unsuccessful with his first two throws and successful with his third.

   i.e. Jack is unsuccessful with his first **and** unsuccessful with his second **and** successful with his third.
   i.e. $P(U, U, S) =$

   (c) By filling in the chart, list all the ways Jack could be successful with his **third** free throw.

   Hence find the probability that Jack is successful with his third free throw.

4 Statistics *through history*

- A relatively modern branch of mathematics
- It involves the (i) collection (ii) organisation (iii) analysis (iv) presentation and interpretation of large amounts of information or data.
- Statistics tries to determine how two sets of data are connected.
- Averages, *mean*, *median* and *mode* give a measure of central location.
- The *range* and the *standard deviation* from the mean give a measure of the variability (or spread) of the data.
- The distribution of data can be categorised as normal, binomial, Poisson etc.

| 1774 AD | **Laplace** said that most errors in scientific observations are small and only a few errors will be large. When the observations are plotted on a graph, they create a bell-shaped curve with a peak at the most likely result or 'norm' in the middle. |

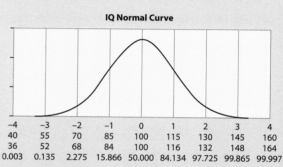

IQ Normal Curve

Standard Deviations	−4	−3	−2	−1	0	1	2	3	4
Wechsler IQ	40	55	70	85	100	115	130	145	160
Stanford–Binet IQ	36	52	68	84	100	116	132	148	164
Cumulative %	0.003	0.135	2.275	15.866	50.000	84.134	97.725	99.865	99.997

When the frequency of IQ scores is plotted, a bell-shaped curve results. 68% of people have an IQ within one standard deviation of the mean.

| 1809 AD | **Carl Friedrich Gauss** noticed that when plotting two variables, like height and weight on a graph, a *scatter* of points is produced that cannot be linked by a straight line. Gauss devised a system called 'least squares' to get the 'line of best fit' for the data. |

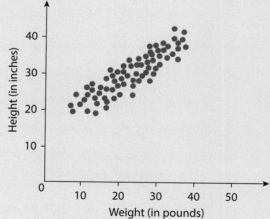

| 1835 AD | **Adolphe Quetelet** suggested that social data such as body mass, weight, height within the human population follow a bell curve shape. He started the concept of the body-mass index. |

| 1880 AD | **Francis Galton** introduced the term correlation (co-relation) to measure how well two quantities such as weight and height are related to each other. The correlation coefficient (r) can vary between -1 and $+1$. A regression line is used to estimate how one variable is connected to a second variable. Regression to the mean shows the tendency of data to even out over time. |

| 1896 AD | **Karl Pearson** developed the key statistical idea of 'standard deviation' which measures how observed values differ from the expected values. |

Part 1: Summary Statistics

- Summary statistics:
    - Measures of *central location* of a set of data.
        - **Mode:** the value that occurs most often
        - **Median:** the middle value of a set of data arranged in order
        - **Mean:** the sum of the values divided by the number of values.
    - Measures of *spread (variability)*.
        - **Range:** the highest value of a set of data minus the lowest value.
- **Frequency tables:** a way of ordering data so that it is easy to read and analyse.

Number of children in a family (x)	1	2	3	4	5	6	7
Number of families (f)	4	11	10	8	6	3	1

- Mean of a frequency table $= \dfrac{\text{Sum of } (f \times x)}{\text{Sum of } f} = \dfrac{\Sigma fx}{\Sigma f}$

Example

Find (i) mean and (ii) range of Jane and Tadgh's maths tests.

Jane: 8, 5, 9, 9, 10, 7, 5, 8, 8, 7.

Tadgh: 6, 4, 7, 8, 8, 8, 10, 10, 3, 9.

Answer:

Jane:

$$\text{Mean} = \frac{8 + 5 + 9 + 9 + 10 + 7 + 5 + 8 + 8 + 7}{10}$$

$$= 7.6$$

Range $= 10 - 4 = 6$

Tadgh:

$$\text{Mean} = \frac{6 + 4 + 7 + 8 + 8 + 8 + 10 + 10 + 3 + 9}{10}$$

$$= 7.3$$

Range $= 10 - 3 = 7$

Example

Find the (i) mode and (ii) mean values of the data table provided.

Number of children in a family (x)	1	2	3	4	5	6	7
Number of families (f)	4	11	10	8	6	3	1

Answer:

(i) The modal number of children is 2 (the value that occurs most often, 11 families had 2 children)

(ii) the mean $= \dfrac{4(1) + 11(2) + 10(3) + 8(4) + 6(5) + 3(6) + 1(7)}{4 + 11 + 10 + 8 + 6 + 3 + 1} = \dfrac{143}{43} = 3.3$ children

…(on average) per family

(Note: the computed mean value (3.3) is not a whole number, it is a statistical number giving us a sense of the central value of the data)

Talking Point

Use of a calculator to find the mean (and later the standard deviation) of a set of data is a very valuable and easy skill to acquire.

Using a Casio *fx-83GT X:*

Step 1. Press **Menu** button

Step 2. Select **2: Statistics** ....statistics mode

Step 3. Select **1: 1 – Variable** ... variables

Step 4. Input values of x, $1=$, $2=$, $3=$, $4=$, $5=$, $6=$, $7=$

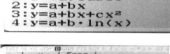

Move the cursor to the top of the **FREQ** column.

Step 5. Input values of **FREQ, *f*** (number of families)
$4=$, $11=$, $10=$, $8=$, $6=$, $3=$, $1=$

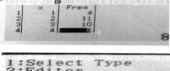

Step 6. Press **OPTN** to get this screen

Step 7. Press **3: 1 – Variable Calc** to get statistical calculations

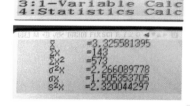

The answer is, $\bar{x} = 3.3$ as before.

Note: If the frequency column is not showing, go to SETUP (Shift menu), toggle down and press 1: Statistics
press 1: On

1.1 Check-up

1. In a maths test, the teacher gave 1 mark for each correct answer. The following table shows the results of his class:
   (i) How many students were in the class?
   (ii) Write down the mode of the data.
   (iii) Calculate the mean mark per student.
   (iv) How many students scored better than the mean mark?

Marks (x)	3	4	5	6	7	8	9
No. of students (f)	3	2	6	10	0	3	1

2. Paula has 5 people in her family. She wondered how many people are in her friends' families. She did a survey among her friends and presented her results in a frequency-table format:

Number in the family (x)	3	4	5	6	7	8	9
Frequency (f)	4	12	8	4	1	1	0

   (i) How many friends did she survey?
   (ii) What was the modal number of people in these families?
   (iii) Calculate the mean of the distribution.

1.2 Check-up

1. Two classes were asked how long it took them to complete their maths homework. The results are presented in table format.
   8 students took between 5 minutes and 15 minutes to complete their maths homework etc.

Minutes (x)	5 – 15	15 – 25	25 – 35	35 – 45
Mid – interval value	10			
No. of students (f)	8	14	28	20

(i) Using Mid interval values $\left(\dfrac{5 + 15}{2} = 10\right)$, estimate the mean time spent by the
students completing their maths homework.
Give your answer correct to 1 place of decimals.

(ii) What was the modal interval of time spent doing the maths homework?

2. The waiting times in a doctor's surgery are shown in this frequency table.

Waiting time (min)	0 – 4	4 – 8	8 – 12	12 – 16	16 – 20
Mid – interval value					
No. of patients (f)	2	6	10	12	8

(i) Find the modal waiting time for this data.

(ii) Copy and complete the table of mid-interval values and use the table to estimate
the mean waiting time correct to 1 place of decimals.

3.

Number of goals scored (x)	0	1	2	3	4	5	6	7	8	9
No. of matches (f) 2018/2019	30	79	99	68	60	24	11	6	2	1
No. of matches (f) 2019/2020	32	82	95	78	48	30	9	6	0	0

The number of goals scored in a football league in two seasons is compared in the table above.
Find the mean number of goals scored for each season correct to 2 places of decimals.

4. Explain why the mean is not a good representative of the following set of data:

$$25, 35, 45, 55, 65, 75, 890.$$

5. Find the mean of the 5 numbers, $a - 2, a - 1, a, a + 1, a + 2$.
If each number in the set of data is multiplied by 3, find the new mean.

6. The following set of data has two modes:

$$2, 3, 4, 5, 6, 7, 8, a, a + 1, 4, 3, 5$$

Find two possible values of a.

Example

$\ll$

Find the median value of each of the following sets of data:

Set A		9	11	11	15*	17	18	100	
Set B		6	10	11	13*	17*	19	25	30
Set C	Variable	0 – 10	10 – 20	20 – 30*	30 – 40	40 – 50			
	Frequency	5	4	6	3	2			

Answer: Set A, the middle value of 7 values is the 4th value
$\Rightarrow$ the median = 15

Set B, the middle value of 8 values is the mean of the middle two values $= \dfrac{13 + 17}{2} = 15$

Set C, there are 20 values $\Rightarrow$ the median is between the 10th and 11th value in order.
The 10th and 11th value are in the (20 – 30) interval.
$\Rightarrow$ the median is in the (20 – 30) interval.

1.3 Check-up

1. Rewrite the following sets of data in order of size and then write down:
   (i) median   (ii) mode   and (iii) calculate the mean.
   (a) 8, 11, 2, 5, 8, 7, 8, 2, 5   (b) 3, 3, 7, 8, 7, 9, 8, 5, 7, 11, 12.

2. The record of attendance at choir practice over 18 weeks was as follows:
   25, 28, 32, 31, 31, 34, 28, 31, 29, 28, 32, 32, 30, 29, 29, 31, 28, 28.
   (i) By arranging the data in order, find the median and mode values.
   (ii) Find the mean of the data correct to 1 place of decimals.

3. The shoe sizes of members of the basketball team are:
   10, 10, 8, 11, 10, 9, 9, 10, 11, 9, 10.
   Find the (i) mean shoe size   (ii) median shoe size   (iii) modal shoe size.

4. Construct a frequency distribution for the following 32 data points:
   5, 7, 5, 3, 1, 4, 5, 4, 3, 2, 1, 3, 4, 5, 7, 6, 8, 4, 3, 1, 5, 3, 5, 7, 3, 2, 4, 2, 6, 5, 2, 2.
   Using the table find:
   (i) the mode and median
   (ii) evaluate the mean correct to 2 places of decimals.

5. A sales representative recorded the distances he covered each day (in kilometres) over a 4-week period as:

   153, 127, 142, 82, 91,   125, 113, 105, 93, 105,
   88, 122, 96, 145, 136,   115, 107, 125, 98, 94.

   Using class intervals of 20, i.e. 80 – 99, 100 – 119, etc complete a grouped frequency chart for the data.
   Find: (i) the mean of the raw data, correct to 1 place of decimals
          (ii) the mean of the grouped frequency table using mid-interval values
          (iii) the modal class of the grouped frequency table
          (iv) the median class of the grouped frequency table.

Part 2: Mean, Median and Mode problems

Looking back
<<

- If the mean of a set of 5 data points is given as, $\dfrac{x_1 + x_2 + x_3 + x_4 + x_5}{5} = 12$
  $\Rightarrow x_1 + x_2 + x_3 + x_4 + x_5 = 5 \times 12 = 60$

Example
<<

The mean of four numbers is 19. Three of the numbers are 21, 25, 16.
Find the fourth number.

Answer: $\dfrac{21 + 25 + 16 + x}{4} = 19$

         $21 + 25 + 16 + x = 4 \times 19$

              $62 + x = 76$

                  $x = 76 - 62 = 14$

2.1 Check-up

<<

1. The mean of the following set of data is 20:

20, 18, c, 24, 23, 13

Find the value of c.

2. Joan rolled a die twenty times and placed her results in a table as shown.

Outcome	1	2	3	4	5	6
Frequency	2	4	a	7	2	3

Given that Joan found that the mean value of her data was 3.6, find the value of a.

Hence find the median and mode of the data.

3. Seán rolled a die thirty times and placed his results in a table as shown.

Outcome	1	2	3	4	5	6
Frequency	4	4	a	3	b	6

The mean value of Seán's data was 3.7, find the values of a and b.
[Hint: simultaneous equations]

4. Simon's marks in his first four tests were 80, 40, 50, 30.
When he completed his 5th and 6th test, he calculated his mean score for all six tests to be 50.
He also noticed that his modal score was 40.
What marks did he get for his 5th and 6th test?

5. The results of the monthly maths test for a class of 30 students were given as follows:
The mean mark of the 20 boys in the class was 17.4
The mean mark of the 10 girls in the class was 13.8
Calculate the mean mark for the whole class.

6. Eight numbers have a mean value of 16.
The first seven numbers have a total value of 130, determine the value of the eighth number.

7. The bar graph shows the distribution of 200 numbers from 1 to 6 inclusive.
Find:
(i) the mean
(ii) the mode
(iii) the median of the data.

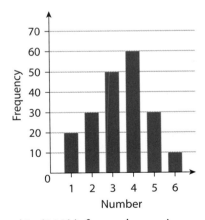

8. The table gives details of the total number in employment, measured in (000's), for each year in the period 2004 to 2013.

2004	2005	2006	2007	2008	2009	2010	2011	2012	2013
1784.8	1867	1954.9	2049.6	2060.4	1903.3	1828.6	1813.4	1773.4	1803.4

Find the (i) median (ii) mean of the data.

9. Using the data set 1, 2, 4, 5, 9, 11 investigate:
(a) if the mean of the squares of the numbers is equal to the square of the mean
(b) if the median of the squares of the numbers is equal to the square of the median.

Part 3: Interquartile range

Looking ahead

- Measures of spread (variability).
  - **Range:** the highest value of a set of data minus the lowest value.
  - **Interquartile range:** when the values are arranged in order, the value $\frac{3}{4}$ of the way up the set of values (upper quartile) **minus** the value $\frac{1}{4}$ of the way up the set of values (lower quartile).
  -
    Lower quartile   Median   Upper quartile

    1, 2, 3, 4, 4, 5, 5, 5, 6, 7, 10, 15, 15, 16, 20, 20, 21, 22, 23, 23, 23, 24, 25.

    Interquartile range

    Interquartile range $= 22 - 5 = 17$
  - If there are 23 data points, the median $= \frac{1}{2}(23 + 1) = 12^{th}$ data point

    the lower quartile $= \frac{1}{4}(23 + 1) = 6^{th}$ data point

    the upper quartile $= \frac{3}{4}(23 + 1) = 18^{th}$ data point

    for n data points the lower quartile $= \frac{1}{4}(n + 1)$, the upper quartile $= \frac{3}{4}(n + 1)$.

Example

>>

The times in minutes of a bus journey to town are:
$$15, 7, 9, 12, 9, 19, 6, 11, 9, 16, 8$$
Find the   (i)   mode   (ii)   median
           (iii)   range   (iv)   interquartile range of the data.

Answer: The data rearranged in order is, 6, 7, 8, 9, 9, 9, 11, 12, 15, 16, 19

     (i)   the mode $= 9$

     (ii)   11 data points, $\Rightarrow$ median $= \frac{1}{2}(n + 1) = \frac{1}{2}(11 + 1) = 6^{th}$ data point $= 9$

     (iii)   range $=$ (highest value $-$ lowest value) $= 19 - 6 = 13$

     (iv)   lower quartile $= \frac{1}{4}(n + 1) = \frac{1}{4}(11 + 1) = 3^{rd}$ data point $= 8$

           upper quartile $= \frac{3}{4}(n + 1) = \frac{3}{4}(11 + 1) = 9^{th}$ data point $= 15$

           The interquartile range $= 15 - 8 = 7$

Talking Point

If $\frac{1}{4}(n + 1)$ results in a fractional answer, take the *mean* value of the integers on either side of the fraction, i.e. $6\frac{1}{2}$ take the mean of the 6th and 7th values

$5\frac{1}{4}$ take the mean of the 5th and 6th values

3.1 Check-up

1. The marks for a Physics test (out of 40) for a class of 19 students are:

    37, 34, 34, 29, 27, 27, 10, 15, 40, 34, 35, 20, 29, 32, 33, 18, 37, 17, 21

    Find: (i)   the range of the marks   (ii)   the median value   (iii)   the lower quartile value
          (iv)   the upper quartile value   (v)   the interquartile range.

2. The systolic blood pressure of 15 smokers and 15 non-smokers are as follows:

Smokers	Non-smokers
122, 146, 120, 114, 124, 126, 118, 128, 130, 134, 116, 130, 135, 129, 140	114, 134, 114, 116, 138, 110, 112, 116, 132, 126, 108, 116, 120, 111, 112

    Compare the blood pressures of both groups by finding:
    (i)   range   (ii)   the median   (iii)   the lower quartile   (iv)   the upper quartile
    (v)   the interquartile range of each set of data.

3. The times taken for a P.E. class to complete an obstacle course (measured in seconds)
    at the beginning of the term and then at mid-term are given below.
    Find (correct to 1 place of decimals):
    (i)   the mean   (ii)   the range   (iii)   the median
    (iv)   the lower quartile   (v)   the upper quartile   (vi)   the interquartile range of each set of data.

    What conclusions can be drawn from the summary statistics?

Mid-term	Start of term
121, 137, 130, 128, 132, 127, 129, 131, 135, 130, 126, 120, 118, 125.	135, 142, 145, 156, 149, 134, 139, 126, 147, 152, 153, 145, 144, 148

4. Amanda played nine rounds of crazy golf while she was on holidays.
    Her scores were:

    51, 53, 50, 41, 59, 54, 66, 65, 50

    Find:
    (i)   the mean
    (ii)   the range
    (iii)   the median
    (iv)   the lower quartile
    (v)   the upper quartile
    (vi)   the interquartile range of her scores.

Talking Point

A calculator can also be used to find:
(i)   median
(ii)   Lower Quartile value (Q_1) and the
(iii)   Upper Quartile value (Q_2).

In the Statistics mode once you have inputted
the data (x), press **OPTN** and select **3** for the **1 – Variable Calc**.

On the bottom of the second page of the table of results,

$Q_1 = 8$, Med $= 9$ and $Q_2 = 15$ are found. (Using the data in the example above.)

5. A doctor recorded the blood sugar levels of a sample of 30 adults attending her surgery. The results of the survey measured in m mol/litre are:

$$3.1, 3.6, 3.7, 2.2, 2.3, 4.0, 4.4, 4.0, 5.1, 4.0, 4.5, 3.7, 3.8, 3.8, 2.3,$$

$$4.6, 4.8, 3.8, 3.9, 2.5, 3.8, 2.7, 3.9, 3.9, 5.5, 2.2, 4.7, 3.2, 3.7, 4.0$$

Arrange the data in order and hence find:
  (i) the mean (ii) the range (iii) the median
  (iv) the lower quartile (v) the upper quartile (vi) the interquartile range of the data.

6. The number of eggs collected on 11 consecutive days on a farm were: 47, 63, 0, 28, 40, 51, a, 77, 0, 13, 35.
The exact value of a was not recorded but it was definitely greater than 100.
Calculate (i) the median number of eggs   (ii) the interquartile range of this data.
Explain why mean, mode and range are not appropriate measures for this data.

Part 4: Standard deviation

Looking ahead
>>

- Standard deviation (σ) measures how much variation there is in a set of data.

  ○ It is the central pillar of all statistical investigations.

  ○ A small standard deviation $\Rightarrow$ values cluster around the mean.

  ○ A large standard deviation $\Rightarrow$ values are spread out over a large range.

  ○ In a large sample of the population, 68% of the data lies within 1 standard deviation of the mean, i.e. in the range $\bar{x} - \sigma$ to $\bar{x} + \sigma$

  ∴ knowing the standard deviation is very important!

  ○ $(x - \bar{x})$ is the deviation (difference) between each data point and the mean ($\bar{x}$).

  ○ $\Sigma(x - \bar{x})^2$ is the sum of the squared (positive) deviations of all the data points from the mean.

  ○ $\dfrac{\Sigma(x - \bar{x})^2}{n}$ = average of the squared deviations of all the data from the mean.

  ○ $\sqrt{\dfrac{\Sigma(x - \bar{x})^2}{n}}$ = the 'standard' deviation of all the data from the mean.

  ○ The symbol used for standard deviation is σ(sigma) $= \sqrt{\dfrac{\Sigma(x - \bar{x})^2}{n}}$

  ○ To calculate the standard deviation σ(sigma), we have to evaluate $\sqrt{\dfrac{\Sigma(x - \bar{x})^2}{n}}$ for the complete set of data in the survey.

Example

>>

The numbers of potatoes in a sample of 2 kg bags were 12, 15, 10, 12, 11, 13, 9, 14.
Find the mean and the standard deviation of the sample data.

Method 1.

Answer: the mean $= \dfrac{12 + 15 + 10 + 12 + 11 + 13 + 9 + 14}{8} = 12$

The standard deviation

$= \sqrt{\dfrac{(12 - 12)^2 + (15 - 12)^2 + (10 - 12)^2 + (12 - 12)^2 + (11 - 12)^2 + (13 - 12)^2 + (9 - 12)^2 + (14 - 12)^2}{8}}$

$= 1.87$

Method 2. (Using a Casio *fx 83GTX*)

> Step 1. Press **Menu** button
> Step 2. Select **2: Statistics** ....statistics mode
> Step 3. Select **1:1 – Variables** ...variables
> Step 4. Input values of x, 12=, 15=, 10=, 12=, 11=, 13=, 9=, 14=
>   (1 is automatically entered under f, if frequency is switched on)
> Step 5. Press **OPTN**
> Step 6. Press **3: 1 – Variable Calc** to get statistical variables
> Step 7. The mean $\bar{x} = 12$
>   The standard deviation $\sigma_x = 1.87$

4.1 Check-up   >>

1. Using your calculator, show that the standard deviation, σ_x is 2.3 and the mean, $\bar{x}$ is 6.1 of the set of 10 numbers, 6, 8, 4, 2, 7, 11, 5, 5, 7, 6.

2. Find the mean and standard deviation of each of the following sets of numbers. Give your answers correct to 1 place of decimals.

  (a) 1, 3, 7, 9, 10   (b) 8, 12, 10, 15   (c) 2, 4, 6, 8, 10, 12, 14

3. The total scores in a series of basketball matches were:

> 215, 224, 182, 200, 229, 219, 209, 217, 195, 162, 210, 213

Find the mean and standard deviation of these results.
Give your answer correct to 2 decimal places.

- To find the standard deviation of a grouped frequency table, we calculate:
  - $(x - \bar{x})$ is the deviation (difference) between each data point and the mean ($\bar{x}$).
  - $\sum f(x - \bar{x})^2$ is the sum of the squared (positive) deviations of all the data points from the mean *multiplied by their frequency*.
  - $\dfrac{\sum f(x - \bar{x})^2}{n}$ = average of the squared deviations of all the data points from the mean.

  $$\therefore \sigma(\text{sigma}) = \sqrt{\frac{\sum f(x - \bar{x})^2}{n}} \text{ for a grouped frequency set of data.}$$

Example

>>

A die is rolled 60 times, giving the following results:

Number (x)	1	2	3	4	5	6
Frequency (f)	6	15	2	4	16	17

Calculate a value for the mean and standard deviation of this data.

Answer:

Step 1. Press **Menu** button
Step 2. Select **2: Statistics** ....statistics mode
Step 3. Select **1:1 – Variables** ...variables
Step 4. Input values of x, 1=, 2=, 3=, 4=, 5=, 6=
Move the cursor to the top of the frequency column
      Input values of f, 6=, 15=, 2=, 4=, 16=, 17=
Step 5. Press **OPTN**
Step 6. Press **3: 1 – Variable Calc** to get statistical variables
Step 7. The mean $\bar{x} = 4$
      The standard deviation $\sigma_x = 1.83$

4.2 Check-up

>>

1. The table below shows the scores of a class quiz.
  (i) How many students took part in the quiz?
  (ii) What was the mean score?
  (iii) Calculate the standard deviation correct to 1 place of decimals.

Score	0	3	4	5	7	9	10
Frequency	1	2	2	4	6	2	3

2. The number of eggs laid by 7 hens per day was recorded over a period of 25 days.

6, 7, 5, 7, 3, 6, 5, 7, 5, 4, 5, 7, 4, 6, 7, 5, 6, 7, 6, 7, 3, 7, 5, 7, 6

  (i) Using the data, complete the frequency table shown.
  (ii) Write down the modal number of eggs laid per day.
  (iii) Find the median number of eggs laid per day.
  (iv) Calculate the mean number of eggs laid per day.
  (v) Calculate the standard deviation of the number of eggs laid per day correct to 2 places of decimals.

Number of eggs	3	4	5	6	7
Frequency					

3. Philip has two routes to get to work.
Both routes have delays due to traffic lights.
He records his time (*in minutes*) for 6 journeys on each separate route as shown in the table.
  (i) Work out the mean time taken for each journey.
  (ii) Calculate the standard deviation for each route.
  (iii) Based on your results, which route would you recommend to Philip?
      Explain your answer.

Route 1	15	15	11	17	14	12
Route 2	11	17	14	15	16	11

4. The marks obtained by 99 students in the summer examination are summarised into intervals in the table below.

Mark range	10 – 19	20 – 29	30 – 39	40 – 49	50 – 59	60 – 69	70 – 79	80 – 89
Mid-interval value (x)	14.5							84.5
Frequency (f)	8	18	25	22	16	6	3	1

Copy and complete the table by adding in the mid interval values.
Using the completed table, find:
   (i)   the modal mark interval
   (ii) the median mark interval
   (iii) the mean mark, correct to 1 place of decimals.
   (iv) the standard deviation of the marks, correct to 1 place of decimals.

5. Compare the standard deviations and the means of the following sets of numbers:
   (A) 2, 4, 5, 7, 9, 12
   (B) 12, 14, 15, 17, 19, 22
   (C) 6, 12, 15, 21, 27, 36
What conclusion can you draw by comparing the sequences and the results in the chart?

	σ_x	$\bar{x}$
A		
B		
C		

6. A local supermarket analysed the amount (€ w) each of its customers spends in the shop and completed the frequency table as shown.

Interval (€)	$0 < w \leq 20$	$20 < w \leq 30$	$30 < w \leq 40$	$40 < w \leq 50$	$50 < w \leq 60$
Mid-interval values					
Frequency	12	23	48	15	3

Copy and complete the table by adding in the mid interval values.
Use the completed table to find (correct to 1 place of decimals where needed):
   (i)   the modal interval of spend
   (ii) the median spend interval
   (iii) the mean amount of money spent by each customer
   (iv) the standard deviation of the amount spent by each customer.

Part 5: The Normal Curve and Standard deviation

Looking ahead

- When a frequency table of the height or weight of a large group of people is plotted in order, from the lowest to the highest values, the results form a bell-shaped curve called the **Normal curve**.

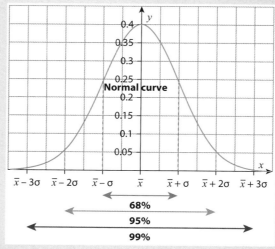

- The values form a peak (maximum point) clustered around the *mean* value $\bar{x}$.
- 68% of the values are within **1 standard deviation** ($\bar{x} - \sigma$ to $\bar{x} + \sigma$) of the mean.
- 95% of the values are within **2 standard deviations** ($\bar{x} - 2\sigma$ to $\bar{x} + 2\sigma$) of the mean.
- 99% of the values are within **3 standard deviations** ($\bar{x} - 3\sigma$ to $\bar{x} + 3\sigma$) of the mean.
- The probability of choosing a value at random from a large sample within 1 standard deviation of the mean i.e. between $\bar{x} - \sigma$ and $\bar{x} + \sigma$, is 68% = 0.68.

Example

The curve represents the normal distribution of a set of values from a survey with a mean $\bar{x} = 40$ and a standard deviation $\sigma = 5$.
If B represents the mean and A represents one standard deviation below and C represents one standard deviation above the mean:
  (i)   Write down the values of A, B and C.
  (ii) What percentage of the data lies under the curve between A and C?
  (iii) If a value is chosen at random, find the probability that it will lie between A and C.

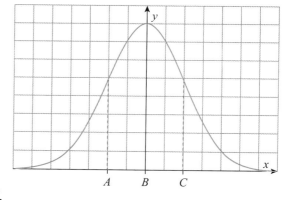

  (iv) If a value is chosen at random, find the probability that it will **not** lie between A and C.
  (v) If a value is chosen at random, find the probability that it will be less than A.

Answer:

  (i) $B = mean = 40$
        $A = $ one standard deviation below the mean $= \bar{x} - \sigma = 40 - 5 = 35$
        $C = $ one standard deviation above the mean $= \bar{x} + \sigma = 40 + 5 = 45$
  (ii) Between A and C (within one standard deviation of the mean) represents 68% of the values of the survey.
  (iii) The probability of picking a value between A and C is 68% = 0.68
  (iv) The probability of picking a value that does **not** come between A and C.
        is 100% − 68% = 32% = 0.32 (i.e. 32% of the values are less than A or greater than C)
  (v)   The probability that it will be less than A = 0.32 ÷ 2 = 0.16

5.1 Check-up

1. (i) What percentage of values of a large sample lie within 1 standard deviation of the mean?
   (ii) 95% of values of a large sample lie within how many standard deviations of the mean?
   (iii) What is the probability of choosing a value at random from a large sample that is within (a) 3 standard deviations of the mean (b) 1 standard deviation of the mean?
   (iv) What is the probability of picking a value from a large sample that is **not** within 2 standard deviations of the mean?

2. In a normal distribution, the mean $\bar{x} = 110$, and the standard deviation $\sigma = 12$.
   (i) Find the limit of the values within which 68% of the values lie.
   (ii) Find the limit of the values within which 99% of the values lie.
   (iii) What is the probability of picking a value at random from a large sample of this data that has a value between 86 and 134?

3. The mean of a large sample of values is 45 and the standard deviation is 4.
   (i) What are the limits of values within 1 standard deviation of the mean? i.e. $[(\bar{x} - \sigma), (\bar{x} + \sigma)]$.
   (ii) Find the limits of values within which 99% of the data lies.
   (iii) If a value is selected at random from the sample, find the probability that it is in within the limits $[(\bar{x} - 2\sigma), (\bar{x} + 2\sigma)]$.

4. A sample survey of plant heights has a standard deviation, $\sigma = 6$ cm
   The normal curve of the distribution is given:
   (i) Write down the value of the mean
   (ii) What percentage of values lie between 44 cm and 56 cm?
   (iii) Write down the values of A and B.

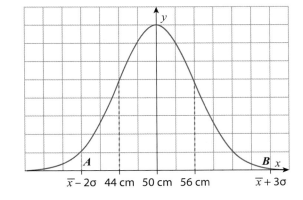

Talking Point

It is important to remember that the area beneath the normal curve represents 100%. If 68% of data lies within *one* standard deviation of the mean, then 32% is evenly distributed beneath the two tails of the curve.

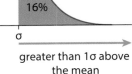

5. The mean speed of vehicles on a given road can be modelled by a normal curve
with a mean of a 54 km/h and a standard deviation of 12 km/h.
What is the speed of a vehicle that is travelling at:
  (i) one standard deviation above the mean
  (ii) two standard deviations below the mean
  (iii) three standard deviations above the mean?
  (iv) What is the probability of a vehicle travelling between 30 km/h and 78 km/h on that road?
  (v) What is the probability of a vehicle travelling between 42 km/h and 66 km/h on that road?
  (vi) What is the probability that a vehicle is travelling at a speed greater than 90 km/h?

6. The manufacturer of a particular brand of car battery
guarantees to replace any battery that does not last 3 years.
If the life of car batteries is **normally** distributed with a mean life
of 4 years and 4 months with a standard deviation of 8 months
approximately, what percentage of batteries would the manufacturer
expect to replace?

7. The distribution of times taken by workers to get
to their place of work can be modelled by a normal
distribution.
The mean time is 40 minutes with a standard
deviation of 12 minutes.
Note: the total area under the curve is 100%.
  (i) What percentage of workers take longer than
      40 minutes to get to work?
  (ii) What percentage of workers take between
      28 min and 52 min?

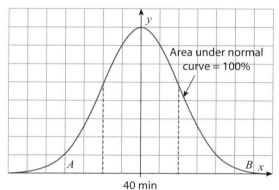

  (iii) What are the limits of the times for 95% of the workers?
By considering the symmetry of the curve find the probability:
  (iv) of selecting a worker who takes *more than* 64 min to get to work
  (v) of selecting a worker who takes *less than* 28 minutes to get to work.

8. The marks awarded in an examination are normally distributed with a mean of 74 marks.
If 95% of the marks are within the limits of [62 marks, 86 marks], work out the standard deviation
of the distribution of the marks.

9. The heights of a random sample of Christmas trees were measured and the results
tabulated as follows: (*h* is the height of the tree)

Height (m)	$0.5 < h \leq 1.0$	$1.0 < h \leq 1.5$	$1.5 < h \leq 2.0$	$2.0 < h \leq 2.5$	$2.5 < h \leq 3.0$
Mid-interval values	0.75				
Frequency	8	26	48	15	3

  (i) Complete the table using the mid-interval values.
  (ii) Calculate the mean and the standard deviation of the sample, correct to 2 places of decimals.
  (iii) Find the height limits for 95% of the trees selected at random from a large sample of trees.

10. Martin said that his box had 45 smarties in it.
If the number of smarties is **normally** distributed with a mean of 40
smarties per box and a standard deviation of 1.5 smarties, what is the
probability of Martin getting 45 smarties in his box?

STATISTICS TEST

1. Find (i) the mean (ii) the median (iii) the mode of the Mia's maths test scores:

5, 5, 6, 6, 7, 7, 7, 7, 9

2. Copy and complete the grouped frequency data table below.

Data	0 – 3	4 – 7	8 – 11	12 – 15	16 – 19
Mid-interval value					
Frequency	2	3	4	9	2

Using the table and a calculator find:
(i) the mean (ii) the median and (iii) the modal class of the data.

3. Find (i) the range (ii) the median (iii) the lower quartile (iv) the upper quartile
and (v) the interquartile range of the following sets of data:
  (a) 3, 3, 4, 5, 5, 6, 6, 6, 8
  (b) 3, 3, 4, 5, 5, 6, 6, 6, 80
Explain the effect of the outlier in set (b)

4. On a school field trip, a quadrat was used to collect the following data about plant life on a local beach.
Find the standard deviation of the data using a calculator:
(Give your answer correct to 2 places of decimals)

$$A = \{7, 8, 9, 9, 11, 12, 13, 13, 13, 14\}.$$

If 3 is added to each of the data points in A, determine how the standard deviation is affected.

5. The heights of young women are normally distributed with a mean $\mu = 160$ cm and a standard deviation $\sigma = 8$ cm.
  (i) What percentage of the women would you expect to have heights:
      (a) between 152 cm and 168 cm?
      (b) greater than 168 cm?
      (c) less than 136 cm?
  (ii) If a woman is chosen at random from a large sample, what is the probability that her height is between 144 cm and 176 cm?

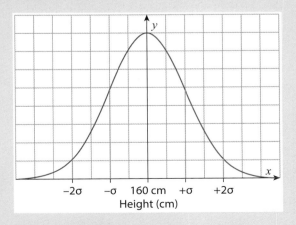

5 Trigonometry *through history*

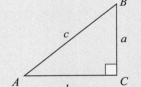

- The mathematics of *angles and triangles.*
- Specialises in the relationships between the length of the sides and the angles of triangles.
- The most used trigonometric ratios are:
  - Sine – Cosine – Tangent.
- $\sin \angle BAC = \dfrac{a}{c}$ $\cos \angle BAC = \dfrac{b}{c}$ $\tan \angle BAC = \dfrac{a}{b}$

300 BC	**Pythagoras** was a Greek philosopher who travelled to Croton in the south of Italy and set up a school of learning. Early records indicate that he was a vegetarian and that his students (*Pythagoreans*) lived a very frugal life and were sworn to secrecy on the teachings of the school. Many discoveries in mathematics and music have been attributed to him and his followers including:

(i) in mathematics for a right-angled triangle,
$$c^2 = a^2 + b^2$$

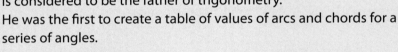

(ii) in music, an instrument tuning system in which the frequency ratios of all intervals are based on the ratio 3:2.

(iii) in astronomy, he identified the morning and evening stars as the planet Venus.

150 BC   **Hipparchus**, a Greek astronomer/mathematician, born in Nicaea, is considered to be the father of trigonometry.
He was the first to create a table of values of arcs and chords for a series of angles.

450 AD   **The Sinddhantas** is a Sanskrit text that contains the earliest surviving tables of sine values, in 3.75° intervals from 0° to 90°, to an accuracy of 4 place of decimals.

1400 AD   **Madhava,** an Indian mathematician/astronomer, created algebraic expansions for sine, cosine and tangent 200 years before his European counterparts Newton and Leibnitz.
Modern day calculators use expansions like this to evaluate the sine of a given angle:
$$\sin x = x - \frac{x^3}{3!} + \frac{x^5}{5!} - \frac{x^7}{7!} + \dots$$

Today   **Modern Trigonometry:** The periodic nature of trigonometric functions is used to study wave motion, in particular the motion of electromagnetic waves used to carry internet signals.

Part 1: Pythagoras's theorem

- In a right-angled triangle:
  Hypothenuse squared = the sum of the squares of the other two sides.
  - Algebra: $c^2 = a^2 + b^2$
  - Geometry: The area of the square on the hypothenuse
    = the sum of the areas of the squares on the other two sides.

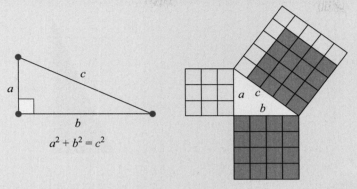

$$a^2 + b^2 = c^2$$

- Knowing the length of any two sides, we can always find the length of the third side:
  - If $a = 3$ and $c = 5$,
    $\therefore c^2 = a^2 + b^2$
    $\therefore 5^2 = 3^2 + b^2$
    $\therefore b^2 = 5^2 - 3^2 = 25 - 9 = 16$
    $\therefore b = \sqrt{16} = 4$

Example

<<

Find the length of the third side marked x, in each of the following triangles:

(i)

7.3 cm   9.5 cm

x cm

(ii)

15 cm   9 cm

x cm

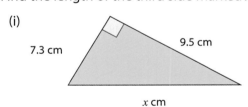

Answer:

$x^2 = 7.3^2 + 9.5^2$
$x^2 = 53.29 + 90.25$
$x^2 = 143.54$
$x = \sqrt{143.54}$
$\quad = 11.98$ cm (2 d. p.)

$15^2 = 9^2 + x^2$
$9^2 + x^2 = 15^2$
$x^2 = 15^2 - 9^2$
$\quad = 225 - 81$
$x^2 = 144$
$x = \sqrt{144} = 12$ cm

Talking Point

In a right-angled triangle, the hypotenuse, c, is the longest side and $c^2 = a^2 + b^2$, where, a and b are the lengths of the other two sides.

If $c^2 > a^2 + b^2$ then $\angle C > 90°$ (obtuse)

If $c^2 < a^2 + b^2$ then $\angle C < 90°$ (acute)

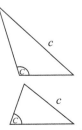

1.1 Check-up

<<

Find the length of the third side in each of the following triangles.
Correct each answer to 1 place of decimals.

1. (i)

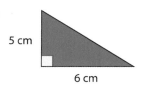

5 cm

6 cm

(ii)

18 mm   16 mm

2. (i)

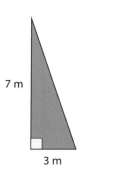

7 m

3 m

(ii)

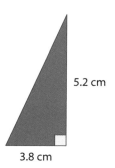

5.2 cm

3.8 cm

3. (i)

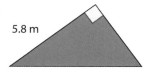

5.8 m

8 m

(ii)

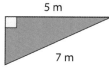

5 m

7 m

4. (i)

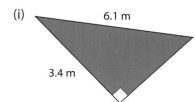

6.1 m

3.4 m

(ii)

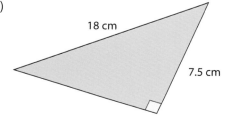

18 cm

7.5 cm

5. Kyle cycled 5 km East before turning and after cycling
North for 4 km he arrived at Jane's house.

The dotted line between A and C shows a cross-country
path Kyle used to cycle home.

How far did Kyle cycle in total?

Give your answer correct to 1 place of decimals.

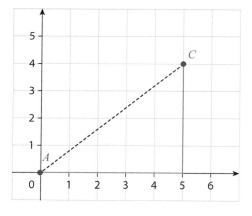

6. Emily has rented the allotment shown.

She wants to fence the perimeter.

Find the length of fencing she needs, give your
answer, correct to the nearest metre.

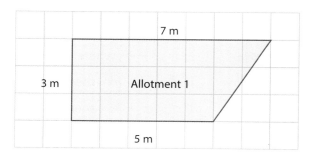

7 m

3 m   Allotment 1

5 m

7. Dave bought a 7 m ladder. The instructions on the ladder said that the base must be placed at a minimum of 1.5 m from the base of a wall.

Find the greatest reach of the ladder on a vertical wall.

Give your answer correct to 1 place of decimals.

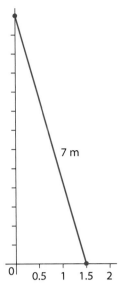

8. Find the values x and y, give your answers correct to 1 place of decimals.

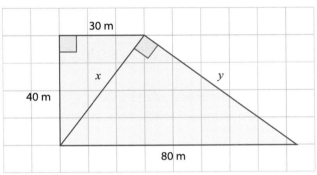

9. A plot of land $EFHG$ has the shape of two right-angled triangles as shown.
  (i) Find the length of the side GH.
  (ii) Find the area of the plot.

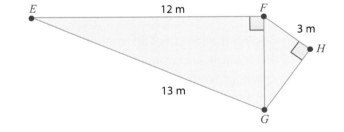

10. Lucy constructed a triangle ABC with the following measurements, $|BC| = 10$ cm, $|AC| = 12$ cm.

When she drew a perpendicular from B to AC it divided the base line in the ratio 1:3.

Find the vertical height of the triangle and hence find the length, l, of the side AB correct to 2 places of decimals.

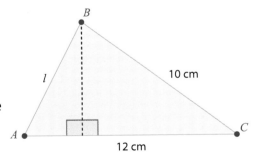

11. A triangle ABC is made by joining two right-angled triangles ABD and BDC together:

(i) Show that the perimeter of the triangle is 78 m

(ii) Prove that the triangle ABC is a right-angled triangle.

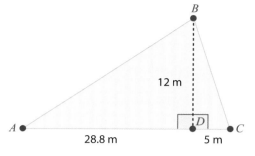

12. Find which of the following sets of measurements form right-angled triangles:

A	12 cm	20 cm	16 cm
B	3 cm	8 cm	7 cm
C	48 cm	14 cm	50 cm
D	17 cm	7 cm	15 cm
E	75 cm	40 cm	85 cm
F	14 cm	20 cm	17 cm
G	17 cm	8 cm	15 cm
H	60 cm	25 cm	65 cm

Talking Point

A *Pythagorean triple* is a set of **whole numbers** that form the lengths of the sides of a right-angled triangle.

e.g. 5 cm, 12 cm, 13 cm.

$$13^2 = 12^2 + 5^2$$

13. Find the perimeter of the shape.
Give your answer to the nearest centimetre.

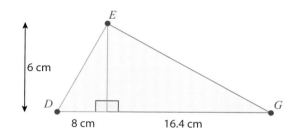

14. By finding the length of all three sides of this triangle and using Pythagoras's theorem, prove that the angle at A is a right angle.

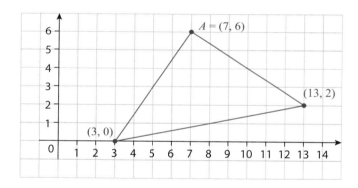

Example

<<

Find the value of x.

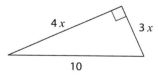

Answer:
$$10^2 = (4x)^2 + (3x)^2$$
$$100 = 16x^2 + 9x^2 = 25x^2$$
$$25x^2 = 100$$
$$x^2 = \frac{100}{25} = 4$$
$$x = \sqrt{4} = 2$$

1.2 Check-up

<<

Find the value of the unknown in each of the following:

1. Given $\angle ABC = 90°$, find the value of x, correct to 1 place of decimals.

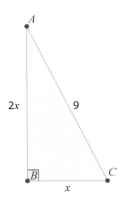

2. The lengths $2y$, $3y$ and 10, where $3y < 10$, form a right-angled triangle. Find the value of y correct to 2 places of decimals.

3. The triangle DEF has a right angle at E.

Find the value of x, correct to 1 place of decimals.

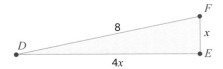

4. While on holidays Alan bought a new putter measuring 92 cm in length. Will the putter fit into his biggest suitcase measuring 80 cm × 50 cm?

1.3 Check-up

<<

1. (i) Find the lengths of the diagonals of a square of side 10 cm. Give your answer correct to 2 places of decimals.
   (ii) It can be shown that the diagonals of a square bisect one another (cut each other in half), using Pythagoras's theorem. Show that the diagonals are also perpendicular to one another.

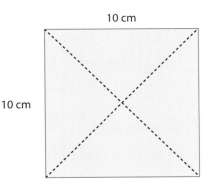

10 cm

10 cm

2. (i) Find the lengths of the diagonals of a rectangle of side 9 cm × 3 cm.
   (ii) It can be shown that the diagonals of a rectangle bisect one another, using Pythagoras's theorem. Show that the diagonals are not perpendicular to one another.

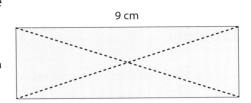

9 cm

3 cm

3. Find the length of the second diagonal of the rhombus shown.
(Rhombus is a quadrilateral with all four sides the same length)

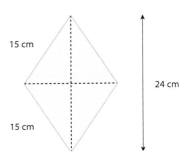

15 cm

15 cm

24 cm

4. Find the lengths of the diagonals of the kite figure shown.
(Correct to 2 places of decimals where needed)

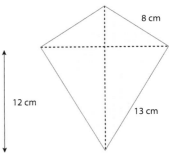

8 cm

12 cm

13 cm

Part 2: Trigonometric ratios

Looking back
<<

- In a right-angled triangle:
  - The sine of an angle is defined as,

$$\frac{\text{the length of the opposite side}}{\text{the length of the hypotenuse}}$$

  - The cosine of an angle is defined as,

$$\frac{\text{the length of the near side}}{\text{the length of the hypotenuse}}$$

  - The tangent of an angle is defined as,

$$\frac{\text{the length of the opposite side}}{\text{the length of the near side}}$$

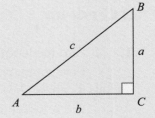

- Using symbols: $\sin\angle BAC = \frac{a}{c}$ $\cos\angle BAC = \frac{b}{c}$ $\tan\angle BAC = \frac{a}{b}$

- A calculator can be used to find:

  - the ratio of sides of a triangle if we know the angle
  - the angle in a triangle if we know the ratio of sides.

Example

<<

Find the trigonometric ratios (i) $\sin A$ (ii) $\tan B$
of the given triangle.

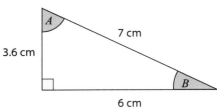

A

7 cm

3.6 cm

B

6 cm

Answer: $\sin\angle A = \dfrac{\text{opposite}}{\text{hypotenuse}} = \dfrac{6}{7} = 0.86$ (correct to 2 places
of decimals)

$\tan\angle B = \dfrac{\text{opposite}}{\text{near}} = \dfrac{3.6}{6} = 0.60$ (correct to 2 places of decimals)

Example

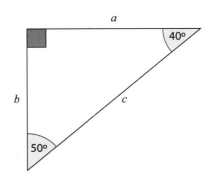

Find the trigonometric ratios (i) cos 40° (ii) tan 50°
of the given triangle.

Answer: (Using a calculator)

$$\cos\angle 40° = \frac{a}{c} = 0.77 \text{ (correct to 2 places of decimals)}$$

$$\tan\angle 50° = \frac{a}{b} = 1.19 \text{ (correct to 2 places of decimals)}$$

Example

Find the lengths of the sides marked with a letter.

(i)

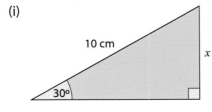

(ii)

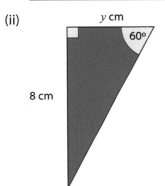

Talking Point

$$\sin 30° = \frac{1}{2}$$

Tells you the **ratio** between the length of the opposite side to the length of the hypotenuse. It does **not** tell you the length of the sides.

$$\sin 30° = \frac{1}{2} \text{ or } \frac{2}{4} \text{ or } \frac{10}{20} \text{ etc.}$$

Answer:

$x \to$ opposite (30°)

10 cm $\to$ hypotenuse

$$\sin 30° = \left[\frac{\text{opp}}{\text{hyp}}\right] = \frac{x}{10} \text{ ...multiply both sides by 10}$$

$$10 \times \sin 30° = x$$

$$x = 10 \times \sin 30°$$

$$x = 10 \times 0.5 = 5.0 \text{ cm}$$

$y \to$ near (60°)

8 cm $\to$ opposite

$$\tan 60° = \left[\frac{\text{opp}}{\text{near}}\right] = \frac{8}{y} \text{ ...multiply both by sides by } y.$$

$$y \times \tan 60° = 8$$

$$y \times 1.732 = 8$$

$$y = \frac{8}{1.732} = 4.62 \text{ (to 2 places of decimals)}$$

2.1 Check-up

1. Find the value of the following trigonometric ratios correct to 2 places of decimals:

(i) sin 35° (ii) cos 55° (iii) tan 65°

(iv) sin 105° (v) cos 280° (vi) tan 385°

2. Niamh was randomly checking values with her calculator.
She keyed in sin 20° and then cos 70° then she experimented with:
   (i) sin 40° and cos 50°
  (ii) sin 10° and cos 80°.
By keying in these pairs into your calculator, state what Niamh had discovered.
Write down two more examples of pairs that would repeat what she
had discovered.
Use the right-angled triangle to explain what she had discovered.

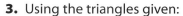

3. Using the triangles given:
   (i) identify the near, opposite and hypotenuse sides
  (ii) find the length of the sides marked with a letter, correct to 2 places of decimals.

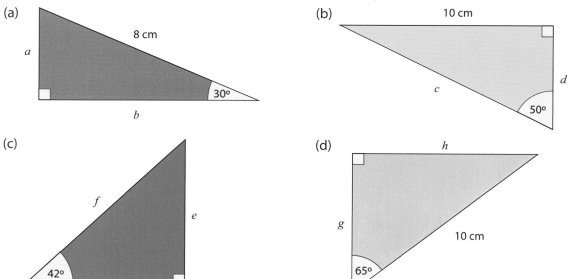

(a)

8 cm

a

30°

b

(b)

10 cm

d

c

50°

(c)

f

e

42°

6 cm

(d)

h

g

10 cm

65°

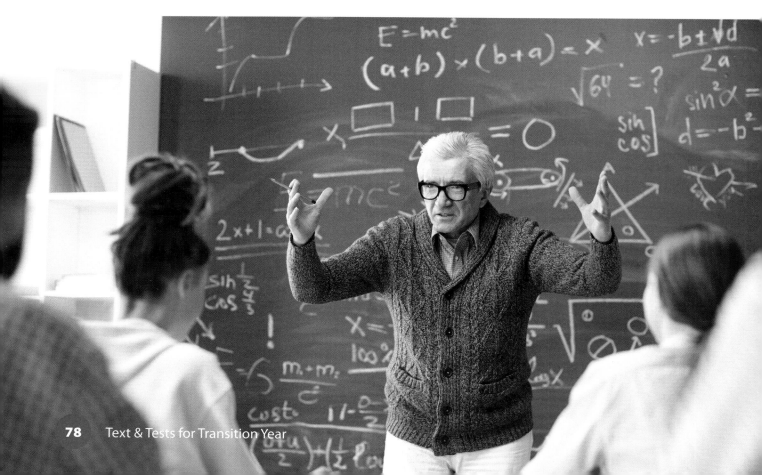

Part 3: Surds

- Surds are expressions containing square roots (or higher roots)
- Many trigonometric ratios can be expressed accurately (not correcting the answers) using surds.
  - $\sin 45° = \dfrac{1}{\sqrt{2}}$
  - $\cos 30° = \dfrac{\sqrt{3}}{2}$
- Calculators give the surd form of a ratio when it is possible.

Example

Find the value of (i) $\tan 30°$ (ii) $\cos 30°$ in surd form.
Hence write down the value of $\tan 30° \times \cos 30°$.

Answer: (i) $\tan 30° = \dfrac{\sqrt{3}}{3}$ (ii) $\cos 30° = \dfrac{\sqrt{3}}{2}$ (Using Casio calculator)

$\tan 30° \times \cos 30° = \dfrac{\sqrt{3}}{3} \times \dfrac{\sqrt{3}}{2} = \dfrac{3}{6} = \dfrac{1}{2}$ (Note this result can be found directly from the calculator)

3.1 Check-up

Find the value of the following in surd form:

1. Find the value of each of the following leaving your answer in surd form:
   (i) $\tan 60°$ (ii) $\cos 135°$
   (iii) $\sin 120°$ (iv) $\cos 30°$
   (v) $\tan 120°$

   Talking Point

   It is normal practice to '*rationalise*' a denominator containing a surd.

   e.g. $\dfrac{2}{\sqrt{3}} = \dfrac{2}{\sqrt{3}} \times \dfrac{\sqrt{3}}{\sqrt{3}} = \dfrac{2\sqrt{3}}{3}$

2. Find the exact value of each of the following:
   (i) $\sin 30° \times \cos 45°$ (ii) $\dfrac{\sin 45°}{\tan 30°}$ (iii) $\sin 135° \times \tan 120°$

3. (i) Using Pythagoras's theorem prove that each of the triangles, ABC and BCD is a right-angled triangle.
   (ii) Using the lengths given in the diagram find the value of each of the following in surd form:
   (a) $\sin 45°$ (b) $\tan 30°$
   (c) $\cos 60°$ (d) $\dfrac{\sin 30°}{\cos 30°}$
   (e) $\dfrac{\sin 60°}{\tan 45°}$ (f) $\sin 45° \times \cos 45°$
   (g) $\dfrac{\cos 30° \times \sin 30°}{\sin 60°}$ (h) $\left(\dfrac{\sin 30° \times \tan 60°}{\tan 45°}\right)^2$

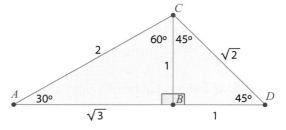

Part 4: Inverse functions

Looking back

<<

- Inverse Trigonometric functions are used to find the angle if the trigonometric ratio is known:

  - If $\sin A = 0.5$, then $A = \sin^{-1}(0.5) = 30°$

  - If $\cos B = \dfrac{1}{\sqrt{2}}$, then $B = \cos^{-1}\left(\dfrac{1}{\sqrt{2}}\right) = 45°$

  - If $\tan C = 1$, then $C = \tan^{-1}(1) = 45°$

Example

<<

Find the angle A, correct to the nearest degree.

Answer: 4 m → opposite

       7 m → near

$$\therefore \tan A = \frac{\text{opposite}}{\text{near}} = \frac{4}{7}$$

$$\therefore A = \tan^{-1}\left(\frac{4}{7}\right) = 29.744 = 30° \text{ (correct to the nearest degree)}$$

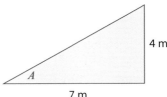

4.1 Check-up

<<

1. Find the angle C, correct to the nearest degree.

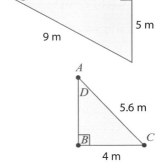

2. Find the angle D, correct to the nearest degree.

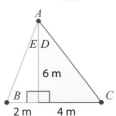

3. A triangle ADC has a base of 6 m as shown and a vertical height of 6 m.
The vertical divides the base in the ratio 2 m : 4 m

Find the value of the angles E and D and hence $E + D$, correct to the nearest degree.

4. A tall building of height h casts a shadow on horizontal ground.

The shadow from a vertical pole 1.5 m high reaches to the end of the shadow 3 m away.
(i) Find the size of the angle of the shadow at the point A.
(ii) Using the answer found in (i) find the height of the building correct to the nearest metre.

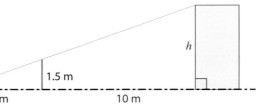

5. Roof beams make an angle of 37° with the horizontal as shown.
If the beams each have a length of 7.5 m, find:
(i) the height h of the roof from the horizontal
(ii) The width w of the roof space.
Give each answer correct to 1 place of decimals.

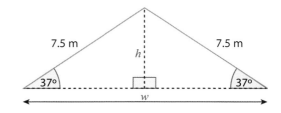

Part 5: Problem solving with trigonometry

- Angle of depression,
  - *look down from the horizontal*

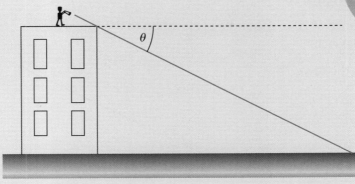

- Angle of elevation,
  - *look up from the horizontal*

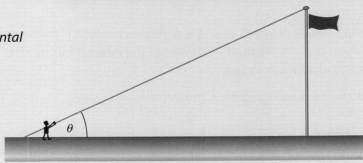

Example

<<

Frank measured the angle of elevation to the top of a vertical tree from a point A on level ground as 52°.

He then measured the distance from A to the base of the tree as 45.5 m.

Find the height of the tree, h.

Give your answer correct to the nearest metre.

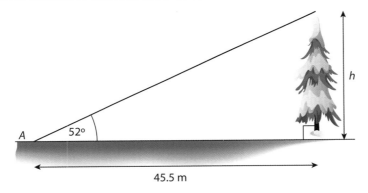

45.5 m

Answer: $h \rightarrow$ opposite (52°)

45.5 m $\rightarrow$ near

$$\tan 52° = \frac{[\text{opp}]}{[\text{near}]} = \frac{h}{45.5}$$

45.5 $\times \tan 52° = h$ …multiplying both sides by 45.5

58.237 m $= h$

Height of tree $= 58$ m

5.1 Check-up

Find the missing lengths:

1. From a distance of 20 m the angle of elevation to the top of a vertical tower is 35°.

How high is the tower?

35°

20 m

2. A straight road slopes down at an angle of depression of 11° to the horizontal. Find the vertical drop in the road, h, correct to the nearest metre, after travelling a distance of 200 m along the road.

(Draw a sketch of the road and fill in the information given.)

3. Ava is flying a kite with a string of length 60 m.

The string is a straight line and makes an angle of 71° with the horizontal.

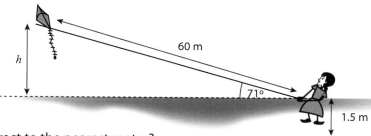

60 m

h

71°

1.5 m

What is the vertical height of the kite above the ground, correct to the nearest metre? Assume that Ava's hand holding the kite is 1.5 m above the ground.

4. An isosceles triangle has sides measuring 10 cm, 10 cm and 5 cm.

Draw a rough sketch of the triangle. Draw a perpendicular line from the top of the triangle to the base forming two right-angled triangles.
Hence find the angle between the two equal sides correct to 2 place of decimals.

5. A plane is taxiing along a runway towards the airport.
An air traffic controller measures the angle of depression of a plane to be 10° and 1 minute later 20° from the top of his 80 m tower.
Find, correct to 1 place of decimals, how far the plane has travelled and its speed during this time.

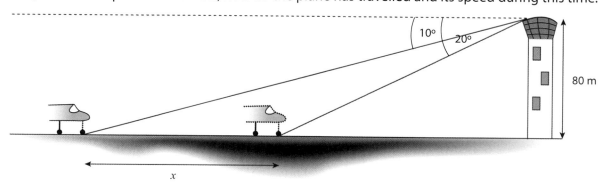

10°
20°

80 m

x

Part 6: Working in 3-Dimensions

Looking ahead >>

- Working in 3-Dimensions requires using:
  - Pythagoras's theorem
  - Trigonometric ratios.
- To solve problems in 3-D you must first locate the right-angles in the shape provided.
  The verticals should be noted in the question.

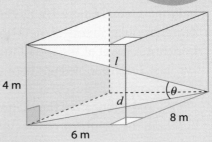

  - d is the hypotenuse of a right-angled triangle with sides, 6 m and 8 m
  - l is the hypotenuse of a right-angled triangle with sides 4 m and d m
  - θ is the angle of elevation to the top of the box.

Example   >>

If the angle of elevation θ to the top of the box in the given diagram is 60° from the base, find:
  (i) the height, h, of the box, and
  (ii) the length l, of the main diagonal, correct to 1 place of decimals.

Answer:

$$d^2 = 6^2 + 9^2$$
$$d^2 = 36 + 81 = 117$$
$$d = \sqrt{117} = 10.82$$

$$\tan 60° = \frac{h}{10.82}$$
$$10.82 \times \tan 60° = h$$
$$18.7 \text{ m} = h$$

$$l^2 = h^2 + d^2$$
$$l^2 = 18.73^2 + 10.82^2$$
$$l^2 = 467.88$$
$$l = \sqrt{467.88} = 21.6 \text{ m}$$

Talking Point

All 3-D problems reduce to a series of connected 2-D right-angled triangles.

The side l connects both right-angled triangles.

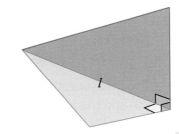

Find the values of the unknowns indicated in the following diagrams:

1. A concrete square base $ABCD$ of side 6 m has a vertical pole of
   height h metres erected at its centre.
   Two triangular sheets of metal inclined at an angle of 70° to the
   horizontal, meet at the top of the pole.
   (i) List 3 right-angles not connected with the corners of the
       square.
   (ii) Find the length of the diagonal, AC, of the base.
   (iii) Find the height, h, of the pole.
   (iv) Find the vertical height of each triangle, GE.
       Give all answers correct to 1 place of decimals.
   It is considered necessary to protect the edges of all the exposed metal [e.g. AE] with tape.
   (v) Find the length of tape needed, correct to the nearest metre.

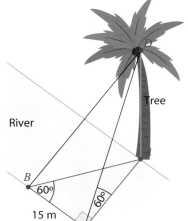

2. Rory stands *directly* across from a tree planted on the bank of a river
   with parallel sides and measures the angle of inclination to the top
   of the tree to be 60°.
   He walks 15 m along the near bank until he measures an angle of
   60° between the base of the tree and the river bank as shown in the
   diagram.
   (i) List 3 right-angles in this diagram.
   (ii) Find the width of the river [AC] in surd form.
   (iii) Find the height of the tree [AD].
   (iv) Find the angle of elevation to the top of the tree from the
        point B.

3. Samantha sits at a conference centre.
   Her eyeline is level with the bottom of the centre of a large
   screen which is 30 m in front of her.

   She measures the angle of elevation to the top of the screen as
   20° and the angle of elevation to the top right-hand corner (D)
   to be 16°.

   Correct to 1 place of decimals find:
   (i) the height of the screen [NR]
   (ii) her distance from the bottom right-hand corner (C) of the screen, $|EC|$
   (iii) the width of the screen.
   (iv) the area of the screen.

4. A cube of side 10 cm is shown.

   Find:
   (i) the lengths of the two main dotted diagonals in surd form
   (ii) the angle between the two diagonals correct to the nearest degree.

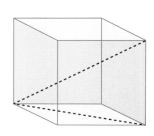

5. Two walls, 10 m × 4 m and 5 m × 4 m, stand vertically to one another as shown.
Find the distance between points B and F, giving your answer in metres correct to 1 place of decimals.
(Hint: Draw a plan of the walls.)

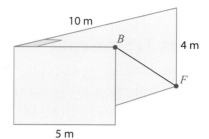

6. (i) Find the vertical height h, of the isosceles triangle shown, using Pythagoras's theorem.

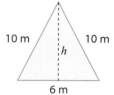

(ii) A shelter is supported by two 4 m and one 6 m pole.
Using the formula, $\frac{1}{2} \times$ base $\times \perp$ height, find the area of the triangular base of the shelter shown.
Hence find the area of the canopy ABC.

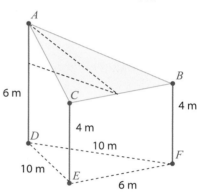

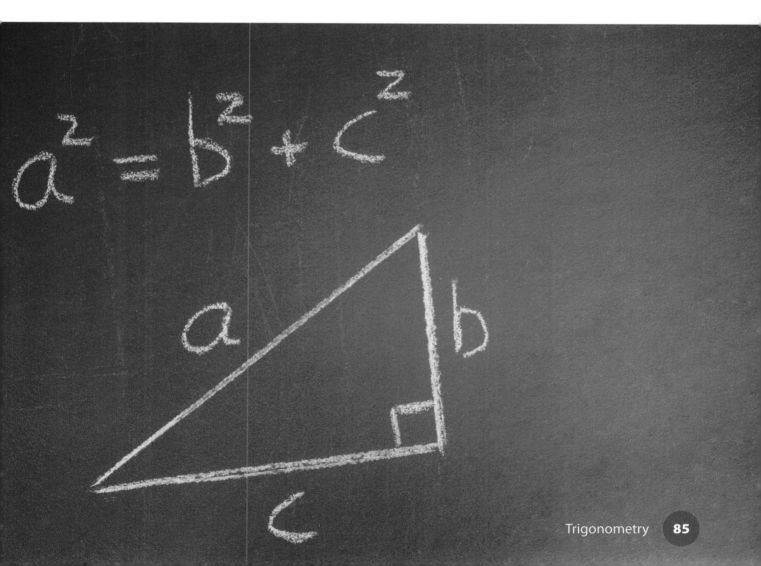

Part 7: Sine rule

Looking ahead >>

- The Sine rule is the first of two very important relationships between the sides and the angles of a triangle.
- The rule applies to **all triangles**.
- As the length of the side of a triangle increases, the angle at the base of the triangle also increases. There is a relationship between an angle and the side opposite.

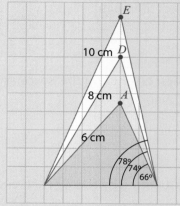

- Given the $\triangle ABC$ with angles A, B, C as shown.
- The sides a, b, and c denote the length of the sides opposite the angles.
- It can be shown that,

$$\frac{a}{\sin A} = \frac{b}{\sin B} = \frac{c}{\sin C}$$

or

$$\frac{\sin A}{a} = \frac{\sin B}{b} = \frac{\sin C}{c}$$

This relationship is called the **Sine Rule.**

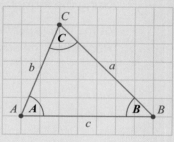

Example

>>

Given the information in the diagram find the length of the side c, correct to 1 place of decimals.

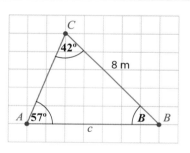

Answer: $\dfrac{c}{\sin C} = \dfrac{a}{\sin A}$

Let $C = 42°$, $A = 57°$ and $a = 8$ m then

$$\frac{c}{\sin 42} = \frac{8}{\sin 57}$$

$$c = \frac{8 \times \sin 42}{\sin 57} \text{ ...using fraction key on calculator}$$

$$= 6.38 \text{ m} = 6.4 \text{ m}$$

Talking Point

If a question requires you to find the length of a **side**, it is best to use the

$$\frac{a}{\sin A} = \frac{b}{\sin B} = \frac{c}{\sin C}$$

version of the rule.

Example

Given the information in the diagram find the size of the angle A, correct to 1 place of decimals.

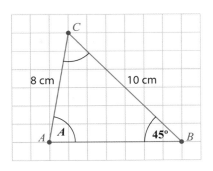

Answer: $\dfrac{\sin A}{a} = \dfrac{\sin B}{b}$

Let $B = 45°$, $a = 10$ cm and $b = 8$ cm then

$\dfrac{\sin A}{10} = \dfrac{\sin 45}{8}$

$\sin A = \dfrac{10 \times \sin 45}{8}$

$= 0.8838$

$\therefore A = \sin^{-1}(0.8838) = 62.1°$

Talking Point

If a question requires you to find the size of an **angle**, it is best to use the

$\dfrac{\sin A}{a} = \dfrac{\sin B}{b} = \dfrac{\sin C}{c}$

version of the rule.

7.1 Check-up

>>

1. (i) Given the information in the diagram, use the sine rule to find length of side b.

   Give your answer correct to 1 place of decimals.

   (ii) Deduce the size of the angle C.

   (iii) Using the sine rule and angle C (or otherwise), find the length of side c, give your answer correct to 1 decimal place.

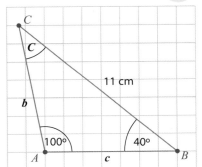

2. Triangle ABC has an angle $B = 60°$ and sides $|AC| = 7.5$ cm, $|AB| = 8$ cm.
   (i) Using the sine rule, find the size of the angle C. Correct your answer to the nearest degree.
   (ii) Find the size of the angle at A and hence find the length of a, correct to 1 place of decimals.

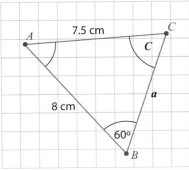

3. In the triangle ABC,
   $|AB| = 22$ cm, $\angle ABC = 46°$ and $\angle BAC = 71°$.
   (i) Determine the size of the angle $\angle BCA$.
   (ii) Using the sine rule, find the lengths of the sides a and b.
   Give your answers correct to 1 place of decimals.

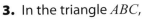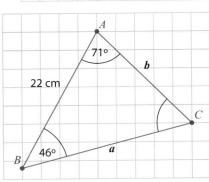

4. (i) Find the size of the angle A in the triangle ABC correct to the nearest degree.

(ii) Find the length of the perimeter of the triangle correct to 1 decimal place.

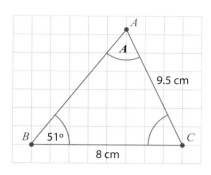

5. Triangle ABJ has sides $|AB| = 6$ cm and $|AJ| = 9.5$ cm.

The point A is joined to a point C on BJ making an angle $\angle ACB = 39°$.

Find (i) $|AC|$ (ii) $|BC|$ (iii) $|CJ|$

Give your answers correct to 1 place of decimals.

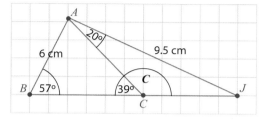

6. Find the length of the perimeter of the triangle RSQ.

Give your answer correct to 1 decimal place.

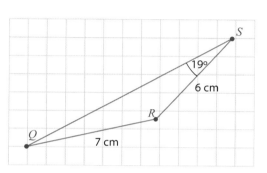

Part 8: Cosine rule

Looking ahead >>

- In the triangle RSQ, the lengths of all the sides are known.
  The sine rule cannot be used to find the size of an angle, since we need to know one of the angles in the triangle to apply it.

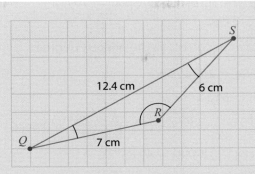

- Also, if we are given the lengths of two sides but not either of the angles opposite these sides, the sine rule again cannot be applied.

- These two examples show the need for the second trigonometric rule.

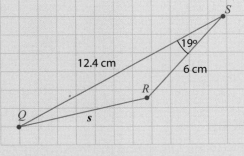

- It can be shown that for any triangle ABC

$$a^2 = b^2 + c^2 - 2bc\cos A$$

where A is the angle contained between b and c.
This relationship is called the **Cosine Rule**.

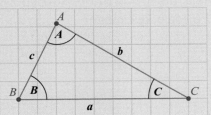

Example

>>

In a triangle RSQ, $|RS| = 6$ cm, $|SQ| = 12.4$ cm and the contained angle $\angle RSQ = 19°$.
Find $|QR| = s$, correct to 1 place of decimals.

Answer:
$a^2 = b^2 + c^2 - 2bc\cos A$
$s^2 = 6^2 + 12.4^2 - 2 \times 6 \times 12.4\cos19°$
$s^2 = 49.067$
$s = \sqrt{49.067} = 7.0$ cm

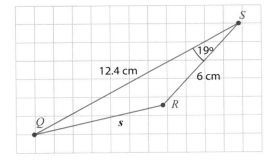

- The cosine rule can be used to find an angle when the lengths of all three sides (a, b, c) are known.

  ○ $a^2 = b^2 + c^2 - 2bc\cos A$
  ○ $2bc\cos A = b^2 + c^2 - a^2$
  ○ $\cos A = \dfrac{b^2 + c^2 - a^2}{2bc}$

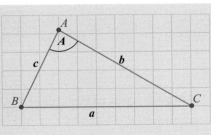

Example

In a triangle ABC, $|AB| = 8$ cm, $|AC| = 10$ cm and $|BC| = 7.8$ cm.

Find $|\angle BAC| = A$, correct to the nearest degree.

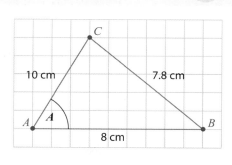

Answer: $a^2 = b^2 + c^2 - 2bc \cos A$

$2bc \cos A = b^2 + c^2 - a^2$

$\cos A = \dfrac{b^2 + c^2 - a^2}{2bc} = \dfrac{8^2 + 10^2 - 7.8^2}{2 \times 8 \times 10} = 0.6448$

$A = \cos^{-1}(0.6448) = 49.85°$

$A = 50°$

Talking Point

If $A = 90°$, $\cos(90°) = 0$ the cosine rule changes to

$$a^2 = b^2 + c^2 - 2bc \cos(90)$$
$$a^2 = b^2 + c^2 - 2bc \times (0)$$
$$a^2 = b^2 + c^2$$

i.e. Pythagoras's theorem

8.1 Check-up

1. Use the cosine rule to find the length of $|CB| = a$, correct to 1 place of decimals.

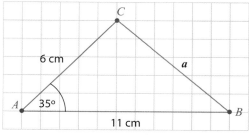

2. The lengths of the three sides of a triangle SQR are 12 cm, 6 cm and 8 cm respectively as shown in the diagram. Use the cosine rule to find the size of $|\angle SRQ|$. Correct your answer to the nearest degree.

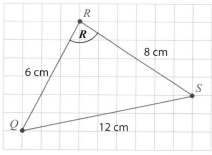

3. Find the length of the perimeter of the triangle ABC correct to 1 place of decimals.

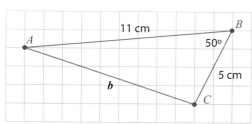

4. The lengths of the sides of the triangle shown are 6 cm, 10 cm and 14 cm. Use the cosine rule to find the size of the largest angle in the triangle.

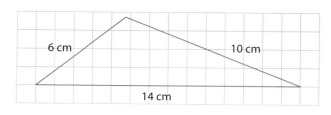

5. Find the length of the side marked b.

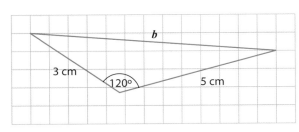

6. The parallelogram $ABCD$ has sides of length 6 cm and 9 cm as shown.
The angle at A measures $60°$.
  (i) Using the cosine rule find the length of the diagonal DB, correct to 1 decimal place.
  (ii) Explain why the angle at B measures $120°$.
  (iii) Using the angle at B, find the length of the diagonal AC, correct to 1 decimal place.

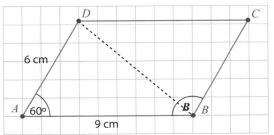

7. Two planes approach an airport.
The air traffic controller in the control tower measures their distances from the airport to be 50 km and 72 km respectively.
She measures the angle between the flight paths as $49°$.
Using the cosine rule calculate the distance between the planes, correct to 1 decimal place.

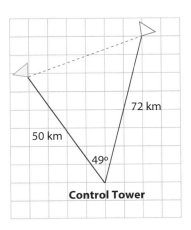

8. A builder wants to erect hoarding around a triangular plot of land PQR.
The length of $[PQ] = 42$ m and the length of $[PR] = 50$ m.
$|\angle QPR| = 72°$.
Calculate the length of hoarding needed by the builder.
Give your answer correct to 1 place of decimals.

Part 9: The Area rule

Looking ahead >>

- Area $= \frac{1}{2} \times$ base $\times \perp$ height

- Area $= \frac{1}{2} \times a \times h$

  ○ $\frac{h}{c} = \sin B$

  ○ $h = c \times \sin B$

- Area $= \frac{1}{2} \times a \times c \times \sin B$

- Area $= \frac{1}{2} \times$ product of any 2 sides $\times \sin$ (angle contained)

Example

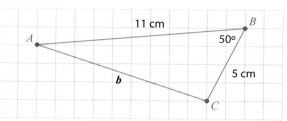

Find the area of the triangle ABC, with $|AB| = 11$ cm and $|BC| = 5$ cm, given that $|\angle ABC| = 50°$.
Give your answer correct to the nearest integer.

Answer: Area $= \dfrac{1}{2} \times a \times c \times \sin B$

Area $= \dfrac{1}{2} \times (11) \times (5) \times \sin 50$

Area $= 21.06$ cm² $= 21$ cm²

Example

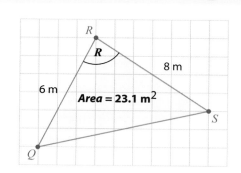

The area of a triangular plot of land QRS, with $|QR| = 6$ m and $|RS| = 8$ m is 23.1 m².

Find the measure of the angle $\angle QRS$ correct to the nearest degree.

Answer: Area $= \dfrac{1}{2} \times a \times c \times \sin B$

$23.1 = \dfrac{1}{2} \times (6) \times (8) \times \sin R$

$23.1 = 24 \times \sin R$

$\sin R = \dfrac{23.1}{24} = 0.9625$

$R = \sin^{-1}(0.9625) = 74°$

Talking Point

These 3 rules work together to give information about the sides, angles and area of **any** triangle.

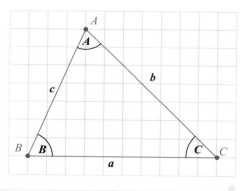

Sine rule: $\quad \dfrac{a}{\sin A} = \dfrac{b}{\sin B} = \dfrac{c}{\sin C}$

Cosine rule: $\quad a^2 = b^2 + c^2 - 2bc \cos A$

Area rule: $\quad$ Area $= \dfrac{1}{2} \times a \times c \times \sin B$

9.1 Check-up

1. Find the area enclosed by a triangle with sides 3 cm and 7 cm as shown, if the angle contained $= 120°$.
Give your answer correct to the nearest integer.
If the angle is changed to 60° how does this affect the area?

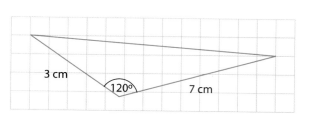

2. (i) Using the sine rule, find the length of the
   side marked c.

   (ii) Hence find the area of the triangle.

   Give your answers correct to one decimal place.

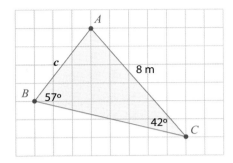

3. Find the lengths of the sides $[AB]$ and $[BC]$
   of the triangle ABC.

   Give your answers correct to the nearest integer.

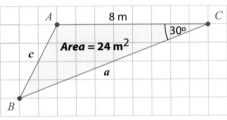

4. In the given triangle, $|AC| = \sqrt{8}$ m,
   $|\angle ABC| = 45°$ and $|\angle ACB| = 30$.

   (i) Find $|AB|$

   (ii) Hence show that the area of the
   $\triangle ABC$ is 2.7 m^2,
   correct to 1 place of decimals.

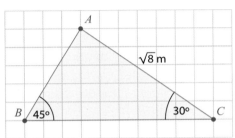

5. The triangle HIJ has $|HI| = 8$ m
   and $|\angle HIJ| = 70°$.

   If the area of the triangle is 26.3 m^2, find:

   (i) $|IJ|$ using the area rule

   (ii) $|HJ|$ using the cosine rule

   (iii) the $|\angle JHI|$.

   Give all your answers correct to 1 place of decimals.

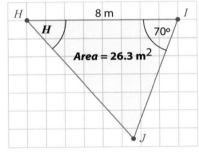

6. In the given triangle $|AO| = |OC| = 5$ cm.
   $|\angle ABC| = 72°$ and $|\angle ACO| = 43°$

   Find: (i) $|AC|$ (ii) $|BO|$,
   correct each answer to 1 place of decimals.

   (Hint: find the size of all the angles first)

   (iii) the ratio of the areas of the
   triangles $ABO : ACO$ to the nearest
   integer.

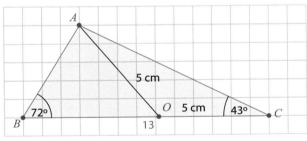

7. $\triangle MBC$ has sides $|MB| = 3$ cm, $|BC| = 7$ cm and $\angle MBC = 60°$

   $\triangle ABC$ has sides $|AB| = 3$ cm, $|BC| = 7$ cm.

   AM is parallel to BC.

   Find the size of $\angle ABC$

   (Hint: the triangles have the same base and
   the same vertical height)

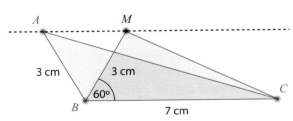

TRIGONOMETRY TEST

1. A ladder leans against a vertical wall as shown.

The base of the ladder is 2 metres from the wall and the vertical reach of the ladder is 6 m.

(i) Find the length of the ladder correct to 1 place of decimals.

(ii) Find the angle of elevation of the ladder correct to the nearest degree.

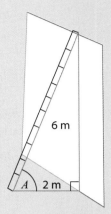

2. A triangular plot of land has a side 18 m long and an angle of 34° as shown. By finding the lengths of the two missing sides, calculate the length of perimeter of the site, correct to 1 place of decimals.

3. (i) Find the length of the side AC using the sine rule.

(ii) By calculating the angle at A, find the area enclosed by the triangle.
Correct each answer to 3 significant figures.

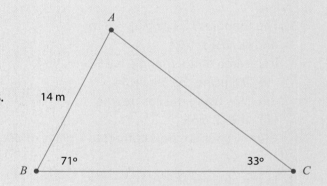

4. A trapezium, as shown in the diagram, has sides $AB = 5$ cm, $BC = 13$ cm, $CD = 6$ cm and $DA = 9$ cm. The angle $ABC = 82°$.

(i) Using the cosine rule, find the length of the diagonal AC. Correct your answer to 1 place of decimals.

(ii) Using the cosine rule again and your answer to part (i), find the size of the angle ADC. Correct your answer to the nearest degree.

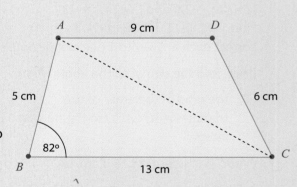

5. Find the size of the longest diagonal, $[AG]$, in a rectangular box with dimensions, 25 cm × 40 cm × 20 cm.
Give your answer correct to 2 places of decimals.

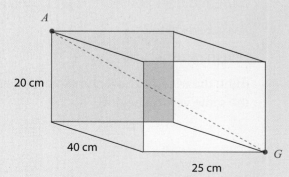

6 Functions and Calculus *through history*

Function: • The mathematics of the relationship between a set of
numbers called a *domain(x)* and a set of numbers called the range.

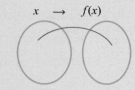

• $y = 3x + 4$ or $f(x) = x^2 - 2x - 5$ are examples of functions.

Calculus: • The mathematics of rates of change → *differential calculus*

• The mathematics of summing up small intervals to find the area
under a curve → *integral calculus*

500 BC	***Zeno*** first introduced infinite series in his Achilles and tortoise paradox.  The tortoise is given a head start of a few metres. During the race, Achilles must first pass a point halfway between himself and the tortoise. But by then the tortoise has moved forward. Achilles must pass a point halfway between himself and the new position of the tortoise. Again, the tortoise has moved forward, the distance between them can be divided an infinite number of times. Therefore, Achilles can never catch the tortoise?
400 BC	***Eudoxus of Cnidus*** introduced the method of exhaustion to determine the area of a circle. 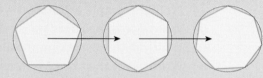 By increasing the number of sides in the polygon the space between the perimeter of the circle and the polygon is almost 'exhausted' to zero. The area of the polygon then approximates to the area of the circle. This approach can be seen as the beginning of *integral calculus*.
1660 AD	***Pierre de Fermat:*** The slope of a curve is changing constantly. By finding the slope of a tangent to a curve at a point (x_1) or (x_2), he approximated the slope of the curve at that point. This was the start of *differential calculus*. 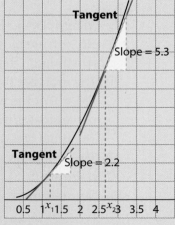
1687 AD	***Newton*** was a renowned English scientist in the fields of optics, mechanics and mathematics. His method of *fluxions* was used to find the slope at any point on a curve, developing the idea of calculus.
1675 AD	***Leibniz***, a German mathematician, independently published a work on differential and integral calculus before Newton, much to Newton's annoyance. This led to a great debate as to who invented calculus first. The Leibniz notation and method of doing calculus is the one in use today.

Functions and Calculus
Part 1: Functions

Looking back

<<

- Functions can also be called Formulas:
  - ○ The set of input numbers is called the **domain.**
  - ○ The actual set of output numbers is called the **range.**
  - ○ The input numbers **map onto** the output numbers using a **rule.**
  - ○ Each input number must have a **distinctive** output number.
- $f(x) = 3x + 4$, $x \in R$ is a function that creates a set of points in a straight line.
- $f(x) = x^2 - 2x + 4$, $x \in R$ is a function that creates a curve called a parabola.
- $v = 5 + 4t$ is a formula (function) for velocity, v, using input values of time t.
- Plots of functions or formulae are called **graphs.**
- The **table function (mode 3)** on a calculator can be used to quickly produce the points needed to plot a graph.

Example

<<

Using a calculator, plot a graph of the function,

$$f(x) = -x^2 + 6x - 4, x \in R, \text{ in the domain } 0 \le x \le 6, x \in R.$$

(i) From the graph, estimate the roots of $f(x)$.
(ii) Write down the coordinates of the maximum point on the graph.
(iii) Write down the maximum value of the function.
(iv) Write down the axis of symmetry of the curve.

Answer: Using a calculator and input values $0 \le x \le 6$, $x \in Z$, the following table is completed.

x	0	1	2	3	4	5	6	Domain values
$f(x)$	-4	1	4	5	4	1	-4	Range values

The points $(0, -4)$, $(1, 1)$, $(2, 4)$, $(3, 5)$, $(4, 4)$, $(5, 1)$, $(6, -4)$ are plotted and a smooth line is drawn through them to include all $x \in R$.

(i) The roots are the values of x so that $f(x) = 0$ or the values of x, where the curve crosses the x-axis.
The roots of $f(x)$ are 0.8 and 5.2.
(ii) The coordinates of the maximum point are $(3, 5)$.
(iii) The maximum *value* of the function is 5.
(iv) The axis of symmetry is $x = 3$.

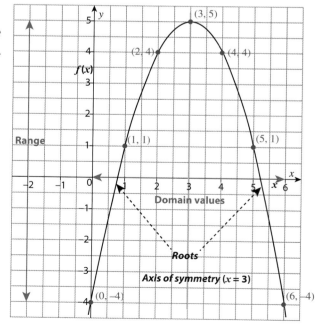

Calculator Steps (Casio fx-83GTX)

Step 1. Press the **Menu** key.

Step 2. Press **3: Table** to create the table of values.
$f(x)$ appears on the screen.

Step 3. Type in function equation, $f(x)$ using the **ALPHA**
and [ )]key each time 'x' is needed to be placed
in the equation.

∴ $f(x) =$ **– ALPHA), $x^{[2]}$, +, 6 ALPHA), – 2** and press **=**

Note: a second function $g(x)$ can now be plotted if needed.

If not press '='again

Step 4. Enter the **Start?** value of the domain ..... 0 and
press =

Step 5. Enter the **End?** value of the domain.... 6 and
press =

Step 6. Enter the **Step?** value between the Start and End
values. The default value is 1, and press =

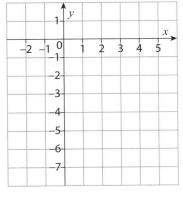

Step 7. Use the cursor to move down through the $f(x)$ values and copy them into the
table.

1.1 Check-up

<<

1. Make a table of values for each of the following functions (use a calculator if possible):
$$f(x) = x^2 - 4x - 2$$
and $g(x) = -x - 2$
in the domain $-1 \le x \le 5, x \in R$.
Plot the points on squared paper as shown and join the points
to form graphs of $f(x)$ and $g(x)$.
Using the graph:

  (i) describe the different shapes of the functions
  (ii) estimate the roots of $f(x)$
  (iii) estimate the root of $g(x)$
  (iv) find the minimum point of $f(x)$
  (v) write down the minimum value of the function $f(x)$
  (vi) write down the x – coordinate of the points of intersection
of the graphs i.e. the values of x so that $f(x) = g(x)$
  (vii) write down the axis of symmetry of $f(x)$.

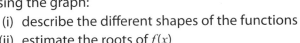

2. Draw a table of values for the function $f(x) = -x^3 + 4x^2 + x - 2$,
in the domain $-1 \le x \le 4, x \in R$ using a calculator.
Copy the grid as shown and plot the points and hence draw a
graph of the function in this domain.
Using your graph estimate the two roots of $f(x)$ in the domain
$-1 \le x \le 4$.

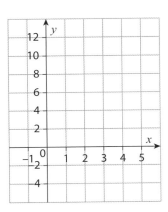

3. A ball is kicked into the air from a point O on the ground, $h(x) = -x^2 + 10x$, approximately describes the path followed by the ball in the air.

$h(x)$ is the height of the ball in metres.

x is the horizontal distance travelled by the ball in metres:

   (i) By trial and error, find two values of x that make, $h(x) = 0$.

  (ii) Explain in words what $h(x) = 0$ means in relation to the flight of the ball.

 (iii) Using a calculator, form a suitable table of values for $h(x) = -x^2 + 10x$ choosing your own domain.

 (iv) Plot the points from your table on squared paper to show the flight of the ball.

  (v) From your graph, find the coordinates of the highest point of the curve.

 (vi) What is the maximum height of the ball?

(vii) On your graph, draw an axis of symmetry for the curve.

Talking Point

The number of possible roots, i.e. values of x that make $f(x) = 0$, forms a pattern. Can you spot it?

	Roots
$f(x) = 4$	0
$f(x) = 2x - 3$	1
$f(x) = x^2 - x + 1$	2
$f(x) = x^3 + 5x - 2x - 4$	3

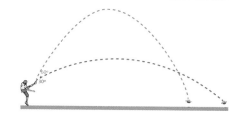

4. A rocket is launched into the air. The height of the rocket, h, can be modelled by the quadratic function $h = -5t^2 + 100t$, where t is measured in seconds.

   (i) Copy and complete the table of values using a calculator [STEP = 2].

t	0	2	4	6	8	10	12	14	16
h									

  (ii) Plot the points from the table on scaled axes, with t on the horizontal axis and h on the vertical axis measured in metres.

        Draw a smooth line through the points to show a graph of the path of the rocket in the first 16 seconds of flight.

 (iii) From the graph, find the maximum height of the rocket.

 (iv) From the graph, find the time at which the maximum height occurs.

5. An equation used to model the distance (d) travelled by a car in emergency stopping on a *dry* road is, $d = 0.01v^2 + 0.7v$ where d is measured in metres (m) and v is measured in km/h

   (i) Copy and complete a table of values for this function using steps of 10 km/h

v(km/h)	10	20	30	40	50	60
d(m)						

  (ii) Plot a graph of the points from the table placing the speed v on the horizontal axis as shown.

 (iii) If the speed limit in an area is changed from 60 km/h to 50 km/h, use your graph to estimate how much stopping distance is saved.

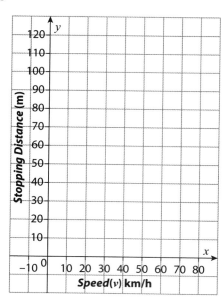

(iv) In *wet* conditions the equation used is $d = 0.015v^2 + 0.7v$. Repeat parts (i) and (ii) using the same axes, to compare stopping distances in wet and dry conditions.

(v) Extending the graphs, compare the stopping distances for wet and dry roads at 80 km/h.

6. A rectangle has a perimeter of 20 m.

(i) Copy and complete the table comparing the length, width and area of the rectangle.

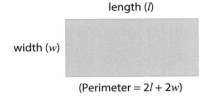

length (*l*)

width (*w*)

(Perimeter = $2l + 2w$)

l(m)	1	2	3	4	5	6	7	8	9
w(m)									
A(m²)									

(ii) Draw a graph of l against A for this rectangle to find the maximum area and when it occurs. (Plot length on the horizontal axis and Area on the vertical axis)

(iii) If the equation for area is represented by $A = a(l)^2 + b(l)$, use two points from the table to form two simultaneous equations in a and b and solve for a and b.

- If $x = 1$ and $x = -4$ are **roots** of $f(x)$.

  then $(x - 1) = 0$ and $(x + 4) = 0$

  are **factors** of the equation.

  then $f(x) = (x - 1)(x + 4) = 0$

  $\therefore f(x) = x^2 + 3x - 4$ is '**a**' function that has roots at $x = 1$ and $x = -4$.

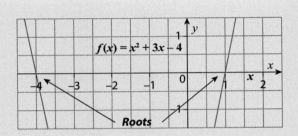

$f(x) = x^2 + 3x - 4$

Roots

---

7. Killian was asked by his teacher to find the roots of the function $f(x) = (x + 1)(x - 2)$ in the domain $-2 \leq x \leq 3, x \in R$.

He first multiplied out the function using a grid as shown and completed a table using his calculator as below.

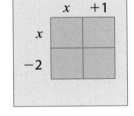

x	-2	-1	0	1	2	3
$f(x)$						

He then plotted the points and drew the graph of $f(x)$.

He said that the roots were $x = -1, x = 2$.

(i) Copy Killian's work and state if the roots were correct.

(ii) Suggest how he might have obtained the roots more easily.

(iii) Using Killian's function show that the point (4, 9) is not on the curve.

(iv) Find the roots of the function $g(x) = (x - 4)(x + 3)$ without plotting the graph.

(v) Find the roots of the function $h(x) = 3(x - 4)(x + 3)$ without plotting the graph.

8. Using a calculator complete the table below for the functions: (a) $f(x) = 1 + 2x - x^2$

(b) $g(x) = 2 + 4x - 2x^2$

(c) $h(x) = 3 + 6x - 3x^2$

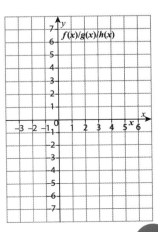

$f(x)/g(x)/h(x)$

x	-1	0	1	2	3
$f(x)$					
$g(x)$					
$h(x)$					

Plot the points on squared paper as shown and hence draw graphs of the three functions when $x \in R$.

(i) What features of each graph are the same?

(ii) $h(x) = k \times f(x)$ and $g(x) = m \times f(x)$, using algebra find the values of k and m.

(iii) Describe the effect of multiplying $f(x)$ by k or m.

(iv) From the graphs write down the maximum points of each graph.

(v) Estimate the roots of the functions.

(vi) Write down a function $c(x)$ that has the same roots as $f(x)$ and a maximum point of $(1, 8)$.

9. Using a calculator draw a table of values in the domain $-2.5 \leq x \leq 1.5, x \in Z$, for the function $f(x) = x^3 + 2x^2 - x - 2$.

Use a **STEP value** of 0.5.

Hence draw a graph of $f(x), x \in R$.

From your graph estimate:

(i) the maximum point of the curve

(ii) the minimum point of the curve

(iii) the roots of the graph.

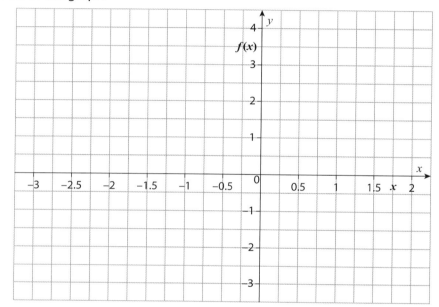

10.

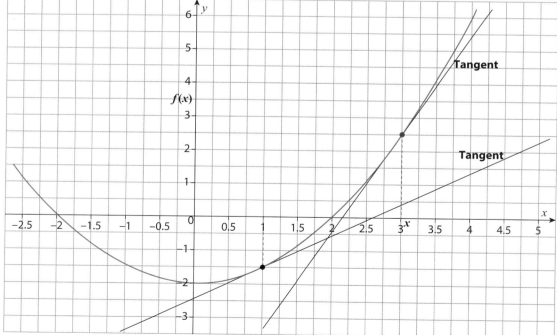

Examine the graph above and:

(i) write down the roots of the function $f(x)$

(ii) using the roots write down the factors of $f(x)$

(iii) using the factors write a possible equation for $f(x)$

(iv) Check if the point $(0, -2)$ is a point on the graph of $f(x)$

(v) Find the value of k so that $kf(x)$ has the same roots and passes through $(0, -2)$

(vi) write down an axis of symmetry for the curve

(vii) using the grid estimate the slope of the tangents to the curve at (a) $x = 3$ (b) $x = 1$

(viii) at what point on the graph could a tangent be drawn that has slope $= 0$?

Talking Point

Slope $= \dfrac{Rise}{Run}$

11. The graph of the function $f(x) = 2x^3 - 27x^2 + 109x - 126$ in the domain $1.5 \leq x \leq 7.5$ is given here.

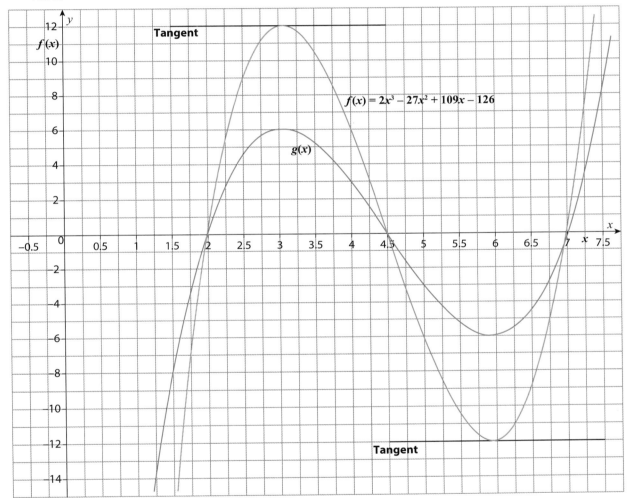

Using the graph find:

(i) the roots of $f(x)$

(ii) the coordinates of the *local* maximum point of $f(x)$

(iii) the coordinates of the *local* minimum point of $f(x)$

Tangents are drawn to the curve at the *local* maximum and minimum points, using the grid find:

(iv) the slope of the tangents.

Talking Point

Cubic graphs have *turning points* that are **local** maximum or **local** minimum points.
The graphs generally have no **absolute** maximum or minimum point

The graph of the function $g(x)$ is also shown and $g(x)$ has the same roots as $f(x)$. Find:

  (v)   the *local* maximum and minimum points of $g(x)$.
  (vi) using $f(x)$ as a guide write an equation for $g(x)$.
  (vii) write $g(x)$ as a product of its factors, $g(x) = (factor\ 1) \times (factor\ 2) \times (factor\ 3)$
  (viii) Verify that the point $(3, 6)$ is on $g(x)$ and find k such that $f(x) = k \times g(x)$.

Talking Point

If $f(x) = k \times g(x)$, k is an **amplification** factor.
By turning the volume control on a sound-system you are changing the value of k, changing the amplitude of the sound.

Part 2: Types and properties of functions

Looking back

<<

Features of a graph:

* Shape

  o **Linear:** $f(x) = ax + b$

    ▪ A straight line with a defined slope, positive, negative or zero

  o **Quadratic:** $f(x) = ax^2 + bx + c$

    ▪ A curve called a parabola

    ▪ A curve with a maximum or minimum turning point

  o **Cubic:** $f(x) = ax^3 + bx^2 + cx + d$

    ▪ A curve with (usually) two turning points a max and a min.

  o **Exponential:** $f(x) = a \times b^x$

    ▪ A curve continually increasing or decreasing.

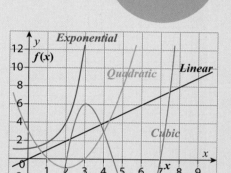

* Properties

  o Positive or negative:

    ▪ A graph is positive if it is above the x-axis

    ▪ A graph is negative if it is below the x-axis

  o Increasing or decreasing:

    ▪ A graph is increasing where the $y - values$ are increasing as we move along the graph from left to right.

       An increasing graph has a *positive* slope.

    ▪ A graph is decreasing where the $y - values$ are decreasing as we move along the graph from left to right.

       A decreasing graph has a *negative* slope.

2.1 Check-up

1. Graphs of a linear function $h(x)$ and a quadratic function $g(x)$ are plotted in the domain
   $-0.5 \leq x \leq 4.5$
   From the graphs find the values of
   x in the given domain for which:

   (i) $g(x)$ is negative
   (ii) $g(x)$ is increasing
   (iii) $g(x)$ is negative **and**
         increasing
   (iv) $g(x)$ is positive **and**
         decreasing
   (v) $h(x)$ positive

   Estimate the values of x for which:

   (vi) $h(x) \geq g(x)$
   (vii) $0 < h(x) < g(x)$

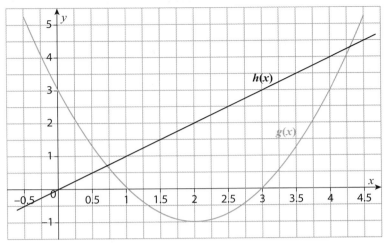

2. Study the graphs of $h(x)$ and $g(x)$ as shown and then complete the following sentences:
   (a) $h(x)$ is an example of a …………… function.
   (b) $g(x)$ is an example of an …………… function.
   In the domain $-1.5 \leq x \leq 3$ estimate the values of x for which:

   (i) $g(x) > 0$
   (ii) $h(x) \geq g(x)$
   (iii) $h(x) \geq g(x) \geq 0$

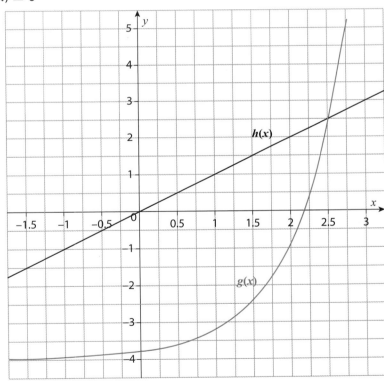

3. Complete the sentences:

   (a) $h(x)$ is an example of a .... function.

   (b) $p(x)$ is an example of a .... function.

   In the domain $-1 \leq x \leq 8$ estimate the values of x for which:

   (i) $h(x) > 0$ (i.e. is positive)

   (ii) $p(x) < 0$ (i.e. is negative)

   (iii) $p(x)$ is positive and decreasing.

   (iv) $p(x)$ is negative and increasing.

   (v) $p(x) = h(x)$

   (vi) $p(x) \geq h(x)$

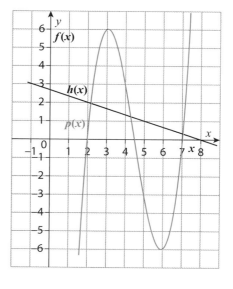

4. From the graph find the values of x in the domain $0 \leq x \leq 7$ for which:

   (i) $h(x)$ is increasing

   (ii) $h(x)$ is positive and increasing

   (iii) $h(x) = 0$

   (iv) $0 \leq h(x) \leq p(x)$

   (v) $p(x) \geq h(x)$

   (vi) $p(x) \geq h(x) \geq 0$

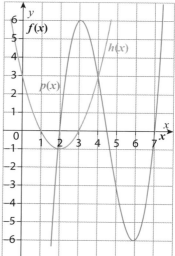

Part 3: Related graphs

Families of graphs:

- Given $f(x)$
  - $f(x) + 3$, creates a function, $+3$ units up from $f(x)$
  - $f(x) - 2$, creates a function, -2 units down from $f(x)$

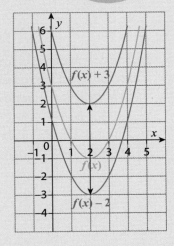

- Given $h(x)$
  - $h(x - 1)$ creates a function,
    1 unit to the right of $h(x)$
  - $h(x + 4)$ creates a function,
    4 units to the left of $h(x)$

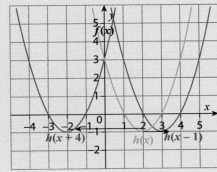

3.1 Check-up

>>

1. Copy the graph of the function, $f(x)$ shown and on the same axes *sketch* a graph of:
   (i) $h(x) = f(x) + 2$
   (ii) $g(x) = f(x) - 3$.
   Label each graph carefully.

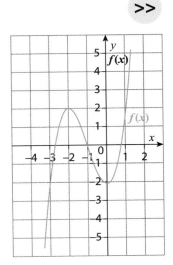

2. Copy the graph of the function, $f(x)$, shown and on the same axes *sketch* a graph of:

   (i) $h(x) = f(x - 4)$

   (ii) $g(x) = f(x + 1)$.

Label each graph carefully.

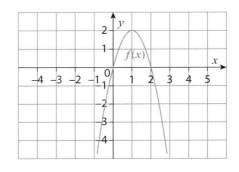

3. The graph of $f(x)$ is plotted as shown.

$h(x)$ and $g(x)$ are translations of $f(x)$.

  (a) Write an equation for:

     (i) $h(x)$ (ii) $g(x)$, in terms of $f(x)$.

  (b) If $f(x) = -x^2 + 2x + 1$ write an equation for:

     (i) $h(x)$ (ii) $g(x)$, in terms of x

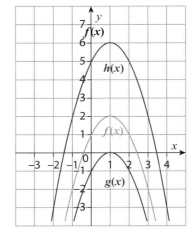

4. $f(x) = x^2 - 4x + 1$ is plotted on the grid as shown. The functions $g(x)$ and $h(x)$ are translations of $f(x)$.

In terms of x, write an equation for

   (i) $g(x)$ (ii) $h(x)$.

Simplify your answer.

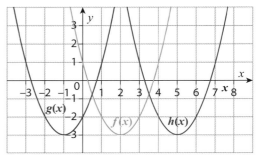

5. Plot a graph of function $y = f(x) = x^2 + 2x, x \in R$ in the domain $-3 \leq x \leq 1$.

Use the graph of y to draw a graph of (i) $y = (x + 3)^2 + 2(x + 3)$

State what effect multiplying each $y -$ value by (-1) has on the shape of the graph.

Hence draw a graph of (ii) $y = -x^2 - 2x$.

Example   >>

The function f is defined by $f(x) = 3x^2 - 2x + 5$

Find expressions for the **related** functions:

  (i) $g(x) = f(x) + 4$ (ii) $h(x) = f(x - 2)$ (iii) $c(x) = f(2x)$ (iv) $r(x) = f(x + 1) - 3$

Answer:

     (i) $g(x) = f(x) + \mathbf{4} = 3x^2 - 2x + 5 + \mathbf{4}$

        $g(x) = 3x^2 - 2x + 9$

     (ii) $h(x) = f(x - 2) = 3(x - 2)^2 - 2(x - 2) + 5$

          $= 3(x^2 - 4x + 4) - 2x + 4 + 5$

          $= 3x^2 - 12x + 12 - 2x + 9$

        $h(x) = 3x^2 - 14x + 21$

	x	-2
x	x^2	$-2x$
-2	$-2x$	$+4$

(iii) $c(x) = f(2x) = 3(2x)^2 - 2(2x) + 5$
$$= 3(4x^2) - 4x + 5$$
$$c(x) = 12x^2 - 4x + 5$$
(iv) $r(x) = f(x + 1) - \mathbf{3} = 3(x + 1)^2 - 2(x + 1) + 5 - \mathbf{3}$
$$= 3(x^2 + 2x + 1) - 2x - 2 + 5 - 3$$
$$= 3x^2 + 6x + 3 - 2x - 2 + 5 - 3$$
$$r(x) = 3x^2 + 4x + 3$$

	x	$+1$
x	x^2	$+x$
$+1$	$+x$	$+1$

3.2 Check-up

1. If $f(x) = 2x^2 - x$, find an expression for each of the following related functions:
   (i) $g(x) = f(x - 3)$ (ii) $h(x) = f(x) + 3$ (iii) $r(x) = f(2x + 1) - 2$.

2. The graph of the function f, defined as:
   $f : x \to x^2 - 2x - 1, x \in R$, is drawn as shown.
   The related graphs of $g(x)$ and $h(x)$ are drawn
   on the same axes.
   Write an equation in terms of $f(x)$ for the
   related functions (a) $g(x)$, (b) $h(x)$.
   Hence write equations in terms of x for
   (a) $g(x)$, (b) $h(x)$.

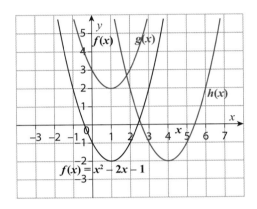

3. Three parallel lines l, m and p are drawn on the same grid.
   l has the equation $y = 1.5x + 2$
   By studying the relationship between the lines in the
   graph, write an equation for m and p.

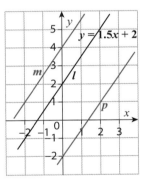

4. Given the function $f(x) = x^2 + 2x + 1$, find in terms of x, an expression for each of the following
   functions:
   (i) $g(x) = f(x) + 3$ (ii) $h(x) = f(x + 2)$
   (iii) $c(x) = f(5x)$ (iv) $t(x) = 3f(x)$ (v) $s(x) = f(x - 2) + 5$

5. Using a calculator, complete the table of points for the functions:
   (i) $f(x) = 2x^2 - 2x$
   (ii) $g(x) = 2x^2 + 6x + 4$
   (iii) $h(x) = 2x^2 - 2x + 5$
   Plot a graph of the three functions on the
   same axes in the domain $-3 \le x \le +3$
   By studying the graphs, write an expression
   for the functions $g(x)$ and $h(x)$ in terms of $f(x)$.
   On the same axes, draw a sketch of the function $c(x) = f(x - 3) - 2$

x	-3	-2	-1	0	1	2	3
$2x^2 - 2x$							
$2x^2 + 6x + 4$							
$2x^2 - 2x + 5$							

Part 4: Differential Calculus

Looking ahead

>>

- The slope of a curve is constantly changing

- Differential calculus is a tool for finding the slope at any point on a curve.

- The symbol for the slope of a function is
  $\dfrac{dy}{dx} = \dfrac{Rise}{Run}$ at a particular point on the curve.

- If a function is written as:
  - $y = \ldots$ then the slope is $\dfrac{dy}{dx} = \ldots$
  - $f(x) = \ldots$ then the slope is $f'(x) = \ldots$

- Finding the slope of a function is also called finding the *derivative* of a function

- The **general** rule: if $y = ax^n$ then the slope 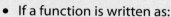 $\dfrac{dy}{dx} = n \times ax^{n-1}$

  In words *'multiply the function by the power **and** reduce the power by 1'*
  - If $y = x^4$ then the slope $\dfrac{dy}{dx} = 4 \times x^{4-1} = 4x^3$
  - If $y = 2x^4$ then the slope $\dfrac{dy}{dx} = 4 \times 2x^{4-1} = 8x^3$
  - If $y = 3x^5 + 2x^2 - 6$ then the slope $\dfrac{dy}{dx} = 5 \times 3x^4 + 2 \times 2x^1 - 0$
    $$= 15x^4 + 4x$$

- If the expression for the slope contains an x then the slope varies with x.

Talking Point

The slope of a constant is zero.

If $y = 6$, then $\dfrac{dy}{dx} = 0$.

Example

>>

Find the slope of each of the following functions:

(a) $y = x^2 + 5x$ (b) $y = 3 - 4x - x^3$ (c) $y = 6x^4 + 5x^2 + 2$

Answer: (a) $y = x^2 + 5x$ $\Rightarrow \dfrac{dy}{dx} = 2x^1 + 5x^0 = 2x + 5$

(b) $y = 3 - 4x - x^3$ $\Rightarrow \dfrac{dy}{dx} = 0 - 4x^0 - 3x^2 = -4 - 3x^2$

(c) $y = 6x^4 + 5x^2 + 2$ $\Rightarrow \dfrac{dy}{dx} = 4 \times 6x^3 + 2 \times 5x^1 + 0$

$$= 24x^3 + 10x$$

Example

Find the slope of $f(x) = x^2 + 2x - 6$ at the points on the curve where:

  (i) $x = 3$

  (ii) $x = 0$

  (iii) $x = -2$

Answer: $f(x) = x^2 + 2x - 6$

         $\Rightarrow f'(x) = 2x + 2,$

  (i) at $x = 3 \Rightarrow f'(3) = 2(3) + 2 = +8$

  (ii) at $x = 0 \Rightarrow f'(0) = 2(0) + 2 = +2$

  (iii) at $x = -2 \Rightarrow f'(-2) = 2(-2) + 2 = -2$

Talking Point

Notice how the slope changes from -2 to $+2$ as the curve passes through a minimum point!

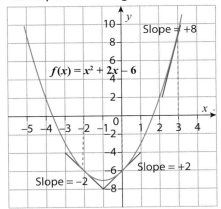

4.1 Check-up

1. Find the slope of:

  (i) $y = 4x^2 - 3x + 5$

  (ii) $y = 2x^3 - x^2 + 6x - 2$

  (iii) $y = x^3 + 5x^2 + 10x$

  (iv) $y = 2 + 4x - 2x^2$

2. Find the slope of the curve $y = 2x^3 - x^2 + 6x - 2$ where $x = 3$

3. Show that the point $(x, y) = (2, 4)$ is on the curve $y = x^2 - 2x + 4$ and find the slope of the curve at this point.

Talking Point

The language of calculus

Three ways of saying the same thing:

- Find the slope of.......

- Find the derivative of .....

- Differentiate ....

4. A graph of the function $y = -x^2 + 2x + 5$ is shown.

Show that the point S(0, 5) is on the curve. Find the slope of the curve at the point (0, 5).

Using the grid, show that the slope of the tangent is the same as the slope of the curve at the point (0, 5).

Hence find the equation of the tangent using the formula $y - y_1 = m(x - x_1)$.

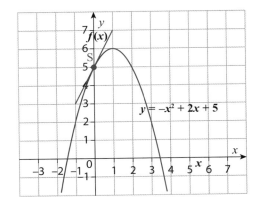

5. Find the derivative of each of the following:
  (i) $f(x) = x^3 + 2x^2 - 3x + 6$ at $x = 3$
  (ii) $f(x) = 2x^3 - 4x^2 + x$ at $x = 2$
  (iii) $f(x) = -5x^2 + 2x + 8$ at $x = -1$
  (iv) $f(x) = x^4 - x^3 + 5x^2 + x - 3$ at $x = 1$

Talking Point

$f'(4)$ is the slope of the function $f(x)$ evaluated at the point where $x = 4$.

6. Find the value of each of the following:
  (i) $f'(3)$ given $f(x) = 5x^2 - 4x + 2$
  (ii) $f'(-1)$ given $f(x) = x^2 - 10x + 6$
  (iii) $f'(-2)$ given $f(x) = 4x^2 + 7x + 2$
  (iv) $f'(4)$ given $f(x) = 3x^3 - 2x^2 + 4x - 1$

7. Differentiate each of the following functions:
  (i) $f(x) = 2x^2 + 3x + 1$ (ii) $f(x) = 4 - 2x - 5x^2$ (iii) $f(x) = 3x^2 - x + 2$

8.

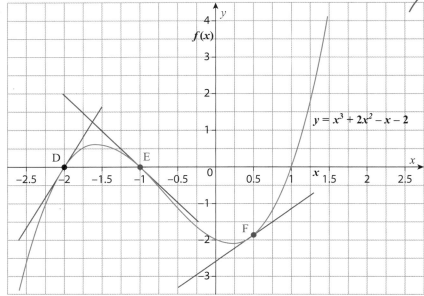

Talking Point

Notice the connection between the slope of the curve and where the graph is increasing and decreasing.
$(+)$ slope $\rightarrow$ increasing
$(-)$ slope $\rightarrow$ decreasing

The graph of $y = x^3 + 2x^2 - x - 2$ in the domain $-2.5 \le x \le 1.5$ is drawn on the axes as shown.

Three tangents are drawn to the curve at the points D, E and F.
  (i) Write down the coordinates of the three points.
  (ii) Find the slope of the curve at the points D, E and F (using calculus).
  (iii) Using the formula, $y - y_1 = m(x - x_1)$, find the equations of the tangents to the curve at these points.

9. Find the slope of the curve $g(x) = -x^2 + 2x$ at the points where:

(i) $x = 0$

(ii) $x = 1$

(iii) $x = 2$

What conclusion can you draw from the slope at the point where $x = 1$?

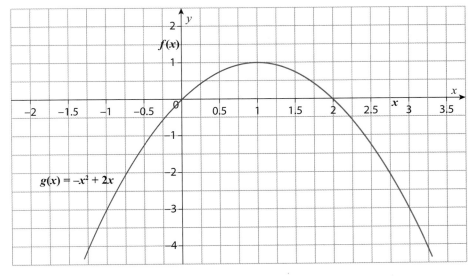

10. Write down the coordinates of the minimum point of $h(x) = x^2 - 4x + 3$.

(i) Find the slope of the tangent to the curve at the minimum point.

(ii) By picking any suitable value of x before the minimum point, show that the slope is negative.

What does a negative slope tell you about the behaviour of the curve at this point?

(iii) By picking a suitable value of x after the minimum point, show that the curve is increasing after that point.

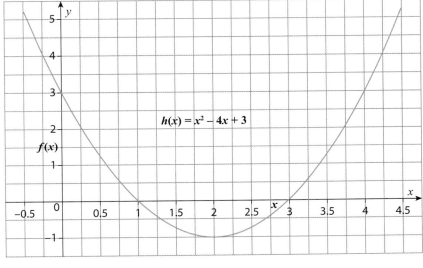

11. Find the derivative of the function
$f(x) = x^2 + 3x - 4, x \in R$.

Show that the slope of the curve is zero when $x = -1.5$.

Find the coordinates of the minimum point of the curve.

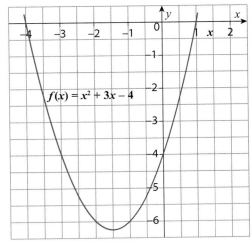

12. Differentiate the function $f(x) = 3x^2 - 6x - 8$, where $x \in R$.

Find the value of x for which the slope $= 0$.

Hence find the coordinates of the minimum point of the curve.

Part 5: Calculus and turning points

Looking ahead >>

- Calculus is used to locate the turning points on a curve.

- The steps involved in finding the maximum and minimum points are:

  ○ *Step 1*. Differentiate the function
  ○ *Step 2*. Equate the derivative to zero
  ○ *Step 3*. Solve the equation to find the $x -$ values of the turning points
  ○ *Step 4*. Use the values of x and the original equation to find the $y -$ coordinates of the turning points.

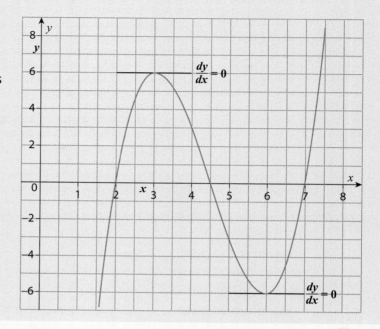

Example

>>

Find the coordinates of the turning point of the function $f(x) = -x^2 + 2x + 5$, where $x \in R$.

Answer: *Step 1.* $f(x) = -x^2 + 2x + 5$

$$\Rightarrow f'(x) = -2x + 2$$

Step 2. Let $f'(x) = -2x + 2 = 0$

Step 3. If $-2x + 2 = 0$

then $2x = 2$

$$x = 1$$

Step 4. If $x = 1, f(1) = -(1)^2 + 2(1) + 5$

$$= 6$$

The turning point of the curve is at $(1, 6)$

Talking Point

It is important to remember that the turning points are located by letting $\dfrac{dy}{dx} = 0$ and solving the equation.

There is still work to do to distinguish the max from the min.

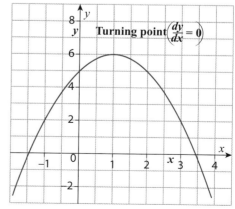

A U-shaped *quadratic curve* must have a minimum point.

An N-shaped *quadratic curve* has a maximum point.

5.1 Check-up

1. The roots of a quadratic function are $x = -2$ and $x = 3$.
   (i) Write down the factors of the function.
   (ii) Use the factors to show that the function can be written in the form
   $$f(x) = ax^2 + bx + c, \text{ where } a, b \text{ and } c \in Z.$$
   (iii) Using calculus, find the slope of the function.
   (iv) Show using your answer to (iii) that the function has a turning point at
   $(x, y) = (0.5, 6.25)$.
   (v) Determine if it is a maximum or minimum turning point.
   Give a reason for your answer.

2. Find the coordinates of turning point of each of the following quadratic curves.
   State if turning point is a maximum or minimum point:
   (i) $y = x^2 + 4x - 8$ (ii) $f(x) = 4x^2 - 4x + 1$ (iii) $y = 7 - 10x - x^2$
   (iv) $y = 10 + 6x - x^2$ (v) $y = 3x^2 - 12x + 1$ (vi) $f(x) = 12x - 3x^2$

3. Show that the three functions:
   (a) $f(x) = -x^2 + 2x$
   (b) $f(x) = -2x^2 + 4x$
   (c) $f(x) = -3x^2 + 6x$, all have the same roots $(0, 2)$
   State which one of the functions above has a graph as shown.
   (i) Using calculus, find the maximum turning point of each of
   the functions.
   (ii) Copy the graph and sketch the remaining two functions on
   the same axes.
   By picking any point before and after the maximum point,
   prove that the curve increases and then decreases.

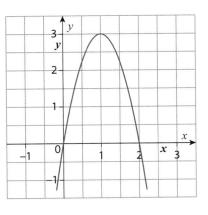

4. (a) Find values for a and b so that $(x + a)(x + b) = x^2 - 3x - 18 = 0, a, b \in Z$.
   (b) Anna plotted a graph of the function $f(x) = -x^3 + 4.5x^2 + 54x$ as shown below:

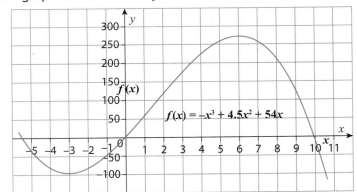

   (i) By differentiation, find the slope of the function and hence find two values of x at which
   turning points occur (your answer to (a) will help).
   (ii) Find the coordinates of the turning points.
   (iii) By choosing a point (a) before (b) between (c) after the turning points, state where the graph
   is increasing or decreasing.

FUNCTIONS AND CALCULUS TEST

1. The graph of $h(x) = x^2 - 2x, x \in R$, is shown in the diagram.
   Copy this diagram and on the same axes sketch the graph of each of
   the following:
   (a) $g(x) = h(x) + 2$
   (b) $g(x) = h(x + 2)$
   Label each graph clearly.
   From the graph find:
   (i) the roots of $h(x)$
   (ii) the axis of symmetry of the curve.

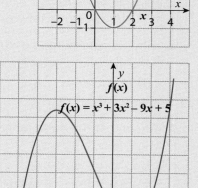

2. The function f is defined as $f : x \rightarrow x^3 + 3x^2 - 9x + 5, x \in R$.
   (i) Find the coordinates of the point where the curve crosses
       the y-axis.
   (ii) Verify that the graph of $f(x)$ cuts the x-axis at $x = -5$.
   (iii) Find the derivative of the function.
   (iv) Using your answer to (iii) show that there is a turning point
        at both $x = 1$ and $x = -3$.
   (v) Find the coordinates of the turning points.
   (vi) The function, $f(x)$, can be written as the product,
        $f(x) = (x + a)(x - b)(x - b)$,
        Find the values of a and b.

3. Find the slope of each of the following functions:
   (i) $y = 17$
   (ii) $y = 6x - 3$
   (iii) $y = x^2 - 2x + 8$.

4. If $f(x) = x^3 + 2x - 6$, find the value of each of the following:
   (i) $f'(2)$
   (ii) $f'(5)$
   (iii) $f'(-1)$

7 Number-Patterns-Sequences
through history

Number systems: The introduction of symbols to denote quantities.

A base 10 system divided into natural, integer, rational, real and complex numbers.

Sequence: An ordered set of numbers. It may be described as a mapping between the set of natural numbers and an ordered set of numbers.

The elements of a sequence are called terms. Term 1 (T_1), Term 2 (T_2), etc.

4000 BC	**Sumerians** were one of the earliest civilisations located in southern Iraq. They developed a system of numbers and counting. Their base unit was 60, a system that persists today in the measurement of rotation and time, 1 rotation = 360°, 60 seconds = 1 minute, 60 minutes = 1 hour. Why 60? One theory is that 60 has so many divisors (10), it made it easier to work with fractions. The number system had just two basic symbols, a unit symbol and a ten symbol.

166 would be written as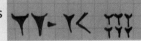

3000 BC   **Hindu-Arabic:** In the Middle East, a place-value system with 10 symbols, 9 digits and a zero was introduced. The twos in the number 2642 have very different values because of their position or place. It is to be noted that it took many centuries before zero was treated as a number.

500 BC to 1000 AD   **Roman / Islamic Art:** Patterns of tiles were used to decorate walls and floors. Patterns are created using different symmetries from geometry, reflection, rotation etc.

Patterns are found in nature particularly in plant growth.

1200 AD   **Fibonnaci**, in 1202, the Italian, Leonardo of Pisa, published his book *Libre Abaci* in which the Hindu Arabic numerals introduced the decimal number system to Western Europe. It also introduced the famous Fibonacci sequence, 1, 1, 2, 3, 5, 8, 13, 21, …etc, where each new term is obtained by adding the two previous terms. This sequence appears many times, in the natural world, in the study of bees in a beehive and petals on a plant.

1900 AD   **Koch**, the Swedish mathematician, generated a snowflake pattern from a triangle. It is an example of a *fractal* curve which has the unusual property that it has a finite area but an infinite circumference. Fractal mathematics is used to study coastlines, clouds and weather systems and the circulatory system.

Part 1: Number systems – Calculation

Looking back <<

Number systems:

- Natural numbers, N, whole positive numbers
  - 1, 2, 3, 4, …
- Integer numbers, Z, positive or negative whole numbers including zero, …
  - …$-3, -2, -1, 0, 1, 3,…$
- Rational numbers, Q, all numbers positive or negative that can be written in the fraction form $\frac{a}{b}$, where a and b are integers and $b \neq 0$.
  - $4 = \frac{4}{1}, \frac{-2}{7}, \frac{1}{3}, \frac{22}{7}$, etc.
- Irrational numbers, all numbers that cannot be written as a fraction.
  - $\sqrt{2}, \sqrt{5}, \pi, …$
- Real numbers, R, the union of the rational and irrational numbers.
- Standard form is used for very large or very small numbers.
  - $a \times 10^n, n \in Z, 1 \leqslant a < 10$
- Numerical calculations:
  - calculators are now used to do complex numerical calculations.
  - most calculators have screens that enable you to check that the calculation is inputted correctly before pressing =.

Example

Find the value of $\sqrt{\dfrac{(1.76 \times 10^3)^3}{4.5}}$ (i) correct to 3 significant figures

          (ii) in standard form correct to 1 decimal place.

Answer:

Carefully key in the data into the calculator.
Always check for errors before pressing '='.
(i) 34 806.69157 = 34 800
(ii) 3.5×10^4

Talking Point   Different models of calculator will have slightly different keying functions. It is very important to become familiar with the procedures connected with your calculator and to be able to use the full range of facilities it offers.

1.1 Check-up

1. Find the value of each of the following correct to 2 significant figures:

   (i) $\sqrt{6.7 \times 10^4}$ (ii) $\dfrac{4.76 \times 10^6}{1.89 \times 10^3}$ (iii) $\dfrac{1}{\sqrt{4.5 \times 3.78}}$

2. Evaluate each of the following:

   (i) $\dfrac{23.7^3}{\sqrt{68.4}}$ (ii) $\sqrt{\dfrac{1.87 \times 10^6}{3.57 \times 10^4}}$ (iii) $\left(\sqrt{2.5 \times 7.3}\right) - \sqrt{4.6 \times 1.6}$

Give each answer (a) correct to 3 significant figures
(b) in standard form correct to one place of decimals.

3. Find the value of the following: (a) in standard form correct to 2 places of decimals
(b) correct to 2 significant figures.

(i) $\sqrt{3.1 \times 10^4} + \dfrac{2.1 \times 10^8}{4.9 \times 10^5}$ 　　(ii) $\dfrac{7.2 \times 10^5}{3 \times 10^2 + 4.1 \times 10^3}$ 　　(iii) $5.25 \times 10^5 - 4.11 \times 10^4$

4. The speed of light in a vacuum is given as 299 792 458 metres per second.
If the distance from the Sun to Earth is given as 149 600 000 km,
find the time taken for the light of the sun to reach Earth.

$$\left(Speed = \frac{Distance}{Time} \right)$$

Give your answer correct to 2 significant figures.
Correct each of the numbers above to 3 significant figures and repeat the calculation.
Find the error involved in correcting the numbers before the calculation takes place.

5. A cylinder of water has a capacity of 3.45×10^6 cm³.
How many cylinders of capacity, 9.76×10^3 cm³, can be filled from the larger cylinder?

6. The mass of the Earth is given by the equation,

$M = \dfrac{g \times R^2}{G}$ where $g = 9.8$, $G = 6.7 \times 10^{-11}$ and $R = 6.4 \times 10^6$

Find, M, giving your answer in standard form correct to one place of decimals.

7. The mass of the sun, M, is related to the distance of the sun from the earth, R,

by the equation $M = \dfrac{4 \times \pi^2 \times R^3}{G \times T^2}$

where $R = 1.5 \times 10^{11} m$, $G = 6.7 \times 10^{-11}$ and $T = 365$ days.
By converting days into seconds, use the equation to find M in standard form correct to 1 place of decimals.

Part 2: Patterns and Sequences

Looking back
<<

- A sequence is a set of numbers with a term-to-term rule:
  - 2, 4, 6, 8,… …
  - each element of a sequence is called a *term*
  - The symbol for the first term is T_1.
  - T_n is the symbol used for the, n^{th}, term
- A sequence can be considered a mapping from the given set to the set of natural numbers
  - $2 \rightarrow T_1, 4 \rightarrow T_2, 6 \rightarrow T_3, 8 \rightarrow T_4 \ldots etc.$
- Geometrical patterns can be described by a set of numbers which form a sequence.

Example

<<

Black and white tiles are arranged in a set
of patterns as shown. Complete the grid below
showing the number sequences creating the
patterns. Extend the patterns to include
Pattern 4 and Pattern 5.

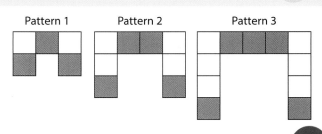

Describe the number patterns formed in words.
How many (i) white (ii) black tiles are needed for Pattern 8?
Will one of the patterns have a total of 30 tiles?

Answer:

	T_1	T_2	T_3	T_4	T_5
White tiles	2	4	6	8	10
Black tiles	3	4	5	6	7
Total number of tiles	5	8	11	14	17

White tiles: The sequence starts with 2 white tiles. 2 extra white tiles are added to each pattern.
Black tiles: The sequence starts with 3 black tiles. 1 extra black tile is added to each pattern.
Total number of tiles: The sequence starts with 5 tiles. 3 extra tiles are added to each pattern.

(i) Since $T_1 = 2$, $T_2 = 4$, $T_3 = 6$, the number of white tiles needed is 2 times the term number
$\times 2 \quad \times 2 \quad \times 2$
$\therefore T_8$ has $2 \times 8 = 16$ white tiles

(ii) Since $T_1 = 3$, $T_2 = 4$, $T_3 = 5$, the number of black tiles is 2 greater than the term
$+2 \quad +2 \quad +2$
number $\therefore T_8$ has $8 + 2 = 10$ black tiles

(iii) Since $T_1 = 5$, $T_2 = 8$, $T_3 = 11$, the total number of tiles increases by 3 for each term.
Using $T_1 = 5$, we need to find a number n so that $2 + 3n = 30$
$$3n = 30 - 2 = 28$$
$$n = \frac{28}{3} = 9\frac{1}{3}$$
$\therefore$ No pattern has exactly 30 tiles.

2.1 Check-up   **<<**

1. The bead pattern is made from 2 different coloured beads as shown.
Complete the table below showing the number of beads needed up to pattern 5.
Explain how to find the total number of beads needed for the nth term.

	T_1	T_2	T_3	T_4	T_5
Blue					
Total					

2.

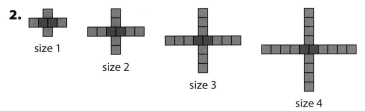

size 1
size 2
size 3
size 4

A pattern of crosses is designed from square tiles as shown.
Describe the sequence created.
Will any of the patterns need 46 tiles? Explain your answer.

3.

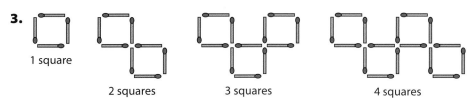

1 square
2 squares
3 squares
4 squares

Complete the chart up to 5 squares.
How many matchsticks will be needed for 12 squares?
Will one of the patterns have 40 matchsticks?

Number of squares	T_1	T_2	T_3	T_4	T_5
Number of matchsticks					

4.

1

2

3

The first three patterns in a sequence of patterns are shown above.

n	Number of black triangles	Number of white triangles	Total number of small triangles
Pattern 1	3	1	4
Pattern 2			
Pattern 3			
Pattern 4			
Pattern 5			

Copy and complete the chart showing the number of white, black and the total number of triangles needed for each pattern.

(i) By studying the pattern, find the number of black triangles that would be needed along the side of the 4th pattern.

(ii) Draw a diagram of the 4th pattern.

(iii) By counting on, find the number of black tiles needed for the 9th pattern.

A formula for the total number of black tiles needed for each pattern is:

Total number of black triangles $= \frac{1}{2}n^2 + \frac{3}{2}n + 1$, where n is the pattern number;

(iv) Verify your answers in the chart using the formula.

(v) Verify your answer for T_9.

5. The first 5 numbers in a sequence are 13, 15, 19, 25, 33, …

By counting on, continue the sequence of numbers by adding in terms T_6, T_7, T_8, T_9.

Verify that the formula $T_n = n^2 - n + 13$ gives the same answers for T_6, T_7, T_8, T_9.

6. By letting $n = 1, 2, 3, …$ etc., write out the first 6 terms of the sequence defined by the formula, $T_n = n^2 + n - 6$.

Part 3: Arithmetic Sequences

Looking back <<

- A sequence that has a *common difference* between consecutive terms is called:

  ○ an *arithmetic* sequence or a

  ○ *linear* sequence

  ○ 3, 6, 9, 12, … is an arithmetic sequence.

  ○ The *common difference* is constant and $= 3$.

- A *rule* for the nth term of an **arithmetic** sequence is

  ○ $T_n = a + (n - 1)d$ where

    ■ a is the first term

    ■ d is the common difference

    ■ n is the term number, the 5th term $\rightarrow n = 5$

Example

Write down the rule for the nth term, T_n of the sequence 8, 15, 22, 29, 36, …
  (i) Use the rule to find T_{20}
  (ii) Which term of the sequence is 211?

Answer: $a = 8$ and
$$(15 - 8) = (22 - 15) = (29 - 22) = 7 = \text{the common}$$
$$\text{difference, } d$$
$$\therefore T_n = a + (n - 1)d = 8 + (n - 1)7$$
$$= 8 + 7n - 7$$
$$T_n = 7n + 1$$
  (i) $T_{20} = 7(20) + 1 = 141$
  (ii) Let $T_n = 7n + 1 = 211$
$$7n = 211 - 1 = 210$$
$$n = \frac{210}{7} = 30$$

> **Talking Point**
>
> For arithmetic sequences
> e.g. 8, 15, 22, 29, etc.
> with common difference = 7
> the nth will be
> $$7n \pm \text{ a number.}$$

3.1 Check-up

1. Find a rule for the nth term, T_n of the sequences:
   (i) 5, 7, 9, 11, 13, …   (ii) 11, 13, 15, 17, ….   (iii) 1, 5, 9, 13, 17, …

2. Find the first four terms in each sequence given the general term, T_n:
   (i) $T_n = 4n + 3$ (ii) $T_n = 6n - 2$ (iii) $T_n = 5 - 2n$

3. Write out the first 5 terms of the sequences (i) $T_n = 4n + 3$ (ii) $T_n = 2 - 5n$.
   Describe the main difference between the sequences formed.

4. Write out the first 5 terms of the sequence defined by the rule $T_n = \dfrac{1}{n + 2}$
   Is the sequence formed arithmetic?

5. Write out T_5 and T_{10} for the sequence $T_n = \dfrac{3n}{5} + 2$.

6. Write out the first 5 terms of the sequence with n^{th} term, $T_n = 3n - 4$.
   Which term of this sequence $= 59$?

7. (i) Write the number sequence for the total number of tiles needed for each of these patterns.
   (ii) Using the formula, $T_n = a + (n - 1)d$, find T_n for the sequence.
   (iii) Hence find the number of tiles needed for Pattern 20.

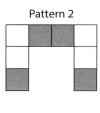
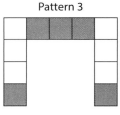

Pattern 1   Pattern 2   Pattern 3

8. The first three stages of a design are shown. Write the number sequence that represents the total number of tiles needed for the first 5 stages of this design.
   Explain why this sequence is not linear(arithmetic).

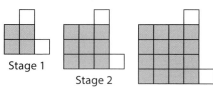

Stage 1   Stage 2   Stage 3

9. The general term of an arithmetic sequence is $T_n = 15 - 2n, n \in N$.
   (i) Write down the first three terms of the sequence.
   (ii) Find the first negative term of the sequence.
   (iii) Find which term of the sequence is -63.

10. In art class, Brian used squares and equilateral triangles to create a pattern. The first 4 parts of his design are shown.

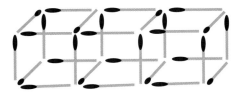

Write a formula for T_n, the nth term of the sequence of squares and T_n, the nth term of the sequence of triangles in his design. If t represents the number of triangles and s represents the number of squares, write a formula connecting t and s.

11. Claire was designing a series of cubes from matchsticks. Complete the table showing the number of matchsticks she will need as the design gets bigger.
Find T_n for the sequence.
If she wants to have 10 cubes in her design how many matchsticks will she need?

n the number of cubes			
number of matchsticks			

Part 4: Arithmetic Series

Looking ahead
>>

- An arithmetic **sequence** with first term a and common difference d can be written as:
  - $a, a + d, a + 2d, a + 3d, a + 4d, \ldots a + (n - 1)d$
  - $T_1, \quad T_2, \quad T_3, \quad T_4, \quad T_5, \quad T_n$
- An arithmetic **series** with first term a and common difference d can be written as:
  - $a + (a + d) + (a + 2d) + \cdots + (a + (n - 1)d)$
  - $T_1 + \quad T_2 \quad + \quad T_3 \quad + \cdots + \quad T_n$
  - a series is created by adding the terms of a sequence.
- It can be shown that the sum of n terms of the **series**, S_n, has the formula:
  - $S_n = \frac{n}{2}\{2a + (n - 1)d\}$

Example

>>

The general term of an arithmetic sequence is, $T_n = 7 - n$, where $n \in N$
  (i) Write out the first 4 terms of the sequence. Hence find values for a and d.
 (ii) Find S_n the sum to n terms of the sequence in terms of n.
(iii) Find the value of n for which the sum of the first n terms is 0.

Answer:
(i) $T_n = 7 - n \Rightarrow T_1 = 7 - 1 = 6$
$\qquad\qquad\qquad T_2 = 7 - 2 = 5$
$\qquad\qquad\qquad T_3 = 7 - 3 = 4$
$\qquad\qquad\qquad T_4 = 7 - 4 = 3$

The first four terms are 6, 5, 4, 3
$\Rightarrow a = 6$ and $d = 5 - 6 = -1$

(ii) $S_n = \frac{n}{2}\{2a + (n - 1)d\}$

$\qquad = \frac{n}{2}\{2(6) + (n - 1)(-1)\}$

$\qquad = \frac{n}{2}\{12 - n + 1\}$

$\qquad = \frac{n}{2}\{13 - n\}$

Talking Point

If the sequence is increasing d is positive.
5, 8, 11, 14, … $d = +3$

If the sequence is decreasing d is negative.
6, 2, -2, -6, … $d = -4$

(iii) Let $S_n = \frac{n}{2}\{13 - n\} = 0$

$\Rightarrow \{13 - n\} = 0 \dots |\, 6 + 5 + 4 + 3 + 2 + 1 + 0 + (-1) + (-2) + (-3) + (-4) + (-5) + (-6) = 0$

$n = 13$ i.e. the sum of the first 13 terms $= 0$

4.1 Check-up

1. Find T_n and S_n for each of the following arithmetic sequences.
   (i) $5, 7, 9, 11, \dots$ (ii) $10, 14, 18, 22, \dots$ (iii) $-4, -1, 2, 5, \dots$ (iv) $11, 6, 1, -4, \dots$

2. The nth term of a sequence is given by $T_n = 4 + 3n$.
   (i) Write out the first 4 terms of the sequence.
   (ii) Find an expression for S_n the sum to n terms of the sequence.
   (iii) Find the sum of the first 20 terms of the sequence, S_{20}.

> **Talking Point**
>
> Solving a quadratic equation to find n, where, n, is a number of terms.
> e.g. If $S_n = n^2 - 5n - 24 = 0$
> Factorising we have $n^2 - 5n - 24 = (n + 3)(n - 8)$
> $\therefore n + 3 = 0 \Rightarrow n = -3$
> or $n - 8 = 0 \Rightarrow n = 8$
> Since $n \in N$, n cannot be negative (-3) $\therefore$ the only valid answer is $n = 8$.
>
> | | n | -8 |
> |-------|-------|--------|
> | n | n^2 | $-8n$ |
> | $+3$ | $+3n$ | -24 |
>
> -24
>
> | 1 | -24 |
> |---|-------|
> | 2 | -12 |
> | 3 | -8 |

3. The first term of an arithmetic sequence is 8 and the common difference is -2.
   (i) Write an equation for the sum of n terms of the sequence, S_n.
   (ii) If the sum of the first n terms, $S_n = 20$, solve the quadratic equation to find the number of terms, n, in the sum.
   Check your answer by writing out the first n terms.

4. The general term of a sequence is $T_n = (n + 1)(n + 4)$.
   (i) Which term of the sequence is 70?
   (ii) Show that the sequence is not arithmetic.

5. The number of mosaic tiles needed for a set of patterns is shown in the table over:

Pattern number	1	2	3	4	5	6	7
Number of tiles	5	8	11				

   (i) Copy and complete the table.
   (ii) Find an expression for the nth term of the sequence, T_n.
   (iii) How many tiles will be needed for the 25th term?
   (iv) Which pattern will have 254 tiles in it?
   (v) Using, $S_n = \frac{n}{2}\{2a + (n - 1)d\}$, find a formula in terms of n for the total number of tiles needed to complete n patterns.
   (vi) How many tiles will the tiler need to complete 30 mosaic patterns?

6. The sum of the first n terms of a series is $S_n = 2n^2 - n$.
   (i) Find values for S_1, S_2, S_3, S_4, S_5.
   (ii) Since $S_1 = T_1$
   and $S_2 = T_1 + T_2$
   and $S_3 = T_1 + T_2 + T_3$ etc.,
   find values for T_1, T_2, T_3, T_4, T_5.

   > **Talking Point**
   >
   > If $S_n = n^2 + n$
   > $\Rightarrow S_1 = 1^2 + 1 = 2 =$ first term (T_1)
   > $\Rightarrow S_2 = 2^2 + 2 = 6 =$ sum of the first two terms $(T_1 + T_2)$
   > $\therefore$ the second term $= 6 - 2 = 4$

   (iii) Show that the sequence is arithmetic and find an expression for T_n.
   (iv) Which term of the sequence $= 101$?

7. The chart below shows the first 5 terms of sequences A, B and C.

(i) Complete the chart.

(ii) The nth term, T_n, of each of the sequences can be written in the form $T_n = n^2 + an + b$, where $a, b \in Z$. Find values of a and b for each sequence.

	T_1	T_2	T_3	T_4	T_5	T_6	T_7
A	6	11	18	27	38		
B	4	9	16	25	36		
C	2	7	14	23	34		

(iii) If T_{n_A} (the nth term of A) $= T_{n_B} + k$, where $k \in Z$, find k.

8. (i) Write down the formula for the sum to n terms, S_n, of an arithmetic sequence.

(ii) Write an equation for S_8 in terms of a and d.

(iii) If the common difference of the series is 3 and $S_8 = 132$, find the value of a.

(iv) Find the first four terms of the sequence and hence find the value for T_{25}.

9. Show that $S_5 - S_4 = T_5$,

where $S_5 =$ the sum of the first five terms of an arithmetic sequence,

$S_4 =$ the sum of the first four terms, and T_5 is the 5th term.

(i) If $S_{11} = 198$ and $S_{10} = 165$ find the value of T_{11}.

(ii) Write simultaneous equations in terms of a and d for (a) T_{11} (b) S_{10}. Solve the equations for a and d.

(iii) Find a value for S_{20}.

10. A start-up company made a loss of €5000 in its first month of trading. This loss reduced by €500 each month that the company traded.

The finances can be represented by a chart as follows:

Month	1	2	3	4	5	6	7
Profit (€)	-5000	-4500	-4000	-3500	...	...	...

(i) Find the nth term of the profit sequence.

(ii) Find the profit in month 20.

(iii) After how many months will the company 'break even'?

(iv) Find S_n, the total profit made by the company after n months.

(v) Hence find the total profit after 2 years.

Talking Point The terms of a sequence are sometimes written as $u_1, u_2, u_3, \ldots u_n$

11. A sequence has a general term $u_n = an + b$

Find a and b given that $u_2 = 0$ and $u_6 = -4$.

Part 5: Quadratic sequences

Looking back <<

- A quadratic sequence is a sequence in which the *second difference* is constant.
  - $T_n = 3n - 1 \rightarrow$ *arithmetic (linear)*

Term	2	5	8	11	14
1st difference	+3	+3	+3	+3	

  - $T_n = n^2 - n + 1 \rightarrow$ *quadratic*

	T_1	T_2	T_3	T_4	T_5
Term	1	3	7	13	21
1st difference	+2	+4	+6	+8	
2nd difference		+2	+2	+2	

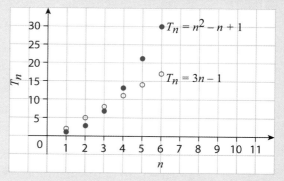

Example

<<

A triangular pattern of dots is part of a design Anna painted onto a long corridor wall.
  (i) Make a table showing the number of dots in the first 6 patterns.
  (ii) Use the table to show that the number of dots forms a quadratic sequence.
  (iii) If $T_n = \frac{1}{2}n^2 + \frac{3}{2}n + 1$, find T_{10} and T_{20}.

Answer:

(i)

	T_1	T_2	T_3	T_4	T_5	T_6
Term	3	6	10	15	21	28
1st difference	+3	+4	+5	+6	+7	
2nd difference		+1	+1	+1	+1	

(ii) The second difference is constant ($= +1$) therefore the sequence is quadratic.

(iii) $T_n = \frac{1}{2}n^2 + \frac{3}{2}n + 1 \Rightarrow T_{10} = \frac{1}{2}10^2 + \frac{3}{2}(10) + 1$

$$= 50 + 15 + 1 = 66$$

$$\Rightarrow T_{20} = \frac{1}{2}(20)^2 + \frac{3}{2}(20) + 1$$

$$= 200 + 30 + 1 = 231$$

5.1 Check-up

1. Using a table format to find 'second-differences', show that each of the following sequences are quadratic:
   - (i) 13, 15, 19, 25, 33, ….
   - (ii) 6, 11, 18, 27, 38, …
   - (iii) 1, 6, 15, 28, 45, …

2. Let $T_n = n^2 + an + b$ be the nth of the quadratic sequence
   4, 9, 16, 25, 36, 49, … where $a, b \in Z$
   - (i) Write an equation in terms of a and b for T_1 and T_2.
   - (ii) Solve the simultaneous equations to find a and b.
   - (iii) Use your equation to find T_{20}.

> **Talking Point**
>
> Simultaneous equations
> If $2a + b = 3$
> and $a + 3b = -1$) $\times 3$
> then $6a + 3b = 9$
> and $a + 3b = -1$ ..subtract
> $\Rightarrow 5a = 10$
> $\Rightarrow a = 2$ and $b = -1$

3. The first three patterns in a sequence of patterns are shown below.

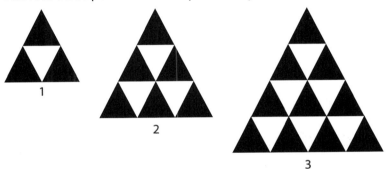

1

2

3

Maurice experimented with a triangular design as part of a graphical competition.
- (i) How many extra triangles does he need for (a) pattern 4 (b) pattern 5.
- (ii) Copy and complete the table showing the number of tiles needed for each pattern.
- (iii) Show using differences that each sequence of numbers is quadratic.
- (iv) If the general term, T_n, for the sequence of black tiles can be written as $T_n = \frac{1}{2}n^2 + an + b$ find the value of a and b using simultaneous equations for T_1 and T_2.
- (v) Repeat part (iv) for the sequence of white tiles.

	T_1	T_2	T_3	T_4	T_5
Black					
1st diff					
2nd diff					
White					
1st diff					
2nd diff					
Total					
1st diff					
2nd diff					

- (vi) The general term, T_n, for the total number of tiles needed for the design can be written as $T_n = n^2 + an + b$, find a and b using simultaneous equations for T_1 and T_2 of the total number of tiles sequence.
- (vii) Show that $T_n(\text{total}) = T_n(\text{black}) + T_n(\text{white})$.

4. Write down the first 7 terms of the sequence,

$S = 2, 7, 16, 29, 46, \ldots$

  (i) Show that the sequence is quadratic.

  (ii) The general term of the sequence is given by,

    $T_n = 2n^2 + an + b$, where $a, b \in Z$. Find the values of a and b.

  (iii) The sequence, $K = 0, 5, 14, 27, 44, \ldots$ is 'related' to the sequence S.
Write down a formula for the nth term of K.

5. Given that $u_n = an^2 + bn$, $u_4 = 28$ and $u_8 = 120$,
find the values of a and b using simultaneous equations.
Hence write out the first five terms of the sequence.

6. $u_n = (2n - 1)(3n + 1)$ is the nth term of a sequence.
If $u_k = 286$ find the value of k.

7. The first three terms of a quadratic sequence are 1, 3, 7,... where the general term of
the sequence is given by $u_n = an^2 + bn + c$.
Find the values of a, b, c, using simultaneous equations with three unknowns.
Use u_n to write out the first 6 terms of the sequence.

8. Show that $n^2 - 8n + 19$ can be written as $(n - 4)^2 + 3$.
Hence show that all the terms of the sequence, $u_n = n^2 - 8n + 19$ are positive.

9. Explain why for $n \in N$, all the terms of the sequence:

  (i) $u_n = 2n$, are even numbers.

  (ii) $u_n = 2n + 1$, are odd numbers.

  If $u_n = 2n - 3$, show that all the terms of the sequence given by $u_{2n + 1}$ are odd numbers.

10. (i) Given the quadratic sequence generated by $u_n = n^2 - 2n - 5$,
find the nth term generated by $u_{3n + 1}$.
Show that 3 is a factor of $u_{3n + 1}$.

  (ii) Write out the first 5 terms of the sequence $u_{3n + 1}$.

11. Find an expression for, S_n, the sum to n terms of 4, 13, 22, 31, ...
The sum of the arithmetic series $4 + 13 + 22 + 31 + \ldots$ is to be greater than 1000. How many
terms are needed to achieve this?

12. Daniel repays a loan over n months:
He repays €150 in the first month, €146 in the second month, €142 in the third month and so on.

  (i) Find how much he repays in the 20th month.

  (ii) Form an equation for the total amount he has repaid in terms of n, the number of months.
Using this equation, find out how much he has repaid in 20 months.

  (iii) If the amount he borrowed was €3000, find out how much was left to be repaid after 3 years.

NUMBER & SEQUENCE TEST

1. Electrons moving in an X-ray tube have a speed given by the equation

   $$v = \sqrt{\frac{2eV}{m}}$$ where m is the mass of the electron, 9×10^{-31} kg

   e is the electronic charge, 1.6×10^{-19} C

   Find the value of the speed v if the potential difference, $V = 10^4$ volts.
   Give your answer in standard form correct to two places of decimals.

2. The fourth and fifth terms of a sequence are 26 and 33.
   if $u_n = an + b$, find the values of the constants a and b.
   Write out the first five terms of the sequence.

3. The nth term of an arithmetic sequence is $T_n = 3n - 2$
   (i) Write down the first five terms of the sequence.
   (ii) State the value of the common difference.
   (iii) Show that the sum of n terms of the series is given by, $S_n = \frac{1}{2}n(3n - 1)$
   Hence find the sum of the first 20 terms.

4. Find the sum of the first 20 terms of the sequence
   $$-23 + (-18) + (-13) + (-8) + \dots$$

5. Alice's godfather gave her an allowance of €500 towards her education on her 11th birthday and
   promised to increase the allowance by €200 each year.
   (i) Write out a list of the monies she received over the first four years.
   (ii) By finding an nth term for the sequence, find out how much of an allowance she received on
   her 18th birthday.
   (iii) Alice decided to save her godfather's generous present in the post office.

   Find the total amount she had saved in the post office up to and including her 18th birthday.
   When the monies she received reached a total of €32 000 the allowance stopped.
   How old was Alice when she received her last allowance?

8 Complex Numbers *through history*

- A special number that has a **real part** (*a*) and an **imaginary part** (*b*).
- All complex numbers take the form $a + bi$
- We usually use *z* to represent a complex number $\therefore z = a + bi$.
- The symbol $i = \sqrt{-1} \Rightarrow i^2 = -1$

1545 AD	***Gerolamo Cardona***, an Italian mathematician, published a book, ***Ars Magna***, which included the sum $(5 + \sqrt{-15}) \times (5 - \sqrt{-15}) = 25 - (-15) = 40$, in an attempt to solve cubic equations. He branded the work '*useless*' because there was at the time no understanding of how to deal with $\sqrt{negative\ number}$.
1572 AD	***Raphael Bombelli***, also an Italian mathematician/engineer, born in Bologna, published his major work in mathematics, ***L'Algebra***, which for the first time set out the rules for dealing with imaginary numbers, e.g. $\sqrt{-9}$. *Remember*, when you square any *real* number the answer is always positive. $(-2) \times (-2) = 4$
1750 AD	***Leonhard Euler***, a Swiss mathematician, gave the name *imaginary unit*, or *i* by which it is known today. Mathematicians of the day including Descartes (of the Cartesian plane) used the term as an insult. 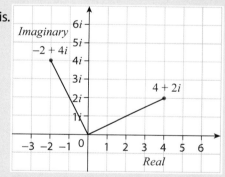 Leonhard Euler
1797 AD	***Carl Friedrich Gauss*** proved that **any** equation built from real numbers could be solved using complex numbers.
1806 AD	***Jean-Robert Argand*** managed a book shop in Paris. He self-published his mathematical work containing the geometrical interpretation of complex numbers. He realised that the *real* number line could not be used to plot a complex number, e.g. $4 + \sqrt{-3}$. He used a rotation of 90° to represent the imaginary part of the complex number. This diagram is still referred to today as an Argand diagram. It is an important mathematical tool which helps us to understand complex numbers. The solutions of *all* equations can be mapped onto the complex plane.
1850 AD	***William Rowan Hamilton***, born in Dublin, extended the idea of a complex number to include 3-dimensional space. He created the idea of a quaternion $\{a + bi + cj + dk\}$ where *j* and *k* are also imaginary. Quaternions are particularly useful in virtual reality technology. 

Part 1: Imaginary numbers

Looking ahead >>

- $\sqrt{-2}$ is an example of an imaginary number.
- $\sqrt{-1}$ is the basic unit of imaginary numbers and is given the symbol i.
  - $\sqrt{-1} = i$
- All imaginary numbers can be written in terms of i.
  - $\sqrt{-2} = \sqrt{2 \times -1} = \sqrt{2} \times \sqrt{-1} = \sqrt{2}i$
  - $\sqrt{-16} = \sqrt{16 \times -1} = \sqrt{16} \times \sqrt{-1} = 4i$

Example

Simplify each of the following, writing each number in terms of i:

(i) $\sqrt{-25}$ (ii) $\sqrt{-20}$ (iii) $\sqrt{-48}$ (iv) $\sqrt{-50}$

Answer:
  (i) $\sqrt{-25} = \sqrt{25 \times -1} = \sqrt{25} \times \sqrt{-1} = 5i$
  (ii) $\sqrt{-20} = \sqrt{20} \times \sqrt{-1} = \sqrt{20}i = \sqrt{4 \times 5}i = \sqrt{4} \times \sqrt{5}i = 2\sqrt{5}i$
  (iii) $\sqrt{-48} = \sqrt{48} \times \sqrt{-1} = \sqrt{48}i = \sqrt{16 \times 3}i = \sqrt{16} \times \sqrt{3}i = 4\sqrt{3}i$
  (iv) $\sqrt{-50} = \sqrt{50 \times -1} = \sqrt{50} \times \sqrt{-1} = \sqrt{50}i$
$$= \sqrt{25 \times 2}i = \sqrt{25} \times \sqrt{2}i$$
$$= 5\sqrt{2}i$$

1.1 Check-up

1. Write each of the following numbers in terms of i:

(i) $\sqrt{-9}$ (ii) $\sqrt{-18}$ (iii) $\sqrt{-72}$ (iv) $\sqrt{-100}$

2. Simplify each of the following:

(i) $\sqrt{-25} + \sqrt{-16}$ (ii) $\sqrt{-40} + \sqrt{-10}$ (iii) $\sqrt{-48} - \sqrt{-12}$ (iv) $\sqrt{-50} + \sqrt{-32}$

3. Once simplified, classify each of the following numbers as:

(a) Imaginary   (b) Rational   (c) Irrational

(i) $\sqrt{16}$ (ii) $\sqrt{-3}$ (iii) $\sqrt{\frac{1}{4}}$ (iv) $\sqrt{\frac{-1}{4}}$ (v) $\sqrt{2}$

(vi) $\sqrt{-49}$ (vii) $\sqrt{20}$ (viii) $\sqrt{9} \times \sqrt{5}$ (ix) $\sqrt{-9} \times \sqrt{-2}$ (x) $\sqrt{-4}$.

Part 2: Complex numbers

Looking ahead >>

- A complex number is written as, $z = a + bi$
  - where a and b are real numbers and $i = \sqrt{-1}$
  - a is the **real part** and b is the **imaginary part** of the complex number
- All numbers can be written in complex form with a real and imaginary part
  - $3 = 3 + 0i$
  - $4i = 0 + 4i$
- All equations have roots that can be written in complex form.

Example

Using the equation, $x = \dfrac{-b \pm \sqrt{b^2 - 4ac}}{2a}$

express the roots of the equation, $x^2 + 2x + 4 = 0$, in complex form.

Talking Point

Answer: $a = 1, b = 2, c = 4$

$$\therefore x = \frac{-b \pm \sqrt{b^2 - 4ac}}{2a}$$

$$= \frac{-(2) \pm \sqrt{(2)^2 - 4 \times (1) \times (4)}}{2 \times (1)}$$

$$= \frac{-2 \pm \sqrt{4 - 16}}{2} = \frac{-2 \pm \sqrt{-12}}{2}$$

$$= \frac{-2 \pm \sqrt{12}i}{2} = \frac{-2 \pm 2\sqrt{3}i}{2}$$

$$= -1 \pm \sqrt{3}i$$

A graph of the function $y = x^2 + 2x + 4$ shows very interesting roots!

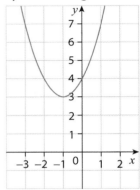

The graph does **not** cross the x – axis.

2.1 Check-up

1. Find the roots of the following equations, expressing each answer in complex form:

   (i) $x^2 + 4x + 5 = 0$ (ii) $2x^2 + 4x + 8 = 0$

   (iii) $x^2 + 3x + 6 = 0$ (iv) $2x^2 - 2x + 4 = 0$

   (v) $3x^2 + 2x + 1 = 0$ (vi) $-2x^2 - 4x - 3 = 0$

   (vii) $x^2 + 3x + 3 = 0$ (viii) $2x^2 + 3x + 4 = 0$

   (ix) $3x^2 + 6x + 8 = 0$ (x) $-2x^2 + 3x - 2 = 0$

   (xi) $3x^2 + 4x + 2 = 0$ (xii) $4x^2 + 2x + 5 = 0$

Part 3: Operations with complex numbers

Looking ahead

- We add/subtract complex numbers by adding/subtracting the real parts and the imaginary parts separately.

  ○ $(3 + 4i) + (2 - 5i) = 3 + 4i + 2 - 5i = 3 + 2 + 4i - 5i = 5 - i$

  ○ $(3 + 4i) - (2 - 5i) = 3 + 4i - 2 + 5i = 3 - 2 + 4i + 5i = 1 + 9i$

- Multiplying by a real number: multiply each part by the real number separately

  ○ $4(2 - 6i) = 8 - 24i$

Example >>

$z_1 = (4 + 3i)$ and $z_2 = (3 - 2i)$
Find (i) $2z_1 + 5z_2$ (ii) $z_2 - 3z_1$

Answer: (i) $2z_1 + 5z_2 = 2(4 + 3i) + 5(3 - 2i)$
$$= 8 + 6i + 15 - 10i$$
$$= 8 + 15 + 6i - 10i = 23 - 4i$$
(ii) $z_2 - 3z_1 = (3 - 2i) - 3(4 + 3i)$
$$= 3 - 2i - 12 - 9i$$
$$= 3 - 12 - 2i - 9i = -9 - 11i$$

3.1 Check-up

1. Express each of the following as a single complex number in the form $a + bi$.
   (i) $(4 + 3i) + (2 - i)$
   (ii) $(3 + 5i) + (1 + 4i)$
   (iii) $(1 - 7i) + (4 - 2i)$
   (iv) $(4 + 4i) + (-3 + 2i)$
   (v) $(-4 + 2i) + (5 - 3i)$
   (vi) $(3 + 8i) - (4 - 2i)$
   (vii) $(-3 + 4i) - (3 - 2i)$
   (viii) $(a + bi) + (c + di)$
   (ix) $(6 - 2i) - (-4 - 3i)$
   (x) $(a + bi) - (c + di)$

2. Write each of the following in the form $a + bi$:
   (i) $3 + \sqrt{-25}$
   (ii) $-2 - \sqrt{-81}$
   (iii) $5 + \sqrt{-12}$
   (iv) $\sqrt{-169}$

3. If $z_1 = 1 + 5i$ and $z_2 = 2 - 3i$, find:
   (i) $4z_1$
   (ii) $3z_1 + z_2$
   (iii) $2z_1 - z_2$
   (iv) $z_1 - 4z_2$
   (v) $5z_1 - 2z_2$
   (vi) $6z_1 - z_2$

4. Simplify $4(2 - 3i) - 3(4 + 5i)$

5. $z_1 = -1 + 3i, z_2 = 2 - i, z_3 = 5 + 2i$, express each of the following in the form $a + bi$:
   (i) $z_1 + z_3$
   (ii) $z_1 - 2z_2$
   (iii) $z_1 + z_2 - z_3$
   (iv) $3z_1 - z_2$
   (v) $4z_2 + z_3 - z_1$
   (vi) $z_1 - 2z_2 + 3z_2$

6. Find a complex number z_1 to satisfy each of the following equations:
   (i) $(3 - i) + z_1 = (4 - 2i)$
   (ii) $z_1 + (1 - i) = 2(4 + i)$
   (iii) $(5 + i) - z_1 = (2 - 3i)$
   (iv) $z_1 - (-3 + i) = 4(2 - 4i)$

Part 4: Multiplying complex numbers

Looking ahead >>

- $i^2 = i \times i = \sqrt{-1} \times \sqrt{-1} = -1$
  - $4i \times 2i = 8i^2 = -8$
  - $(2 + 3i)(1 - 4i) = 2 - 5i - 12i^2 \dots i^2 = -1$
    $$= 2 - 5i + 12$$
    $$= 14 - 5i$$

	2	+3i
1	2	+3i
−4i	−8i	−12i²

Example >>

Simplify: (i) $4i(3 - 5i)$ (ii) $(1 + 2i)(3 - i)$

Answer:

(i) $4i(3 - 5i) = 12i - 20i^2$
$\qquad\qquad = 12i - 20(-1) \ldots i^2 = -1$
$\qquad\qquad = 12i + 20$
$\qquad\qquad = 20 + 12i$

(ii) $(1 + 2i)(3 - i) = 3 + 5i - 2i^2$
$\qquad\qquad\qquad = 3 + 5i - 2(-1) \ldots i^2 = -1$
$\qquad\qquad\qquad = 3 + 5i + 2$
$\qquad\qquad\qquad = 5 + 5i$

	1	$+2i$
3	3	$+6i$
$-i$	$-i$	$-2i^2$

4.1 Check-up >>

Multiply each of the following complex numbers and express your answers in the form $a + bi$.

1. (i) $i(2 + 4i)$
   (ii) $i(-3 + 2i)$
   (iii) $2i(5 - i)$
   (iv) $-3i(-7 - 3i)$

Multiply each of the following complex numbers and express your answers in the form $a + bi$:

2. (i) $(1 + i)(2 + 5i)$
   (ii) $(3 - i)(2 + 2i)$
   (iii) $(6 + i)(1 - i)$

3. (i) $(4 + 4i)(2 - 3i)$
   (ii) $(6 - i)(4 + i)$
   (iii) $(8 - 2i)(5 + 4i)$

4. (i) $(-1 + 5i)(3 + 6i)$
   (ii) $(-2 - 7i)(3 + 4i)$
   (iii) $(3 + i)(3 - i)$

5. (i) $(3 + 2i)^2$
   (ii) $(5 - i)^2$
   (iii) $(-2 + 4i)^2$

4.2 Check-up >>

1. If $z_1 = 2 + 3i, z_2 = 4 - i, z_3 = -1 + 2i$, express each of the following in the form $a + bi$:
   (i) $z_1.z_2$
   (ii) $z_3.z_1$
   (iii) $z_3.z_2$
   (iv) $z_1.z_2.z_3$

2. The complex number, $z_1 = 3 - i, z_2 = 5 + 2i, z_3 = -4 + i$, express the following complex numbers in the form $a + bi$:
   (i) $i.z_1z_2$
   (ii) $z_1(z_1 - z_3)$
   (iii) $z_3(z_2 + z_1)$
   (iv) $i(z_2 - z_3)$

3. The complex number, $u = (3 + i)$, $v = (2 - 5i)$, $w = (1 + 3i)$, find in the form $a + bi$,
   (i) $u.v + v.w$
   (ii) $(v - u).w$
   (iii) $u^2 + v^2$
   (iv) $w.(v + u)$
   (v) $(v + u)(w + v)$
   (vi) $(v - u)(v + w)$

4. If $z_1 = a + bi$ and $z_2 = c + di$, find $z_1.z_2$ in the form $a + bi$.

5. Write each of the following as a single complex number:
   (i) $(3 + 2i)(2 + i) + (2 - i)(4 + 2i)$
   (ii) $(5 - i)(2 + 2i) - 4(3 - 2i)$
   (iii) $i(4 + 2i) + 6(2 + i)$
   (iv) $i(5 - i) - i(3 + 2i)$
   (v) $5(3 - i) + 4i(2 + i)$
   (vi) $6i(2 - i) - 5(3 - 3i)$

4.3 Check-up >>

Simplify each of the following products:

1. $(4 + 3i)(4 - 3i)$
2. $(2 - 5i)(2 + 5i)$

3. $(-1 + 4i)(-1 - 4i)$
4. $(a + bi)(a - bi)$

	a	$+bi$
a	a^2	$+abi$
$-bi$	$-abi$	$-b^2i^2$

Talking Point

$(a - bi)$ is the **complex conjugate** of $(a + bi)$ for all a and $b \in R$.

$(a + bi) \times (a - bi)$ is equal to $a^2 + b^2$, a real number.

Part 5: Dividing complex numbers

Looking ahead >>

- $\dfrac{6 + 5i}{2}$ is a complex number divided by a real number

- $\dfrac{6 + 5i}{2} = 3 + \dfrac{5}{2}i$ is a complex number

- $\dfrac{4 + 5i}{2 - 3i}$ **cannot** be divided directly

- To divide complex numbers, we eliminate the complex number denominator by multiplying above and below by the *complex conjugate* of the denominator.

- $\dfrac{4 + 5i}{2 - 3i} \times \dfrac{2 + 3i}{2 + 3i} = \dfrac{(4 + 5i)(2 + 3i)}{2^2 + 3^2} = \dfrac{-7 + 22i}{13} = \dfrac{-7}{13} + \dfrac{22}{13}i$

  —— complex conjugate

- $\bar{z}$ is the symbol for the complex conjugate,

  - if $z = (2 + 5i)$ then $\bar{z} = (2 - 5i)$

  - if $z = (1 - 4i)$ then $\bar{z} = (1 + 4i)$

Example

>>

Divide (i) $\dfrac{14 + 5i}{2}$ (ii) $\dfrac{3 - i}{4 + 5i}$

Answer:

(i) $\dfrac{14 + 5i}{2}$

$= 7 + \dfrac{5}{2}i$

(ii) $\dfrac{3 - i}{4 + 5i} = \dfrac{3 - i}{4 + 5i} \times \dfrac{4 - 5i}{4 - 5i}$

$= \dfrac{(3 - i)(4 - 5i)}{4^2 + 5^2}$

$= \dfrac{12 - 19i + 5i^2}{41}$

$= \dfrac{12 - 19i - 5}{41}$

$= \dfrac{7 - 19i}{41}$

$= \dfrac{7}{41} - \dfrac{19}{41}i$

Talking Point

$(3 + 8i)(3 - 8i)$
$= 3^2 + 8^2$

	3	$-i$
4	12	$-4i$
$-5i$	$-15i$	$+5i^2$

5.1 Check-up

>>

1. Write down the complex conjugate of the following complex numbers:
   - (i) $z = (2 + 6i)$
   - (ii) $z = (5 - 5i)$
   - (iii) $z = (-2 + i)$
   - (iv) $z = (-3 - 2i)$

2. If $z = (6 + 2i)$ write each of the following in the form of $a + bi$:
   - (i) $3\bar{z}$
   - (ii) $z + \bar{z}$
   - (iii) $z - \bar{z}$
   - (iv) $z\bar{z}$

3. $z_1 = 5 - 4i$ and $z_2 = 2 + 3i$ simplify each of the following:
   - (i) $\bar{z}_1 + z_2$
   - (ii) $3z_1 + \bar{z}_2$
   - (iii) $\bar{z}_1 \bar{z}_2$
   - (iv) $\bar{z}_1 - \bar{z}_2$

4. Write each of the following as a complex number in the form $a + bi$:
   - (i) $\dfrac{12 - 16i}{4}$
   - (ii) $\dfrac{10 + 15i}{5}$
   - (iii) $\dfrac{12 - 24i}{8}$
   - (iv) $\dfrac{-2 + 5i}{3}$

5. Divide each of the following complex numbers:

(i) $\dfrac{2-i}{4+i}$ 　　(ii) $\dfrac{2+4i}{1-i}$ 　　(iii) $\dfrac{4+2i}{2+3i}$ 　　(iv) $\dfrac{5+3i}{-2+i}$

6. If $z_1 = 2 + 5i$, $z_2 = 3 - i$ and $z_3 = 6 + 2i$, express in the form $a + bi$:
(remember to find the complex conjugate $\bar{z}$ where needed before dividing)

(i) $\dfrac{z_1}{z_2}$ 　　(ii) $\dfrac{z_3}{z_2}$ 　　(iii) $\dfrac{z_1}{\bar{z}_2}$

(iv) $\dfrac{\bar{z}_2}{\bar{z}_3}$ 　　(v) $\dfrac{z_1 - z_3}{z_2}$ 　　(vi) $\dfrac{z_3}{iz_1}$

(vii) $\dfrac{z_1 + z_3}{\bar{z}_2}$ 　　(viii) $\dfrac{z_1 + z_3}{z_2 + z_3}$ 　　(ix) $\dfrac{\overline{(z_2 + z_3)}}{(z_1 + z_2)}$

Part 6: The Argand diagram

Looking ahead

- We use the Argand diagram to plot complex numbers.
- The horizontal axis is used to plot the real part
  - it is called the **Real axis (Re)**.
- The vertical axis is used to plot the imaginary part
  - it is called the **Imaginary axis (Im)**.
- The complex numbers $z_1 = 4 + i$ and $z_2 = -2 - 3i$ and their conjugates are plotted below.

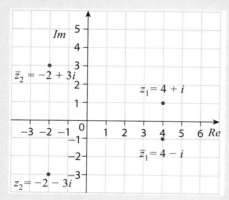

6.1 Check-up

>>

Draw an Argand diagram and use it plot the following sets of complex numbers:

1. (i) $4 + i$ 　(ii) $4 - 2i$ 　(iii) $3 + 3i$ 　(iv) $-2 - i$

2. (i) $2 - 3i$ 　(ii) $-4 + 4i$ 　(iii) 3 　(iv) $2i$

Use a separate Argand diagram to plot the complex numbers in 3. and 4.
(express (iii) as a single complex number, $a + bi$, before plotting it):

3. (i) $2 + i$ 　(ii) $1 + 3i$ 　(iii) $(2 + i) + (1 + 3i)$

4. (i) $-1 - 2i$ 　(ii) $-2 + 2i$ 　(iii) $(-1 - 2i) + (-2 + 2i)$

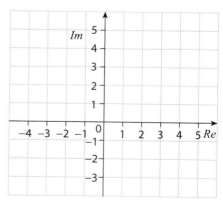

Talking Point　To plot a **real** number, a number line (one dimension) is needed.

To plot a **complex** number, two dimensions are needed.

6.2 Check-up

1. Given $z_1 = 3 + 2i$ and $z_2 = -1 + 3i$, plot each of the following complex number on an Argand diagram:

   (i) z_1 (ii) z_2 (iii) $z_1 + z_2$

   (iv) $2z_1$ (v) $2z_2$ (vi) $2(z_1 + z_2)$

2. Copy the following Argand diagram. Write down the complex numbers A, B and C.

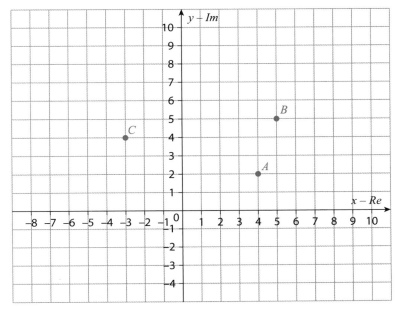

   On the same diagram, plot the complex numbers:

   (i) $A + B$ (ii) $A + C$ (iii) $A - B$ (iv) $A - C$.

   Join the complex numbers   (a) $0 + 0i, A, A + B, B, 0 + 0i$.

                                   (b) $0 + 0i, A, A + C, C, 0 + 0i$.

   Write down a geometrical interpretation of (a) and (b).

3. (i) Write down any complex number, z.

   (ii) Write down the complex conjugate of the complex number, $\bar{z}$.

   (iii) Write down the sum of $z + \bar{z}$.

   (iv) Plot all three answers on an Argand diagram.

4. Simplify each of the following complex numbers and plot the results on an Argand diagram:

   (i) i (ii) i^2 (iii) i^3 (iv) i^4 (v) i^5

   Describe what would happen if the pattern above is continued i.e. i^6, i^7 etc.

5. Write each of the following complex numbers in the form of $a + bi$ and plot the results on an Argand diagram:

   (i) $z_1 = 4 + i$ (ii) $z_2 = i(4 + i)$ (iii) $z_3 = i^2(4 + i)$ (iv) $z_4 = i^3(4 + i)$

   Describe the effect of multiplying a complex number by i.

Part 7: Complex numbers and transformations

- A complex number multiplied by a real number:

  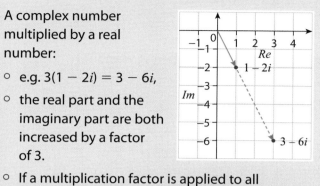
  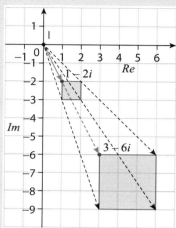

  - e.g. $3(1 - 2i) = 3 - 6i$,
  - the real part and the imaginary part are both increased by a factor of 3.
  - If a multiplication factor is applied to all the numbers forming a geometrical shape then an enlargement of that shape occurs with $(0, 0)$ as the centre of the enlargement.

- A complex number can be considered as a *translation* between, $0 + 0i$ and the complex number:

  - Adding a complex number to a point or a set of points causes a translation of the point or set of points

  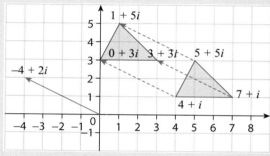

  - $-4 + 2i$ can be considered a translation between $0 + 0i$ and $-4 + 2i$
    $$5 + 3i + (-4 + 2i) = 1 + 5i$$
    $$7 + i + (-4 + 2i) = 3 + 3i$$
    $$4 + i + (-4 + 2i) = 0 + 3i$$

  - the triangle is translated 4 units to the left (-4) and 2 units up $(+2)$ the complex plane.

- A complex number multiplied by i causes a rotation about the origin $(0 + 0i)$:

  - $i \times (3 - i) = 3i - i^2$
    $$= 3i + 1$$
    $$= 1 + 3i$$
  - $i^2 \times (3 - i) = 3i^2 - i^3$
    $$= -3 - i(-1)$$
    $$= -3 + i$$
  - $i^3 \times (3 - i) = 3i^3 - i^4$
    $$= -3i - (-1)^2$$
    $$= -3i - 1$$
    $$= -1 - 3i$$

  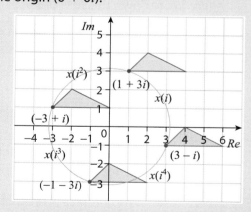

  - $z \times i$ causes an anticlockwise rotation of 90°
  - $z \times i^2$ causes an anticlockwise rotation of 180°
  - $z \times i^3$ causes an anticlockwise rotation of 270°
  - $z \times i^4$ causes an anticlockwise rotation of 360°

Example

Write down the complex numbers, z_1, z_2, z_3, z_4, z_5 using the Argand diagram below:
  (i) Given that $z_2 = kz_1$ find the value of k.
  (ii) Find the translation z that maps z_3 onto z_4.
  (iii) Find a relationship between z_3, z_4 and z_5.

Answer:

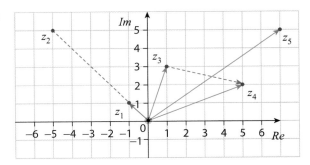

$z_1 = (-1 + i), z_2 = (-5 + 5i), z_3 = (1 + 3i), z_4 = (5 + 2i), z_5 = (6 + 5i)$

  (i) $z_2 = kz_1 \Rightarrow (-5 + 5i) = k(-1 + i) \quad \therefore k = 5$
  (ii) $z_3 + z = z_4$
        $\therefore (1 + 3i) + z = (5 + 2i)$
        $\qquad\qquad z = (5 + 2i) - (1 + 3i)$
        $\qquad\qquad z = 4 - i \quad$ (4 units to the right and 1 unit down)
  (iii) $z_5 = z_3 + z_4 \Rightarrow 6 + 5i = (1 + 3i) + (5 + 2i)$

7.1 Check-up

1. Using the Argand diagram shown:
  (i) Write down the complex numbers
       z_1 and z_2.
  (ii) Plot and join the complex numbers
        $3z_1$ and $3z_2$.
  (iii) Find the value of k so that
         $0.5 + i = k(z_1)$.

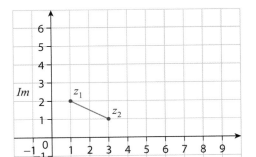

2. Draw an Argand diagram with *Real-axis* from -4 to $+4$ and *Imaginary axis* from -4 to $+4$.
Plot the complex numbers: (i) $z_1 = 3 + 2i$ (ii) $z_2 = -2 + i$ (iii) $z_3 = -4 - 3i$ (iv) $z_4 = 1 - 4i$.
Plot the complex conjugates of each number on the same diagram, $\bar{z}_1, \bar{z}_2, \bar{z}_3$ and $\bar{z}_4$.
State the symmetry used to get the complex conjugate of a complex number.

3. The diagram shows the plot of the complex
numbers z_1, z_2, z_3 which when joined form the
blue triangle.
  (a) Find the complex number $z = x + yi$ which when
       added to z_1, z_2 and z_3 would translate it to the:
       (i) red triangle position (z_4)
       (ii) purple triangle position (z_5)?
  (b) Write down the complex numbers of the images
       of z_1, z_2 and z_3 by axial symmetry in:
       (i) the real axis i.e. S_{Re}
       (ii) the imaginary axis i.e. S_{Im}.

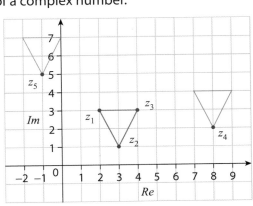

4. On an Argand diagram of the complex plane, plot the complex numbers.

$z_1 = 5 + 3i$ and $z_2 = -1 + 2i$

Plot the image of the complex numbers by the following rotations:

(i) $i(z_1)$ (ii) $i^2(z_1)$ (iii) $-i(z_1)$ (iv) $-i(z_2)$ (v) $i^3(z_2)$ (vi) $i(z_2)$

State the rotation used in each case.

5. (i) Write down the coordinates of the vertices of the triangle ABC in the complex plane, in the form, $x + yi$.

(ii) Find the coordinates of the image of the triangle ABC under the translation $(x + yi) + z_1$ where $z_1 = 3 + 2i$

(iii) Find the coordinates of the image of the triangle ABC under the translation $(x + yi) + z_2$, where $z_2 = -1 + 4i$

(iv) Find the coordinates of the image of the triangle ABC under the translation $(x + yi) + (z_1 + z_2)$.

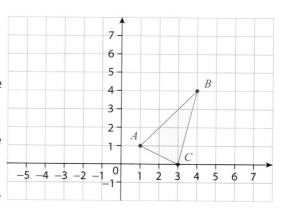

6. If $z_1 = 3 + 2i$ and $z_2 = 1 + 4i$, find the complex number $z_1 + z_2$ in the form $a + bi$.

On an Argand, plot the complex numbers z_1 and z_2.

Complete a parallelogram with $(0 + 0i)$ to z_1 and $(0 + 0i)$ to z_2 as the two adjacent sides.

What relationship has the complex number $(z_1 + z_2)$ to the parallelogram?

7. When a complex number is multiplied by i, an anticlockwise rotation of 90° occurs.

When a complex number is multiplied by i^2, an anticlockwise rotation of 180° occurs.

Copy and complete the table showing the connection between the real and imaginary parts of the object and image complex numbers.

By plotting column 1 and column 3 on an Argand diagram, determine what other symmetry is equivalent to a rotation of 180°.

1	2	3
z	$\times i$	$\times i^2$
$3 + i$		
$4 - i$		
$-2 + 3i$		
$-4 - 2i$		
$x + yi$		

8. By using the coordinates or otherwise, state the relationship between:

(i) z_1 and z_2 (ii) z_1 and z_3 (iii) z_1 and z_4 (iv) z_2 and z_3 and z_5.

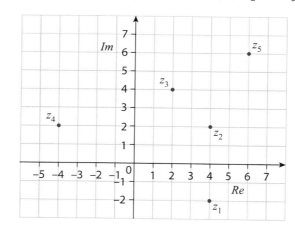

9. Ewa and Peter's project was to write a program for a rocket launching vertically from a surface and then rotating 90° until it was horizontal with the original surface.

They used, $z = 0 + 8i$, to launch the rocket and zi to rotate the rocket into a horizontal plane.

Using the initial coordinates in the complex plane as given, find the coordinates of final position of the rocket P, Q, R, S, T.

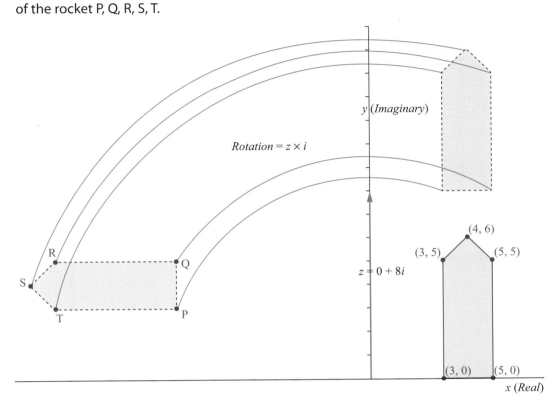

COMPLEX NUMBER TEST

1. If $z = 3 - 3i$ and $w = 2 + 4i$ find in the form $x + yi$ each of the following complex numbers:

   (i) $z + w$ (ii) $z - w$ (iii) $3z + \overline{w}$ (iv) $\overline{z} + \overline{w}$

2. Write each of the following as a single complex number in the form of $a + bi$:

   (i) $i(3 + 7i)$

   (ii) $4(1 - 2i) + 5(1 + i)$

   (iii) $i^2(-3 + 7i)$

3. Multiply the complex numbers $(5 - 2i)$ and $(1 + 4i)$.

4. Given $z_1 = 6 + 2i$ and $z_2 = 3 - i$, find:

   (i) $\dfrac{z_1}{z_2}$

   (ii) $\dfrac{z_2}{z_1}$ as a single complex number in the form $a + bi$.

5. In the diagram shown,

   (i) $z_2 = kz_1$

        find z_1, z_2 and a value for k.

   (ii) $z_4 = 4z_3$, find z_4.

   (iii) $z_5 = z_4 - z_2$, find z_5.

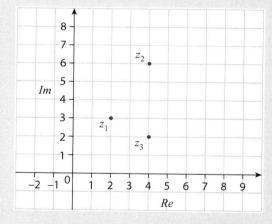

6. A line segment is drawn between the complex numbers z_1 and z_2 on the Argand diagram shown:

   (i) Find the complex numbers z_3 and z_4 which are the end points of the line segment under the translation $z = 3 - 3i$

   (ii) Find the complex numbers z_5 and z_6 which are the end points of the line segment under an anticlockwise rotation of 90°.

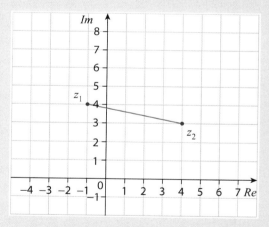

Answers

1. Algebra

Part 1

1.1 Check-up (page 2)

1. (i) 2   (ii) 7   (iii) $\frac{15}{6} = 2.5$
2. (i) 8   (ii) 12   (iii) 6
3. (i) $\frac{1}{5}$ (ii) $\frac{1}{5}$ (iii) 2
4. (i) 8   (ii) 1.5   (iii) 1

1.2 Check-up (page 3)

1. (i) 9   (ii) 8   (iii) 1
2. (i) -1 (ii) $\frac{1}{2}$ (iii) 6
3. (i) 3.5   (ii) $-1\frac{5}{7}$ (iii) 6

Part 2

2.1 Check-up (page 4)

1. (i) $x = \frac{c-y}{d}$, 1   (ii) $x = \frac{h-a}{g}$, -5
   (iii) $x = \frac{c-a-b}{d}$, 0
2. (i) $x = \frac{a^2-d}{b}$, $-\frac{1}{4}$ (ii) $x = \frac{h}{y^2-y}$, 1
   (iii) $x = \frac{ab-c}{a}$, -1
3. (i) $x = \frac{h-bm}{b}$, $-\frac{1}{4}$ (ii) $x = \frac{\sqrt{(b-g)}}{a}$, $\sqrt{5}$
   (iii) $x = \frac{c}{-g^2-3+y^2}$, 1
4. $a = \frac{v^2-u^2}{2s}$, 3.575
5. $g = \frac{4\pi^2 l}{T^2}$, 9.8
6. $v = \frac{fu}{u-f}$, 2.76
7. (i) CoP $= 4$ (ii) because $Q_h > Q_h - Q_c$
   (iii) because $W < Q_h$ (iv) Proof
   (v) $\eta = 25\%$ (vi) 125J

2.2 Check-up (page 5)

1. (i) $12(2x + 7y)$ (ii) $3(4a - 2b + 3c)$
   (iii) $3x(3 + 2y - x)$
2. (i) $\pi r(r + 2)$ (ii) $\pi r(4r + h)$
   (iii) $5(4x^2 - 3y^2)$
3. (i) $3t(1 + 3t)$ (ii) $4x(x^2 + 3x + 2)$
   (iii) $xy(a + by)$

2.3 Check-up (page 5)

1. (i) $x = -4, 2$ (ii) $x = 3, 5$ (iii) $y = -\frac{1}{2}, -4$
2. (i) $x = \frac{1}{3}, -4$ (ii) $x = 1, \frac{-5}{2}$ (iii) $t = -6, \frac{3}{2}$
3. (i) $x = 1, -\frac{2}{5}$ (ii) $t = \frac{1}{4}, \frac{3}{2}$ (iii) $v = -4, 9$
4. (i) $\frac{x+3}{x+5}$ (ii) $\frac{x-2}{x+1}$

Part 3

3.1 Check-up (page 6)

1. $C(-1, -6), D(3, 10)$
2. $A(0, 1), B(-2, -4), C(6, 16)$
3. $A(2.5, 0), C\left(5, \frac{-5}{4}\right), D\left(0, \frac{5}{4}\right)$
4. $A(2, 4), C(4, 5), D(-6, 0)$
5. l, k, n 6. $(2, 16)$ and $(3, 18)$ do not satisfy the equation.

3.2 Check-up (page 7)

1. $a = 3$ 2. $c = -14$ 3. $b = 5$
4. $f = -2$ 5. $g = 9$ 6. $b = 3$
7. $a = 1$ 8. $a = -7, b = 8$ 9. Proof
10. $(1, -4), (-1, 2)$ 11. $a = -13$

Part 4

4.1 Check-up (page 8)

1. $(x, y) = (3, 1)$ 2. $(x, y) = (2, -1)$
3. $(a, b) = (2, -4)$ 4. $(m, n) = (6, 3)$
5. $(a, b) = \left(4\frac{1}{2}, -4\frac{1}{2}\right)$ 6. $(x, y) = (4, 0)$
7. $4 = -2a + b, 1 = 4a + b$
   $(a, b) = -\frac{1}{2}, 3$
8. $m = -3, c = 4$ 9. $y = 2x + 4$
10. $3x + 2y - 18 = 0$
    $3x - 5y + 3 = 0$

Part 5

5.1 Check-up (page 10)

1. $(a, b, c) = (1, 2, 4)$ 2. $(x, y, z) = (2, -1, 1)$
3. $(r, s, t) = (2, 1, 0)$ 4. $(a, b, c) = (4, 1, -1)$
5. $(x, y, z) = (3, -5, 1)$
7. $(a, b, c) = (1, -4, 1)$ 6. $(r, s, t) = (3, 4, -5)$
8. $(a, b, c) = (2, -5, 2)$ 9. Marcus

Part 6

6.1 Check-up (page 11/12)

1. length $= 7$ cm, width $= 4$ cm   2. 10, 35
3. €18.75   4. $x = 9$, Area $= 1140\,u^2$
5. $\frac{3}{7}$ 6. $x = 76$
7. $x = 70°$(smaller), $110°$(larger)
8. $n = 123, n + 2 = 125$ 9. 5 m

Part 7

7.1 Check-up (page 13/14)

1. $3\frac{3}{7}$ hours
2. (i) $\frac{d}{18}$ (ii) $\frac{d}{16}$ (iii) Proof
3. (i) $\frac{1}{36}$ (ii) 36 min
4. 50 kg

Part 8

8.1 Check-up (page 15)
1. 2, 4   2. 23

8.2 Check-up (page 15/16)
1. 17 rows of 25 seats, 8 rows of 15 seats
2. $x = 5, y = 2$
3. 535 adults, 265 students   4. $x = 8, y = 2$
5. (i) 850 loaves   (ii) 5 days
6. $\dfrac{42}{147}, \dfrac{45}{150}$
7. 40 m²   8. 1561   9. € 170   10. 112

Part 9

9.1 Check-up (page 18)
1. $(a, b, c) = (1, -1, 2)$ 2. $(x, y, z) = (40, 35, 50)$
3. $x^2 + y^2 - 2x - 2y + 1 = 0$ 4. $(x, y, z) = 4, 3, 6$

Part 10

10.1 Check-up (page 20)
1. $A: (x + 7)^2$
   $B: (x + 2)^2$
   $C: (x - 4.5)^2$
   $D: (x - 6)^2$

2. $(x - 6)^2 \rightarrow E$
   $(x + 1)^2 \rightarrow B$
   $(x - 2.5)^2 \rightarrow C$
   $-(x - 3)^2 \rightarrow D$
   $-(x + 4)^2 \rightarrow A$

10.2 Check-up (page 21)
1. (i) $x = (10, -4)$
   (iv) $x = \left(\dfrac{3}{2}, -\dfrac{9}{2}\right)$
   (iii) $x = (6, -4)$
   (vi) $x = \dfrac{1 \pm \sqrt{5}}{2}$
   (v) $x = \left(\dfrac{8}{3}, 0\right)$
   (ii) $x = (0, -4)$

2. (i) $(11, -1)$ (ii) $\left(\dfrac{9}{5}, -\dfrac{11}{5}\right)$ (iii) $\left(0, -\dfrac{7}{2}\right)$

3. (i) $(x + 2)^2 - 4$ (ii) $(x - 2)^2 - 4$
   (iii) $(x + 8)^2 - 64$ (iv) $(x + 6)^2 - 36$
   (v) $(x - 10)^2 - 100$ (vi) $\left(x + \dfrac{5}{2}\right)^2 - \dfrac{25}{4}$

10.3 Check-up (page 21)
1. (i) $x = -5, 1$ (ii) $x = 2 \pm \sqrt{5}$
   (iii) $x = -6 \pm \sqrt{42}$ (iv) $x = -4 \pm 3\sqrt{2}$
   (v) $x = -2 \pm \sqrt{3}$ (vi) $x = 2 \pm \sqrt{6}$
   (vii) $x = \dfrac{-5 \pm \sqrt{29}}{2}$

Test (page 22)
1. $6 + x$
2. $3x^2 - 10x - 8 = (3x + 2)(x - 4)$
   (i) $g(x) = 3x + 2$ (ii) $h(x) = -3x - 2$
3. $(x, y) = (4, 2)$,   Area $= \dfrac{11}{3}$ 4. $x = -5 \pm 3\sqrt{2}$
5. $(a, b, c) = (-1, 5, -3)$
6. 11 years of age, 41 years of age
7. (i) $x = 1 \pm \sqrt{6}$ (ii) $x = 5 \pm 2\sqrt{7}$ (iii) $x = \dfrac{5 \pm \sqrt{29}}{2}$

8.

2. Geometry

Part 1

1.1 Check-up (page 25)
1. $y = 4x - 12$ 2. $y = \dfrac{1}{2}x - \dfrac{9}{2}$
3. $y = \dfrac{1}{2}x - 2$ 4. $y = -4x + 16$
5. $y = 6x + 9$ 6. $y = -2x + \dfrac{9}{2}$
7. $y = 2x - 6$ 8. $y = \dfrac{1}{3}x + 5$
9. $y = -6x + 8$

1.2 Check-up (page 25)
1. 2   2. -3 3. $\dfrac{1}{2}$
4. -3 5. 5   6. 4
7. $-\dfrac{1}{5}$ 8. 5   9. -12

1.3 Check-up (page 25)
1. 4, 1   2. $-\dfrac{5}{3}, -3$ 3. $-1, -1$
4. $-\dfrac{3}{2}, \dfrac{9}{2}$ 5. $\dfrac{1}{3}, 0$ 6. $\dfrac{2}{3}, 1$

1.4 Check-up (page 25/26)
1. $3x - y - 2 = 0$ 2. $x + y - 3 = 0$
3. $x - 2y + 1 = 0$ 4. $5x - y + 2 = 0$
5. $3x - y - 1 = 0$ 6. $2x - 3y - 10 = 0$
7. $x + 6y + 3 = 0$

1.5 Check-up (page 26)
1. $AD \quad x - y + 1 = 0$ 2. $AB \quad x - 4y + 13 = 0$
3. $AC \quad x + y - 7 = 0$ 4. $DB \quad x + y - 17 = 0$
5. $BC \quad x - y - 5 = 0$

Part 2

2.1 Check-up (page 28)
1. $A \quad 2x + y - 4 = 0$ 2. $B \quad x - 2y + 10 = 0$
3. $C \quad 4x - y - 3 = 0$ 4. $D \quad 4x - y - 6 = 0$
5. $E \quad x + 2y - 2 = 0$ 6. $F \quad x - y + 3 = 0$

2.2 Check-up (page 28)

Parallel $[CH]$, $[LI]$

Perpendicular $[CD]$, $[FG]$, $[AB]$, $[JK]$, $[H, D]$, $[E, I]$, $[E, L]$

2.3 Check-up (page 28)

1. $x - y - 6 = 0$ 2. Proof

Part 3

3.1 Check-up (page 30)

1. 0.4   2. 2.7   3. 4.9   4. 4.0
5. 0.7   6. 2.8   7. 2.1   8. 2.1
9. (i) $\dfrac{6}{15}$ (ii) $6x - 15y + 27 = 0$

(iii) No, they are equidistant.

Part 4

4.1 Check-up (page 32)

1. $x^2 + y^2 = 4$ 2. $x^2 + y^2 = 25$
3. $4x^2 + 4y^2 = 49$ 4. $x^2 + y^2 = 3$
5. $4x^2 + 4y^2 = 1$ 6. $9x^2 + 9y^2 = 49$
7. $x^2 + y^2 = 18$ 8. $9x^2 + 9y^2 = 5$

4.2 Check-up (page 32)

1. 5   2. 1   3. $4\sqrt{3}$
4. $\dfrac{5}{2}$ 5. $\dfrac{2}{3}$ 6. $\dfrac{2\sqrt{3}}{5}$

4.3 Check-up (page 32)

1. $x^2 + y^2 = 17$ 2. $x^2 + y^2 = 29$
3. $x^2 + y^2 = 18$ 4. $x^2 + y^2 = 8$

4.4 Check-up (page 32)

1. $x^2 + y^2 = 18$ 2. $4x^2 + 4y^2 = 81$

Part 5

5.1 Check-up (page 33/34)

1. (i) $\sqrt{5}$ (ii) $x^2 + y^2 = 5$
2. $x^2 + y^2 = 25$ 3. $x^2 + y^2 = 20$,   Yes
4. (i) Proof   (ii) $-\dfrac{1}{2}$ (iii) $2x - y - 10 = 0$
5. $x + y - 4 = 0$ 6. Proof
7. (i) $x^2 + y^2 = 25$ (ii) $3x + 4y - 25 = 0$ (iii) $3x + 4y = 0$
8. (i) $x^2 + y^2 = 9$ (ii) Proof   (iii) $\dfrac{15}{4}$

(iv) (a) $-\dfrac{15}{4}$ (b) $3x + 4y + 15 = 0$

(v) $m : 4x - 3y + 15 = 0$
   $n : 4x - 3y - 15 = 0$

Part 6

6.1 Check-up (page 35/36)

1. (i) $x = 60°$ (ii) $x = 30°, y = 40°$
   (iii) $x = 75°, y = 80°$ (iv) $x = 50°, y = 65°$
2. $a = 28°$ 3. $c = 55°, d = 125°, x = 218°$
4. $c = 116°, a = 64°$ 5. $26°$
6. Proof   7. $x = 22.5°$

6.2 Check-up (page 37/38)

1. (a) All the sides have the same length.
       All the angles are 90°.
       Opposite sides are parallel.
       Diagonals are equal in length.
       Diagonal bisect each other at 90°.

(b) All angles are 90°.
    Opposite sides are equal in length.
    Opposite sides are parallel.
    Diagonals are equal in length.
    Diagonals bisect each other.

(c) All the sides have the same length.
    Opposite sides are parallel.
    Opposite angles are equal.
    Diagonal bisect the angles of the rhombus.
    Diagonal bisect each other at 90°.

(d) Opposite sides are equal in length.
    Opposite sides are parallel.
    Opposite angles are equal.
    Diagonal bisect each other.

(e) One pair of opposite sides are parallel.

(f) Two pairs of adjacent sides are equal in length.
    Two isosceles triangles are formed by a diagonal.
    Diagonal intersect at 90°.

2. (a) False: A rhombus does not need to have right angles.
   (b) True: Opposite sides are parallel
       Opposite sides are equal in length
       Opposite angles are equal to 90°
   (c) True: Opposite sides are parallel.
   (d) False: because diagonals do not make angles of 45°
       with the base.
   (e) True : Opposite sides are parallel.
   (f) False: It only has one pair of parallel sides.
3. (a) $x = 75°, y = 105°$ (d) $l = 150°$
   (b) $a = 54°, b = 90°$ (e) $f = 80°, g = 105°$
   (c) $c = 45°$ (f) $n = 60°.$

Test (page 39)

1. $3x - y - 2 = 0$ 4. $\dfrac{2}{5}$
3. $3x - y - 2 = 0$ 6. $x^2 + y^2 = 25$
5. 0.4   8. $x - 3y + 18 = 0$
7. $x^2 + y^2 = 20$ 10. Proof
9. $x = 15°$
2. $x + 3y - 11 = 0$

3. Probability

Part 1

1.1 Check-up (page 42/43)

1. (i) $\dfrac{4}{5}$ (ii) $\dfrac{1}{5}$ 2. (i) $\dfrac{1}{6}$ (ii) $\dfrac{1}{3}$
3. (i) $\dfrac{3}{10}$ (ii) $\dfrac{2}{5}$ (iii) $\dfrac{3}{5}$
4. (i) $\dfrac{11}{20}$ (ii) $\dfrac{7}{10}$ (iii) $\dfrac{17}{20}$ (iv) $\dfrac{9}{20}, \dfrac{5}{19}$
5. (i) $\dfrac{3}{10}$ (ii) $\dfrac{1}{2}$ (iii) $\dfrac{1}{2}$ (iv) $\dfrac{4}{25}$ (v) $\dfrac{3}{10}$

6.

Coin 1	Coin 2	Coin 3
H	H	H
H	H	T
H	T	H
T	H	H
H	T	T
T	H	T
T	T	H
T	T	T

(i) $\dfrac{3}{8}$ (ii) $\dfrac{1}{4}$ (iii) $\dfrac{1}{2}$

7. $P(\text{silver}) = \dfrac{x}{5+x}$, 10

8. $(a\,b\,c)$, $(a\,c\,b)$, $(b\,a\,c)$, $(b\,c\,a)$, $(c\,a\,b)$, $(c\,b\,a)$.

   (i) $\dfrac{1}{3}$ (ii) $\dfrac{1}{6}$ (iii) $\dfrac{1}{3}$

9. $\dfrac{2}{3}$ **10.** $\dfrac{1}{5}$

Part 2

2.1 Check-up (page 45)

1. (i) $\dfrac{1}{2}$ (ii) $\dfrac{2}{15}$ (iii) $\dfrac{1}{6}$

2. (i) $\dfrac{9}{10}$ (ii) $\dfrac{3}{10}$ (iii) $\dfrac{1}{5}$

3. (i) $\dfrac{1}{10}$ (ii) $\dfrac{7}{20}$ (iii) $\dfrac{9}{20}$ (iv) $\dfrac{1}{2}$ (v) $\dfrac{3}{20}$

4. $\dfrac{1}{12}$

$U = 24$

$C(6)$ $D(5)$

4   2   3

15

5. 110,

  (i) $\dfrac{1}{11}$ (ii) $\dfrac{28}{55}$ (iii) $\dfrac{22}{55}$ (iv) $\dfrac{4}{55}$ (v) $\dfrac{3}{55}$

  (vi) $\dfrac{1}{55}$ (vii) $\dfrac{10}{11}$ (viii) $\dfrac{2}{55}$ (ix) $\dfrac{34}{55}$

Part 3

3.1 Check-up (page 47/48)

1. 0.4   **2.** $\dfrac{2}{13}$ **3.** $\dfrac{9}{25}$

4. (i) $\dfrac{1}{4}$ (ii) $\dfrac{1}{13}$ (iii) $\dfrac{1}{52}$

   (iv) $\dfrac{1}{2}$ (v) $\dfrac{1}{13}$ (vi) $\dfrac{4}{13}$

5. (i) $\dfrac{2}{9}$ (ii) $\dfrac{5}{9}$ (iii) $\dfrac{1}{18}$ (iv) $\dfrac{1}{2}$

6. $\dfrac{3}{5}$

7. (i) $\dfrac{9}{25}$ (ii) $\dfrac{16}{25}$ (iii) $\dfrac{4}{5}$

8. (i) $\dfrac{4}{25}$ (ii) $\dfrac{1}{2}$ (iii) $\dfrac{47}{50}$

   (iv) $\dfrac{21}{25}$ (v) $\dfrac{33}{50}$

9.

Coin 1	Coin 2
H	H
H	T
T	H
T	T

$, \dfrac{1}{2}$

10. (i) $\dfrac{1}{6}$ (ii) $\dfrac{5}{36}$ (iii) $\dfrac{5}{18}$ (iv) $\dfrac{1}{3}$

11. (i) $\dfrac{2}{9}$ (ii) $\dfrac{1}{9}$ (iii) $\dfrac{2}{3}$ (iv) $\dfrac{8}{9}$

Part 4

4.1 Check-up (page 49/50)

1. (i) $\dfrac{1}{2}$ (ii) $\dfrac{1}{4}$ **2.** 0.16

3. (i) 12   (ii) $\dfrac{1}{2}$ (iii) $\dfrac{1}{2}$ (iv) $\dfrac{1}{4}$ (v) $\dfrac{1}{4}$

4. $\dfrac{1}{36}$ **5.** $\dfrac{1}{8}$

6. $\dfrac{5}{6}$ (i) $\dfrac{5}{36}$ (ii) $\dfrac{25}{216}$

7. (i) $\dfrac{1}{4}$ (ii) $\dfrac{1}{169}$ (iii) $\dfrac{1}{104}$

8. (i) 0.504   (ii) 0.006

9.

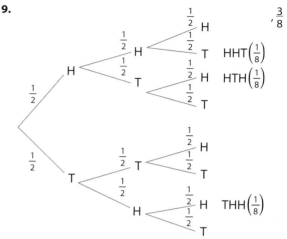

$, \dfrac{3}{8}$

4.2 Check-up (page 51/52)

1. $\dfrac{5}{18}$

2. (i) $\dfrac{9}{25}$ (ii) $\dfrac{6}{25}$ (iii) $\dfrac{6}{25}$ (iv) $\dfrac{4}{25}$ (v) $\dfrac{13}{25}$

3. (i) 0.014 (ii) 0.014 (iii) 0.014 (iv) 0.041

4. (i) 0.28 (ii) 0.063 (iii) 0.25 (iv) 0.096

5. $\dfrac{1}{6}$

6. (i) $\dfrac{125}{216}$ (ii) $\dfrac{25}{72}$ (iii) $\dfrac{91}{216}, \dfrac{1}{36}$

7. (i) 0.630 (ii) 0.315 (iii) 0.370

8. (i) $\dfrac{1}{64}$ (ii) $\dfrac{9}{64}$ (iii) $\dfrac{27}{64}$

9. 0.834

Test (page 53)

1. (a) $U = 168$

$C(34)$ $D(69)$

20   14   55

79

  (b) (i) $\dfrac{5}{42}$ (ii) $\dfrac{1}{12}$

2. $\dfrac{12}{49}$

3. (a) 0.448
  (b) 0.072
  (c) 0.748

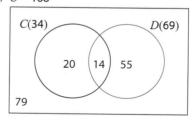

4. Statistics

Part 1

1.1 Check-up (page 56)

1. (i) 25   (ii) 6   (iii) 5.6   (iv) 14
2. (i) 30   (ii) 4   (iii) 4.6

1.2 Check-up (page 56/57)

1. (i) 28.6 hours   (ii) 25–35 hours

Minutes (x)	5–15	15–25	25–35	35–45
Mid – interval value	10	20	30	40
No. of students(f)	8	14	28	20

2. (i) 12–16 minutes   (ii) 11.9 min
3. (2018/19) 2.56 goals (2019/2020) 2.48 goals
4. Because the outlier value 890 distorts the data set.
5. $a, 3a$ **6.** 3, 4

1.3 Check-up (page 58)

1. (a) (i) 7   (ii) 8   (iii) $6\frac{2}{9}$

    (b) (i) 7   (ii) 7   (iii) $7\frac{3}{11}$

2. (i) median $= 29.5$, mode $= 28$ (ii) 29.8
3. (i) 9.7   (ii) 10   (iii) 10

4.

x	1	2	3	4	5	6	7	8
f	3	5	6	5	7	2	3	1

    (i) mode $= 5$, median $= 4$ (ii) mean 3.97

5.

X	80–99	100–119	120–139	140–160
F	7	5	5	3

    (i) 113.1 km   (ii) 113.5 km
    (iii) 80–99 km   (iv) 100–119 km

Part 2

2.1 Check-up (page 59)

1. 22   **2.** $a = 2$, median $= 4$, mode $= 4$
3. $a = 7, b = 6$ **4.** 40, 60
5. 16.2   **6.** -2
7. (i) 3.4   (ii) 4   (iii) 3.5
8. (i) 1 847 800   (ii) 1 883 880
9. (a) mean of squares $= 41.3$
       square of the mean $= 28.4$, No
    (b) median of the squares $= 20.25$
       square of the median $= 20.5$, No

Part 3

3.1 Check-up (page 61/62)

1. (i) 30   (ii) 29   (iii) 20   (iv) 34   (v) 14
2. Smokers   (i) 32   (ii) 128   (iii) 120
                (iv) 134   (v) 14
    Non-smokers   (i) 30   (ii) 116   (iii) 112
                (iv) 126   (v) 14
3. Midterm   (i) 127.8   (ii) 19   (iii) 128.5
                (iv) 123   (v) 131.5   (vi) 8.5
    Start of term   (i) 143.9   (ii) 30   (iii) 145
                (iv) 137   (v) 150.5   (vi) 13.5
    A general improvement in fitness.
4. (i) $54\frac{1}{3}$ (ii) 25   (iii) 53   (iv) 50
    (v) 62   (vi) 12

---

5. (i) 3.723   (ii) 3.3   (iii) 3.8   (iv) 3.2
    (v) 4.2   (vi) 1.05
6. (i) 40eggs   (ii) 50eggs
    Outlier distorts the mean and the range values.
    A mode of zero does not represent the centre of the data

Part 4

4.1 Check-up (page 63)

2. (a) $\bar{x} = 6, \sigma = 3.5$
    (b) $\bar{x} = 11.3, \sigma = 2.6$
    (c) $\bar{x} = 8, \sigma = 4$
3. $\bar{x} = 206.25, \sigma = 18.18$

4.2 Check-up (page 64/65)

1. (i) 20   (ii) 6.2   (iii) 2.6
2. (i)

Number of eggs	3	4	5	6	7
Frequency	2	2	6	6	9

    (ii) 7   (iii) 6
    (iv) 5.72   (v) 1.25
3. (i) Route 1, $\bar{x} = 14$. Route 2, $\bar{x} = 14$.
    (ii) Route 1, $\sigma = 2$. Route 2, $\sigma = 2.3$.
    (iii) Route 1 has a smaller σ, therefore more reliable.

4.

Mark range	10–19	20–29	30–39	40–49	50–59	60–69	70–79	80–89
Mid-interval value (x)	14.5	24.5	34.5	44.5	54.5	64.5	74.5	84.5
Frequency (f)	8	18	25	22	16	6	3	1

    (i) Modal interval $= 30$–39
    (ii) Median mark interval $= 30$–39
    (iii) Mean $= 40.01$
    (iv) $\sigma = 15.3$

5.

	σ_x	$\bar{x}$
A	3.3	6.5
B	3.3	16.5
C	9.9	19.5

6.

Interval (€)	$0 < w \le 20$	$20 < w \le 30$	$30 < w \le 40$	$40 < w \le 50$	$50 < w \le 60$
Mid-interval values	10	25	35	45	55
Frequency	12	23	48	15	3

    (i) €30–€40   (ii) €30–€40
    (iii) €31.83   (iv) €10.66

Part 5

5.1 Check-up (page 67/68)

1. (i) 68%   (ii) 2 standard deviations
    (iii) (a) 0.99   (b) 0.68   (iv) 0.05
2. (i) 98–122   (ii) 74–146   (iii) 0.95
3. (i) 41, 49   (ii) 33, 57   (iii) 0.95
4. (i) 50 cm   (ii) 68%
    (iii) $A = 38$ cm , $B = 68$ cm
5. (i) 66 km/h   (ii) 30 km/h   (iii) 90 km/h
    (iv) 0.95   (v) 0.68   (vi) 0.005
6. 2.5%
7. (i) 50%   (ii) 68%   (iii) 16 min, 64 min
    (iv) 0.025   (v) 0.16

8. $\sigma = 6$ marks

9. (i)

Height (m)	$0.5 < h \leq 1.0$	$1.0 < h \leq 1.5$	$1.5 < h \leq 2.0$	$2.0 < h \leq 2.5$	$2.5 < h \leq 3.0$
Mid-interval values	0.75	1.25	1.75	2.25	2.75
Frequency	8	26	48	15	3

(ii) $\bar{x} = 1.65, \sigma = 0.45$ (iii) 0.75 m, 2.55 m

10. Less than 0.005

Test (page 69)

1. (i) 6.5   (ii) 6.5   (iii) 7

2.

Data	0–3	4–7	8–11	12–15	16–19
Mid-interval value	1.5	5.5	9.5	13.5	17.5
Frequency	2	3	4	9	2

(i) 10.7   (ii) 12–15   (iii) 12–15

3. (a) (i) 5   (ii) 5   (iii) 3.5   (iv) 6   (v) 2.5
   (b) (i) 77   (ii) 5   (iii) 3.5   (iv) 6   (v) 2.5
   It only affects the range and no effect on the median or quartiles / interquartile range.

4. $\sigma = 2.34$
   $\sigma = 2.34$, therefore no change.

5. (i) (a) 68%   (b) 16%   (c) 0.5%
   (ii) 95%.

5. Trigonometry

Part 1

1.1 Check-up (page 72/73/74)

1. (i) 7.8   (ii) 24.1   **2.** (i) 7.6   (ii) 6.4
3. (i) 5.5   (ii) 4.9   **4.** (i) 5.1   (ii) 16.4
5. 15.4 km   **6.** 18.6 m
7. 6.8 m   **8.** $x = 50$ m, $y = 62.4$ m
9. (i) 4 m   (ii) 36 m^2
10. height = 4.36 cm,   length = 5.29 cm
11. (i) Proof   (ii) Proof   **12.** A, C, E, G, H.
13. 52 cm.   **14.** Proof

1.2 Check-up (page 75)

1. 4.0   **2.** 2.77   **3.** 1.6   **4.** Yes

1.3 Check-up (page 75/76)

1. (i) 14.14 cm (ii) Proof   **2.** (i) $3\sqrt{10}$ cm (ii) Proof
3. 18 cm   **4.** 10 cm, 18.24 cm

Part 2

2.1 Check-up (page 77/78)

1. (i) 0.57   (ii) 0.57   (iii) 2.14   (iv) 0.97
   (v) 0.17   (vi) 0.47

2. $\sin(A) = \cos(90° - A)$ for all A.
   sin 20°, cos 70°
   sin 35°, cos 55°

3. (a) (i) a = Opposite, b = Near
      8 cm = Hypotenuse
      (ii) $a = 4$ cm, $b = 6.93$ cm
   (b) (i) 10 cm = Opposite, d = Near
      c = Hypotenuse
      (ii) $c = 13.05$ cm, $d = 8.39$ cm

(c) (i) e = Opposite,   6 cm = Near
   f = Hypotenuse
   (ii) $e = 5.40$ cm, $f = 8.07$ cm
(d) (i) h = Opposite, g = Near
   10 cm = Hypotenuse
   (ii) $h = 9.06$ cm, $g = 4.23$ cm

Part 3

3.1 Check-up (page 79)

1. (i) $\sqrt{3}$ (ii) $\dfrac{-\sqrt{2}}{2}$ (iii) $\dfrac{\sqrt{3}}{2}$ (iv) $\dfrac{\sqrt{3}}{2}$ (v) $-\sqrt{3}$

2. (i) $\dfrac{\sqrt{2}}{4}$ (ii) $\dfrac{\sqrt{6}}{2}$ (iii) $\dfrac{-\sqrt{6}}{2}$

3. (i) Proof
   (ii) (a) $\dfrac{\sqrt{2}}{2}$ (b) $\dfrac{\sqrt{3}}{3}$ (c) $\dfrac{1}{2}$ (d) $\dfrac{\sqrt{3}}{3}$
      (e) $\dfrac{\sqrt{3}}{2}$ (f) $\dfrac{1}{2}$ (g) $\dfrac{1}{2}$ (h) $\dfrac{3}{4}$

Part 4

4.1 Check-up (page 80)

1. 34°   **2.** 46°   **3.** $E = 18°, D = 34°, E + D = 52°$.
4. (i) 26.57° (ii) 6.5 m   **5.** (i) 4.5 m   (ii) 12.0 m

Part 5

5.1 Check-up (page 82)

1. 14 m   **2.** 38 m   **3.** 58 m
4. 28.96°   **5.** 233.9 m, 14 km/h

Part 6

6.1 Check-up (page 84/85)

1. (i) $\angle EFG, \angle EFD, \angle EFA$ (ii) 8.5 m
   (iii) 8.2 m   (iv) 8.8 m   (v) 37.2 m
2. (i) $\angle CAD, \angle BAD, \angle BCA$ (ii) $15\sqrt{3}$ m
   (iii) 45 m   (iv) 56.3°
3. (i) 10.9 m   (ii) 38.1 m   (iii) 46.9 m
   (iv) 511.2 m^2
4. (i) $10\sqrt{2}$ cm, $10\sqrt{3}$ cm   (ii) 35°
5. $|BF| = 11.9$ m
6. (i) $\sqrt{91}$ m   (ii) $3\sqrt{91}$ m^2, $3\sqrt{95}$ m^2

Part 7

7.1 Check-up (page 87/88)

1. (i) 7.2 cm   (ii) 40°   (iii) 7.2 cm
2. (i) 67°   (ii) 6.9 cm
3. (i) 63°   (ii) $a = 23.3$ cm, $b = 17.8$ cm
4. (i) 41°   (ii) 29.7 cm
5. (i) 8 cm   (ii) 9.5 cm   (iii) 5.2 cm
6. 25.4 cm

Part 8

8.1 Check-up (page 90/91)

1. 7.0 cm   **2.** 117°   **3.** 24.7 cm
4. 120°   **5.** 7 cm
6. (i) 7.9 cm   (ii) Proof   (iii) 13.1 cm
7. 54.4 km   **8.** 146.5 m

Part 9

9.1 Check-up (page 92/93)

1. 9 cm^2, the area does not change.

2. (i) 6.4 m   (ii) 25.3 m²
3. $|AB| = 6$ m $|BC| = 12$ m
4. (i) 2 m   (ii) Proof
5. (i) 7.0 m   (ii) 8.6 m   (iii) 49.9°
6. (i) 7.3 cm   (ii) 2.0 cm   (iii) 2:5
7. 120°

Test (page 94)

1. (i) 6.3 m   (ii) 72°   **2.** 76.9 m
3. (i) 24.3 m   (ii) 165 m²
4. (i) 13.3 cm   (ii) 124°.   **5.** 51.23 cm

6. Functions

Part 1

1.1 Check-up (page 97/98/99/100/101)

1. (i) $f(x)$ is quadratic, $g(x)$ is linear   (ii) 4.4, −0.4
(iii) −2   (iv) (2, −6)
(v) −6   (vi) $x = 0, 3$
(vii) $x = 2$

2.

x	−1	0	1	2	3	4
$f(x)$	2	−2	2	8	10	2

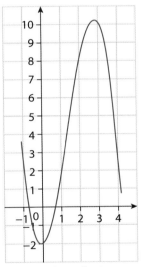

Roots: −0.8, 0.6

3. An n-shaped quadratic curve.
(i) 0, 10 m
(ii) Where the ball is on the ground.
(iii)

x	0	1	2	3	4	5	6	7	8	9
$f(x)$	0	9	16	21	24	25	24	21	16	9

(iv)

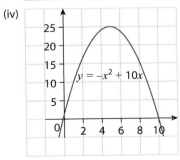

(v) (5, 25)   (vi) 25 m   (vii) $x = 5$ m

4. (i)

x	0	2	4	6	8	10	12	14	16
$f(x)$	0	180	320	420	480	500	480	420	320

(ii)

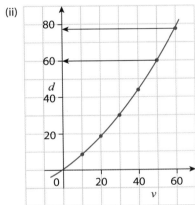

$h = -5t^2 + 100t$

(iii) 500 m   (iv) 10 s

5. (i)

v	10	20	30	40	50	60
d (dry)	8	18	30	44	60	78
d (wet)	8.5	20	34.5	52	72.5	96

(ii)

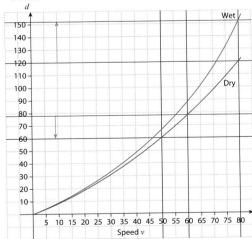

(iii) Approximately 18m.
(iv)

(v) Dry 120 m,   Wet 153 m

6. (i)

l	1	2	3	4	5	6	7	8	9
w	9	8	7	6	5	4	3	2	1
A	9	16	21	24	25	24	21	16	9

(ii)

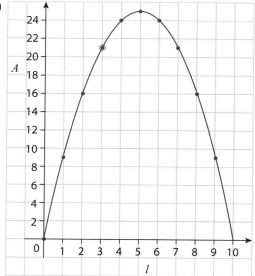

Max Area = 25 m² at $l = 5$

(iii) $A = -l^2 + 10l$

7.

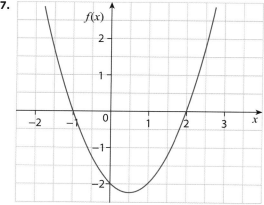

(i) Yes, the roots were correct.

(ii) Let $(x + 1) = 0, x = -1$
Let $(x - 2) = 0, x = +2$

(iii) proof

(iv) $x = 4, x = -3$

(v) $x = 4, x = -3$

8.

x	−1	0	1	2	3
$f(x)$	−2	1	2	1	−2
$g(x)$	−4	2	4	2	−4
$h(x)$	−6	3	6	3	−6

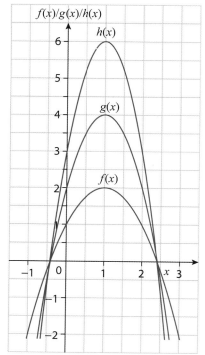

(i) the roots

(ii) $k = 3, m = 2$

(iii) they amplify the graphs

(iv) $(1, 2), (1, 4), (1, 6)$

(v) $-0.4, 2.4$

(vi) $c(x) = 4 + 8x - 4x^2$

9.

x	−2.5	−2	−1.5	−1	−0.5	0	0.5	1	1.5
$f(x)$	−2.625	0	0.625	0	−1.125	−2	−1.875	0	4.375

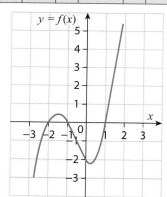

(i) Max $(-1.5, 0.7)$

(ii) Min $(0.25, -2.125)$

(iii) Roots $-2, -1, 1$

10. (i) $-2, 2$ (ii) $(x + 2), (x - 2)$
   (iii) $f(x) = x^2 - 4$ (iv) No
   (v) $k = \dfrac{1}{2}$ (vi) $x = 0$
   (vii) (a) 3 (b) 1 (viii) at $x = 0$

11. (i) $2, 4.5, 7$ (ii) $(3.1, 12)$
   (iii) $(5.9, -12)$ (iv) Slope $= 0,$
   (v) $(3, 6), (6, -6)$
   (vi) $g(x) = x^3 - 13.5x^2 + 104.5x - 63$
   (vii) $g(x) = (x - 2)(x - 4.5)(x - 7)$
   (viii) Proof, $k = 2$

Part 2

2.1 Check-up (page 103/104)

1. (i) $1 < x < 3$ (ii) $2 < x \leq 4.5$
   (iii) $2 < x < 3$ (iv) $-0.5 \leq x < 1$
   (v) $0 < x \leq 4.5$ (vi) $0.7 \leq x \leq 4.3$
   (vii) $x > 4.25$ (vii) $0 < x < 0.7$ and
     $4.3 < x \leq 4.5$

2. (a) linear (b) exponential
   (i) $2.2 < x \leq 3$
   (ii) $-1.5 \leq x \leq 2.5$
   (iii) $0 \leq x \leq 2.5$

3. (a) linear (b) cubic
   (i) $-1 \leq x < 8$
   (ii) $-1 \leq x < 2$ and $4.5 < x < 7$
   (iii) $3 \leq x < 4.5$
   (iv) $-1 \leq x < 2$ and $6 < x < 7$
   (v) $x = 2.2, 4.3, 7.1$
   (vi) $2.1 \leq x \leq 4.25$ and $7.1 \leq x \leq 8$

4. (i) $2 < x \leq 7$ (ii) $3 < x \leq 7$
   (iii) $x = 1, 3$ (iv) $3 \leq x \leq 4$
   (v) $1.9 \leq x \leq 4$ (vi) $3 \leq x \leq 4$

Part 3

3.1 Check-up (page 105/106)

1.

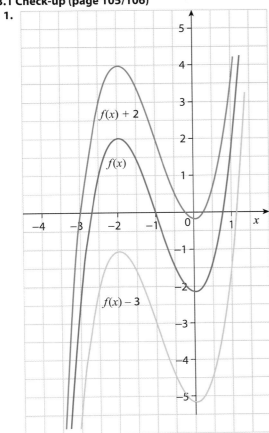

2.

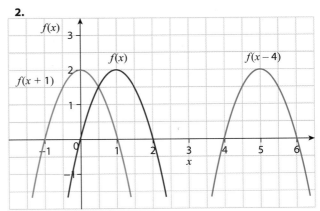

3. (a) (i) $h(x) = f(x) + 4$
   (ii) $g(x) = f(x) - 2$
   (b) (i) $h(x) = -x^2 + 2x + 5$
   (ii) $g(x) = -x^2 + 2x - 1$

4. (i) $g(x) = x^2 + 2x - 2$
   (ii) $h(x) = x^2 - 10x + 22$

5.

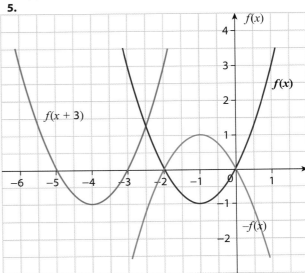

the graph is reflected in the x-axis.

3.2 Check-up (page 107)

1. (i) $g(x) = 2x^2 - 13x + 21$ (ii) $h(x) = 2x^2 - x + 3$
   (iii) $r(x) = 8x^2 + 6x - 1$

2. (a) $g(x) = f(x) + 4$
     $= x^2 - 2x + 3$
     $h(x) = f(x - 3)$
     $= x^2 - 8x + 14$

3. $m : y = 1.5x + 4$
   $p : y = 1.5x - 2$

4. (i) $g(x) = x^2 + 2x + 4$ (ii) $h(x) = x^2 + 6x + 9$
   (iii) $c(x) = 25x^2 + 10x + 1$ (iv) $t(x) = 3x^2 + 6x + 3$
   (v) $s(x) = x^2 - 2x + 6$

5.

x	-3	-2	-1	0	1	2	3
$2x^2 - 2x$	24	12	4	0	0	4	12
$2x^2 + 6x + 4$	24	13	6	3	4	9	18
$2x^2 - 2x + 5$	29	17	9	5	5	9	17

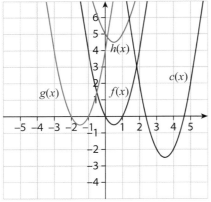

$g(x) = f(x + 2)$
$h(x) = f(x) + 5$
$c(x) = f(x - 3) - 2$

Part 4

4.1 Check-up (page 109/110/111)

1. (i) $8x - 3$ (ii) $6x^2 - 2x + 6$
(iii) $3x^2 + 10x + 10$ (iv) $4 - 4x$
2. Slope $= 54$
3. Slope $= 2$
4. Slope $= 2$, $2x - y + 5 = 0$
5. (i) $f'(3) = 36$ **6.** (i) $f'(3) = 26$
(ii) $f'(2) = 9$ (ii) $f'(-1) = -12$
(iii) $f'(-1) = 12$ (iii) $f'(-2) = -9$
(iv) $f'(1) = 12$ (iv) $f'(4) = 12$
7. (i) $f'(x) = 4x + 3$
(ii) $f'(x) = -2 - 10x$
(iii) $f'(x) = 6x - 1$
8. (i) $D: (-2, 0)$, $E: (-1, 0)$ $F: (0.5, -2)$
(ii) D: Slope $= 3$, E: Slope $= -2$, F: Slope $= \dfrac{7}{4}$
(iii) $D: 3x - y + 6 = 0$
$E: 2x + y + 2 = 0$
$F: 14x - 8y - 23 = 0$
9. (i) $+2$ (ii) 0 (iii) -2
The slope is zero at a turning point.
10. Minimum point $= (2, -1)$
(i) Slope $= 0$
(ii) Negative slope indicates a decreasing curve.
11. $f'(x) = 2x + 3$
Min pt. $= (-1.5, -6.25)$
12. $f'(x) = 6x - 6, x = 1, (1, -11)$

Part 5

5.1 Check-up (page 113)

1. (i) $(x + 2), (x - 3)$ (ii) $x^2 - x - 6$
(iii) $f'(x) = 2x - 1$ (iv) Proof
(v) Minimum – U shaped curve
2. (i) $(-2, -12)$ Min   (iv) $(3, 19)$ Max
(iii) $(-5, 32)$ Max   (vi) $(2, 12)$ Max
(v) $(2, -11)$ Min
(ii) $\left(\dfrac{1}{2}, 0\right)$ Min
3. $f(x) = -3x^2 + 6x$
(i) $(1, 1), (1, 2), (1, 3)$

(ii)

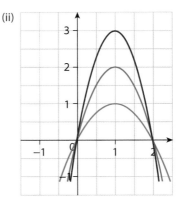

4. (a) $a = -6, b = 3$
(b) (i) $x = -3, 6$
(ii) $(-3, -94.5), (6, 270)$
(iii) Decreasing, Increasing, Decreasing.

Test (page 114)

1. (i) Roots $= 0, 2$
(ii) Axis of symmetry: $x = 1$.

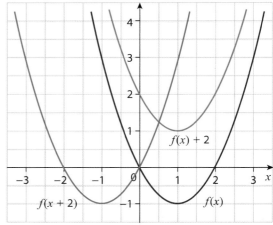

2. (i) $(0, 5)$ (ii) Proof
(iii) $f'(x) = 3x^2 + 6x - 9$ (iv) Proof
(v) $(1, 0), (-3, 32)$ (vi) $a = -3, b = 1$
3. (i) 0 (ii) 6 (iii) $2x - 2$

7. Patterns & Sequences

Part 1

1.1 Check-up (page 116/117)

1. (i) 260   (ii) 2500   (iii) 0.24
2. (i) (a) 1610   (b) 1.6×10^3
(ii) (a) 7.24   (b) 7.2×10^0
(iii) (a) 1.56   (b) 1.56×10^0
3. (i) (a) 6.05×10^2 (b) 600
(ii) (a) 1.64×10^2 (b) 160
(iii) (a) 4.84×10^5 (b) 480 000
4. 500 seconds, 500 seconds, No error
5. 353   **6.** 6.0×10^{24} kg   **7.** 2.0×10^{30} kg

Part 2

2.1 Check-up (page 118/119)

1.

	T_1	T_2	T_3	T_4	T_5
Blue	3	6	9	12	15
Total	4	7	10	13	16

$4 + 3n$ beads needed for the nth term.

2. 6, 10, 14, 18, … the pattern is increasing by 4 tiles for each pattern.

Yes, the eleventh term, $2 + 4n = 46$

3.

Number of squares	T_1	T_2	T_3	T_4	T_5
Number of matchsticks	4	8	12	16	20

48, Yes

4.

n	Number of black triangles	Number of white triangles	Total number of small triangles
Pattern 1	3	1	4
Pattern 2	6	3	9
Pattern 3	10	6	16
Pattern 4	15	10	25
Pattern 5	21	15	36

  (i) 5 black triangles   (iii) 55 black triangles
(iv) Proof   (v) Proof

5. 43, 55, 69, 85

6. -4, 0, 6, 14, 24, 36

Part 3

3.1 Check-up (page 120/121)

1. (i) $T_n = 2n + 3$ **2.** (i) 7, 11, 15, 19, …
  (ii) $T_n = 2n + 9$ (ii) 4, 10, 16, 22, …
  (iii) $T_n = 4n - 3$ (iii) 3, 1, -1, -3, …

3. (i) 7, 11, 15, 19, 23, …
  (ii) -3, -8, -13, -18, -23, …
      (i) is increasing
      (ii) is decreasing

4. $\dfrac{1}{3}, \dfrac{1}{4}, \dfrac{1}{5}, \dfrac{1}{6}, \dfrac{1}{7}$ … No.   **5.** $T_5 = 5, T_{10} = 8$

6. -1, 2, 5, 8, 11, … $n = 21$

7. (i) 5, 8, 11   (ii) $T_n = 3n + 2$ (iii) 62

8. 6, 11, 18, 27, 38, …
No common difference between terms.

9. (i) 13, 11, 9, …   (ii) -1 (iii) $n = 39$

10. $T_{squares} = n + 2$, $T_{triangles} = n$
  $t = s - 2$

11.

n the number of cubes	1	2	3
number of matchsticks	12	20	28

$T_n = 8n + 4$, 84 matchsticks

Part 4

4.1 Check-up (page 122/123)

1. (i) $T_n = 2n + 3$, $S_n = n^2 + 4n$
  (ii) $T_n = 4n + 6$, $S_n = 2n^2 + 8n$
  (iii) $T_n = 3n - 7$, $S_n = \dfrac{3n^2}{2} - \dfrac{11n}{2}$
  (iv) $T_n = 16 - 5n$, $S_n = \dfrac{27n}{2} - \dfrac{5n^2}{2}$

2. (i) 7, 10, 13, 16, …   (ii) $S_n = \dfrac{3n^2}{2} + \dfrac{11n}{2}$
  (iii) $S_{20} = 710$

3. (i) $S_n = -n^2 + 9n$ **4.** (i) $n = 6$
  (ii) $n = 4$ or 5   (ii) Proof

5. (i)

Pattern number	1	2	3	4	5	6	7
Number of tiles	5	8	11	14	17	20	23

  (ii) $T_n = 3n + 2$ (iii) 77 tiles
  (iv) $n = 84$ (v) $S_n = \dfrac{3n^2}{2} + \dfrac{7n}{2}$
  (vi) 1455

6. (i) $S_1 = 1, S_2 = 6, S_3 = 15,$ (ii) $T_1 = 1, T_2 = 5, T_3 = 9,$
     $S_4 = 28, S_5 = 45$ $T_4 = 13, T_5 = 17$
  (iii) $T_n = 4n - 3$ (iv) $n = 26$

7. (i)

	T_1	T_2	T_3	T_4	T_5	T_6	T_7
A	6	11	18	27	38	51	66
B	4	9	16	25	36	49	64
C	2	7	14	23	34	47	62

  (ii) A: $T_n = n^2 + 2n + 3$
     B: $T_n = n^2 + 2n + 1$
     C: $T_n = n^2 + 2n - 1$
  (iii) $k = 2$

8. (i) $S_n = \dfrac{n}{2}(2a + (n - 1)d)$ (ii) $S_8 = 8a + 28d$
  (iii) $a = 6$ (iv) 6, 9, 12, 15, … $T_{25} = 78$

9. (i) $T_{11} = 33$ (ii) $a = 3, d = 3$ (iii) 630

10. (i) $T_n = 500n - 5500$ (ii) €4500
  (iii) $n = 11$ (iv) $S_n = \dfrac{500n^2}{2} - 5250n$
  (v) €18 000

11. $a = -1, b = 2$

Part 5

5.1 Check-up (page 125/126)

1. Proof

2. (i) $T_1: a + b = 3$, $T_2: 2a + b = 5$
  (ii) $a = 2, b = 1$
  (iii) $T_{20} = 441$

3. (i) (a) 9   (b) 11
  (ii) Proof

	T_1	T_2	T_3	T_4	T_5
Black	3	6	10	15	21
1st diff		3	4	5	6
2nd diff			1	1	1
White	1	3	6	10	15
1st diff		2	3	4	5
2nd diff			1	1	1
Total	4	9	16	25	36
1st diff		5	7	9	11
2nd diff			2	2	2

  (iii) 2nd difference is constant   (iv) $a = \dfrac{3}{2}, b = 1$
  (v) $a = \dfrac{1}{2}, b = 0$ (vi) $a = 2, b = 1$
  (vii) Proof

4. 2, 7, 16, 29, 46, 67, 91, …
  (i) Proof   (ii) $a = -1, b = 1$ (iii) $T_n = 2n^2 - n - 1$

5. $a = 2, b = -1$
  1, 6, 15, 28, 45, …

6. $k = 7$

7. $a = 1, b = -1, c = 1$
  1, 3, 7, 13, 21, 31, …

Maths Extra (page 126)

8. Proof

9. (i) doubling a number $\Rightarrow$ 2 is a factor $\therefore$ an even number
  (ii) Since $2n$ must be even
         $2n + 1$ must be odd

10. (i) $9n^2 - 6$
  (ii) 3, 30, 75, 138, 219, …

11. $S_n = \dfrac{9n^2}{2} - \dfrac{n}{2}$, 15 terms

12. (i) €74

   (ii) $S_n = 152n - 2n^2$, €2240

   (iii) €120

Test (page 127)

1. 5.96×10^7 m/s

2. $a = 7, b = -2$; 5, 12, 19, 26, 33

3. (i) 1, 4, 7, 10, 13, … (ii) $d = 3$

   (iii) Proof, 590

4. 490

5. (i) €500, €700, €900, €1100, …

   (ii) €1900

   (iii) €9600; 26 years

8. Complex numbers

Part 1

1.1 Check-up (page 129)

1. (i) $3i$

   (ii) $3\sqrt{2}i$

   (iii) $6\sqrt{2}i$

   (iv) $10i$

2. (i) $9i$

   (ii) $3\sqrt{10}i$

   (iii) $2\sqrt{3}i$

   (iv) $9\sqrt{2}i$

3. (i) Rational (ii) Imaginary

   (iii) Rational (iv) Imaginary

   (v) Irrational (vi) Imaginary

   (vii) Irrational (viii) Irrational

   (ix) Irrational (x) Imaginary

Part 2

2.1 Check-up (page 130)

1. (i) $-2 \pm i$ (ii) $-1 \pm \sqrt{3}i$ (iii) $\frac{-3}{2} \pm \frac{\sqrt{15}}{2}i$

   (iv) $\frac{1}{2} \pm \frac{\sqrt{7}}{2}i$ (v) $\frac{-1}{3} \pm \frac{\sqrt{2}}{3}i$ (vi) $-1 \pm \frac{\sqrt{2}}{2}i$

   (vii) $\frac{-3}{2} \pm \frac{\sqrt{3}}{2}i$ (viii) $\frac{-3}{4} \pm \frac{\sqrt{23}}{4}i$ (ix) $-1 \pm \frac{\sqrt{15}}{3}i$

   (x) $\frac{3}{4} \pm \frac{\sqrt{7}}{4}i$ (xi) $\frac{-2}{3} \pm \frac{\sqrt{2}}{3}i$ (xii) $\frac{-1}{4} \pm \frac{\sqrt{19}}{4}i$

Part 3

3.1 Check-up (page 131)

1. (i) $6 + 2i$ (ii) $4 + 9i$

   (iii) $5 - 9i$ (iv) $1 + 6i$

   (v) $1 - i$ (vi) $-1 + 10i$

   (vii) $-6 + 6i$ (viii) $(a + c) + (b + d)i$

   (ix) $10 + i$ (x) $(a - c) + (b - d)i$

2. (i) $3 + 5i$ (ii) $-2 - 9i$

   (iii) $5 + 2\sqrt{3}i$ (iv) $0 + 13i$

3. (i) $4 + 20i$ (ii) $5 + 12i$ (iii) $13i$

   (iv) $-7 + 17i$ (v) $1 + 31i$ (vi) $4 + 33i$

4. $-4 - 27i$

5. (i) $4 + 5i$ (ii) $-5 + 5i$ (iii) $-4 + 0i$

   (iv) $-5 + 10i$ (v) $14 - 5i$ (vi) $10 + 11i$

6. (i) $1 - i$ (ii) $7 + 3i$

   (iii) $3 + 4i$ (iv) $5 - 15i$

Part 4

4.1 Check-up (page 132)

1. (i) $-4 + 2i$ (ii) $-2 - 3i$

   (iii) $2 + 10i$ (iv) $-9 + 21i$

2. (i) $-3 + 7i$ (ii) $8 + 4i$ (iii) $7 - 5i$

3. (i) $20 - 4i$ (ii) $25 + 2i$ (iii) $48 + 22i$

4. (i) $-33 + 9i$ (ii) $22 - 29i$ (iii) $10 + 0i$

5. (i) $5 + 12i$ (ii) $24 - 10i$ (iii) $-12 - 16i$

4.2 Check-up (page 132)

1. (i) $11 + 10i$ (ii) $-8 + i$

   (iii) $-2 + 9i$ (iv) $-31 + 12i$

2. (i) $-1 + 17i$ (ii) $19 - 13i$

   (iii) $-33 + 4i$ (iv) $-1 + 9i$

3. (i) $28 - 12i$ (ii) $17 - 9i$ (iii) $-13 - 14i$

   (iv) $17 + 11i$ (v) $7 - 22i$ (vi) $-15 - 16i$

4. $(ac - bd) + (bc + ad)i$

5. (i) $14 + 7i$ (ii) $16i$ (iii) $10 + 10i$

   (iv) $3 + 2i$ (v) $11 + 3i$ (vi) $-9 + 27i$

4.3 Check-up (page 132)

1. 25 **2.** 29 **3.** 17 **4.** $a^2 + b^2$

Part 5

5.1 Check-up (page 133/134)

1. (i) $2 - 6i$ (ii) $5 + 5i$

   (iii) $-2 - i$ (iv) $-3 + 2i$

2. (i) $18 - 6i$ (ii) $12 + 0i$

   (iii) $0 + 4i$ (iv) $40 + 0i$

3. (i) $7 + 7i$ (ii) $17 - 15i$

   (iii) $22 - 7i$ (iv) $3 + 7i$

4. (i) $3 - 4i$ (ii) $2 + 3i$

   (iii) $\frac{3}{2} - 3i$ (iv) $\frac{-2}{3} + \frac{5}{3}i$

5. (i) $\frac{7}{17} - \frac{6}{17}i$ (ii) $-1 + 3i$

   (iii) $\frac{14}{13} - \frac{8}{13}i$ (iv) $\frac{-7}{5} - \frac{11}{5}i$

6. (i) $\frac{1}{10} + \frac{17}{10}i$ (ii) $\frac{8}{5} + \frac{6}{5}i$ (iii) $\frac{11}{10} + \frac{13}{10}i$

   (iv) $\frac{2}{5} + \frac{3}{10}i$ (v) $\frac{-3}{2} + \frac{1}{2}i$ (vi) $\frac{-26}{29} - \frac{22}{29}i$

   (vii) $\frac{31}{10} + \frac{13}{10}i$ (viii) $\frac{79}{82} + \frac{55}{82}i$ (ix) $\frac{49}{41} + \frac{31}{41}i$

Part 6

6.1 Check-up (page 134)

1.

2.

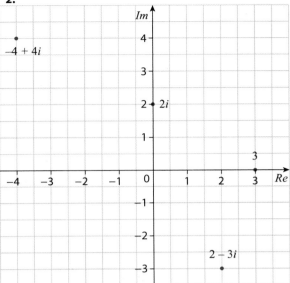

1.

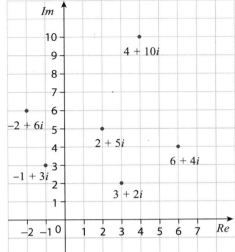

3.

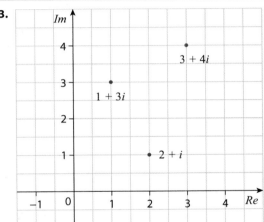

4.

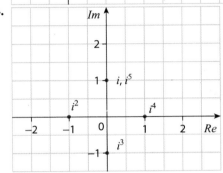

The numbers would rotate onto i^2, i^3 etc.

4.

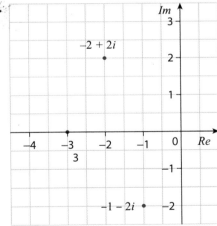

5.

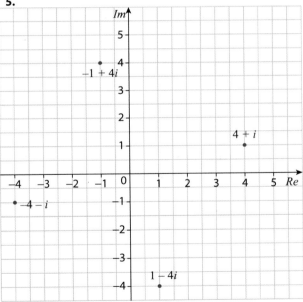

The complex number rotates about the origin.

7.1 Check-up (page 137/138/139)

1. (i) $z_1 = 1 + 2i, z_2 = 3 + i$
   (ii)

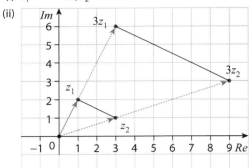

   (iii) $k = \dfrac{1}{2}$

2.

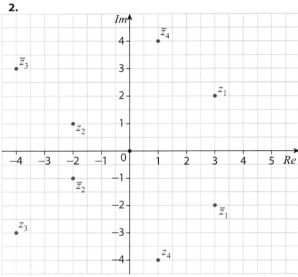

   Axial Symmetry (Reflection) in the x-axis

3. (a) (i) $z = 5 + i$ (ii) $z = -4 + 4i$
   (b) (i) $2 - 3i, 3 - i, 4 - 3i$
       (ii) $-2 + 3i, -3 + i, -4 + 3i$

4.

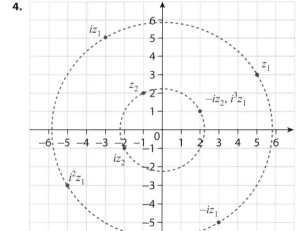

   (i) Anti-clockwise rotation 90°
   (ii) Anti-clockwise rotation 180°
   (iii) Clockwise rotation 90°
   (iv) Clockwise rotation 90°

   (v) Clockwise rotation 90° or Anti-clockwise rotation 270°
   (vi) Anti-clockwise rotation 90°

5. $A: 1 + i, B: 4 + 4i, C: 3 + 0i$
   (i) $A': 4 + 3i, B': 7 + 6i, C': 6 + 2i$
   (ii) $A': 0 + 5i, B': 3 + 8i, C': 2 + 4i$
   (iii) $A': 3 + 7i, B': 6 + 10i, C': 5 + 6i$

6.

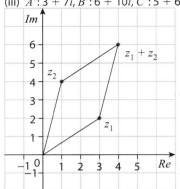

   $4 + 6i$ is the 4th vertex of the parallelogram.

7.

1	2	3
z	$\times i$	$\times i^2$
$3 + i$	$-1 + 3i$	$-3 - i$
$4 - i$	$+1 + 4i$	$-4 + i$
$-2 + 3i$	$-3 - 2i$	$+2 - 3i$
$-4 - 2i$	$+2 - 4i$	$+4 + 2i$
$x + yi$	$-y + xi$	$-x - yi$

   Central symmetry (Reflection) through the origin.

8. (i) Image in the Real-axis
   (ii) Image due to Anti-clockwise rotation 90°
   (iii) Image due to Anti-clockwise rotation 180° or Reflection through the origin.
   (iv) $z_5 = z_3 + z_2$

9. $P(-8 + 5i), Q(-8 + 5i), R(-13 + 5i), S(-14 + 4i),$
   $T(-13 + 3i)$

Test (page 140)

1. (i) $5 + i$ (ii) $1 - 7i$
   (iii) $11 - 13i$ (iv) $5 - i$

2. (i) $-7 + 3i$ (ii) $9 - 3i$ (iii) $3 - 7i$

3. $13 + 18i$

4. (i) $\dfrac{8}{5} + \left(\dfrac{6}{5}\right)i$ (ii) $\dfrac{2}{5} - \dfrac{3}{10}i$

5. (i) $z_1 = 2 + 3i, z_2 = 4 + 6i, k = 2$
   (ii) $16 + 8i$ (iii) $12 + 2i$

6. (i) $z_3 = 7 + 0i, z_4 = 2 + i$
   (ii) $z_5 = -3 + 4i, z_6 = -4 - i$